THE
HUNDRED YEARS

PHILIP GUEDALLA

THE HUNDRED YEARS

If it be romance, if it be contrast,
if it be heroism that we require,
what was Troy town to this?
—STEVENSON.

Je ne blâme ni n'approuve: je raconte.
—TALLEYRAND.

THE LITERARY GUILD, INC.
New York   1937

PRINTED AT THE *Country Life Press*, GARDEN CITY, N. Y., U. S. A.

To
N. G.
Lovingly

Author's Note

ONE HUNDRED YEARS AGO *next June the world heard for the first time of Queen Victoria; and the world we live in is largely the result of that eventful century. To write its history in full would be a despairing enterprise for anything short of a syndicate of centipedes with a pen in every hand. But the task undertaken in the present volume is not beyond the powers of an individual. It is an attempt to describe the leading moments of the century as they affected the leading units of the Western world. These may be located without difficulty in Great Britain, France, Russia, Germany, and (since the modern world is not confined to one shore of the Atlantic) the United States. For as the ancient world consisted principally of the shores of the Mediterranean, its modern counterpart lies on both sides of the Atlantic. That is why a fair proportion of its chief events have been American.*

This is not, as I have indicated, an effort to compress a

hundred years of European and American history into a single volume, but merely to present the reader with a series of its leading moments. I have not tried to cover the whole area of the century with a complete and continuous chronicle of its crowded course, but rather to throw a light bridge of selected narrative across the chasm of a hundred years. Its method is apparently discontinuous. But I can assure the reader that its plan, which engaged me for two years of thought and reading before I began to write this book in 1934, is quite consecutive. A mosaic is no less a picture because it is made up of separate pieces. The selection is, of course, my own; but, though personal, it is by no means arbitrary, since I have tried to throw upon the screen those pictures which appear to be the most significant. Following this principle, I have preferred, in dealing with the World War, to concentrate upon its consequences rather than the mere drama of its course. For that reason I have chosen for projection the year 1917, since the collapse of Russia and the intervention of the United States are events of more immediate significance to the contemporary world than the causal days of 1914.

Those are the principles on which my scenes have been selected. It will be found, I hope, that they are not an arbitrary peepshow of picturesque events, but an unwinding panorama in the last scene of which we are still living. Within the strictest limits of historical precision I have done my best to make them live; and if there are no pictures in this book except those which I have painted, I have tried to see each of them through the eyes of contemporary witnesses, and I have been at pains to visit almost every back-

AUTHOR'S NOTE

ground that I found it necessary to describe at any length. For this purpose a normal course of European travel has been supplemented by extensive visits to the United States, Mexico, the chief battlefields of the American Civil War and those scenes of the Russian Revolution which lie in and round Leningrad; and, above all, to whom I am indebted for counsel and co-operation in a considerable undertaking, my thanks belong to my unwearied fellow-traveller.

P. G.

July, 1936.

Contents

[xi]

CONTENTS

CONTENTS

[xiii]

EIGHTEEN
THIRTY–SEVEN

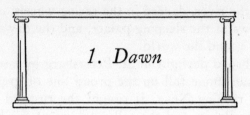

1. Dawn

THE SUMMER DAWN came through the trees at Kensington, and the first light of a June morning caught the windows of a little palace sleeping in its garden. Nothing stirred about the house, as daylight crept through the shutters and moved silently across the empty rooms. The palace slept in the summer dawn, and there was nothing stirring in the little courtyard or on the green outside. The world was still asleep; the little streets were empty; and beyond the quiet fields the gleaming reaches of the river crept towards London in the sunrise. All its streets and squares were still in shadow as the light touched the housetops, and the great city hardly stirred. But carriage-wheels, bearing two anxious gentlemen, were racing through the dawn towards the sleeping palace. They had left Windsor in the dim blue of a June night, and at daybreak they were still clattering through sleeping villages. But half the journey was behind them now. The road in front was paling fast between the tall midsummer hedgerows outlined against the dawn; and as the day came up, light flooded all the empty

[3]

fields, looked down the silent streets, gleamed in the bright curves of the river, danced in the racing wheels, and caught the windows of the sleeping palace, and the dawn of a new day swept round the world.

It was broad daylight in St. Petersburg by now, and the morning sun shone full on the proud line of great façades along the rushing Neva. It caught the rust-red rococo of the Winter Palace and the tall windows of the Hermitage beyond; and the slim spire of the Admiralty hung like a golden ghost in the pale summer sky. Churches, palaces, and prisons stood ranged in order beneath their gilded pinnacles and behind their colonnades; and as the sentries paced outside the palace gates in their tight uniforms, more sentries stood on guard at Peterhof beside the sea and the square towers of Gatchina and still more beneath the trees at Czarskoye Selo. It was a summer morning; and the guard was almost ready for the morning relief, while behind guarded doors the tall imperial figure of the Czar was strapped and buckled into one more uniform for one more review. He looked well in uniform. Indeed, he rarely left it after the eventful morning a few years earlier, when he had faced a roaring square of mutineers wearing the tunic of the Ismailovski Guards with a broad blue ribbon. That had been the day of his accession; and as he left the Winter Palace, the great square was black with soldiers cheering contumaciously for the Grand Duke Constantine and *Constituzia* (whom they hazily believed to be his wife). There was some scattered shooting, as the Czar shouted his commands. A charge of cavalry skated uncertainly across the freezing cobbles; and as the winter dusk was falling, he raked the crowded square with grape-shot. The rebels broke; the quays were black with frightened men running to safety by the frozen river towards the Islands and the Fortress of St. Peter and St. Paul that crouched behind its

[4]

bastions with the spectral finger of its slender spire pointing skywards in a perpetual warning. The brief Dekabrist attempt was over; and in the hush that followed the reign of Nicholas I began. That had been twelve years ago; and as the reign went on, the silence deepened. There was a deathly hush in Warsaw; and the busy fingers of the Third Section stopped the ears of Russia against the more disturbing sounds of Europe. School-children chanted their catechism—"What does religion teach us as our duty to the Czar? Worship, fidelity, the payment of taxes, service, love, and prayer; the whole being comprised in the words worship and fidelity"—and his barracks rang with the unpleasant rhythm of the *palka* (they called him Nicholas *Palkin*), as the Russian rod imposed the Russian discipline. Three thousand miles from east to west his faithful Cossacks swung their *nagaikas,* his *chinovniki* wrote their interminable reports on his devoted subjects, and his sentries stood at the palace gates in their tight uniforms, as the morning sun of 1837 looked down on St. Petersburg.

Westwards across the world the day was not yet high above Vienna. The Hofburg was still half in shadow, and Prince Metternich's obedient sovereign reposed among the trees at Schönbrunn. His capital was largely occupied that summer in applauding Fanny Elssler in the new *cachuca;* she gave five performances, at which she danced it more than twenty times, and had half Vienna serenading gratefully beneath her windows. Prince Metternich at sixty-five had passed a charming birthday, although the music afterwards had been a trifle overpowering and his advancing years made his young wife quite anxious, as she prayed heaven to preserve him for herself and for the whole world as well. The Prince was slightly anxious too; but that paladin of the *status quo* was nearly always anxious in a world that obstinately declined to stand completely still. Mankind with rare perversity refused to see that he had fixed its destiny once and for all nearly a quarter of a century ago in the peace-treaties of Vienna; and, what was worse, the intolerable Lord Palmerston seemed to abet it. For even peace-treaties are mortal; and those in question, if the truth must be confessed, were beginning to show signs of age, a painful thought for those among their authors who were still alive and felt as young as ever. The Poles were restless; the Italians were highly explosive; the forbidden tricolour floated over France once more with certain genteel reservations; and a series of alarming detonations from the Peninsula announced the rising temper of the Spaniards. But the Viennese viewed these alarms with equanimity amounting almost to complete unconcern. Largely untroubled by their imperial destinies, a taste for music and certain combinations of cream with coffee appeared to serve them as an agreeable substitute for a public mind; and their parochial felicity was undisturbed. Nothing stirred that morning in their little world, where elegance was represented by the dusty alleys of the Prater and art by the roulades of a galaxy of operatic talent. The trim sentries were on guard in their white uniforms; the Empire was at peace under the double-eagle on its yellow ground from depressing Polish villages along the Russian frontier to dusty garrisons eight hundred miles away in the Italian sunshine; and as the day came up, their bugles rang down the streets of Mantua, sounded in the deep shadow of the cathedral at Milan, and echoed over the lagoon at Venice.

The reveille went northwards across Germany. Buglecalls rang out in barrack yards, as Prussia called to Bavaria, Bavaria to Baden, Baden to Hesse-Cassel, Hesse-Cassel to Saxe-Weimar, and Saxe-Weimar to Saxe-Coburg-Gotha; and sentries paced outside the gates of every *Residenz* in uniforms of every colour. This military spectrum honoured

[6]

the diverse loyalties of that uncomfortable mosaic, the Germanic Confederation, where little kingdoms elbowed one another on a crowded background of grand-duchies, duchies, and still smaller units of Teutonic dignity. All the way across the Continent from the Tyrol to the Baltic sandhills the little towns of Germany began to stir in the first light of day. Wheels rattled over cobbles; shops were opening; shutters were being taken down; and the narrow streets began to stir again after the silence of the night.

Beyond the Rhine, beyond the long roads and the quiet fields of France the dawn broke over Paris. It caught the great loop of the river and the white shoulder of the new Arc de Triomphe and gleamed in the ranged windows of the Tuileries. The King was at the Château, where his sons, his daughters, his unmeaning smile, his moderation, and his domestic happiness alternately inspired and depressed his less judicious subjects. For it was the gay, the slightly rakish Paris of the *Comédie Humaine;* and the sober paces of King Louis Philippe were in imperfect harmony with that unrestful scene. Elegance, fighting a losing battle with the most unbecoming fashions, nightly reclined in easy attitudes on furniture of steadily increasing complication. Smiles and ringlets jostled high finance in anterooms; dishevelled poets perorated to untidy painters; and young Romantics, whose carefully disordered costume breathed a conscientious pursuit of the bizarre, made splendid gestures in attics on the heights beyond the river. Political exiles conspired in every language; victimised but strident, they announced the woes of Poland or the griefs of Italy, until the sympathetic French caught something of their tone and began to view a blameless monarch with resentment worthy of a sterner tyrant. That mirror of strictly constitutional propriety presided with a faint, but growing, uneasiness over the rising effervescence of his capital, where paving-stones were apt

[7]

to become barricades upon the least excuse. But now the streets were silent, as the piled roofs of Paris came up against the dawn beneath a forest of fantastic chimneypots. A few early workers hurried along empty pavements; red-trousered sentries lounged outside the Tuileries; and as the *diane* began to sound behind high barrack walls, the city stirred again in the first light of a June morning. On every side of it, mile after mile, the life of France resumed. Drovers plodded along country roads; mail-coaches rattled by; stray locomotives shrieked; clocks struck; windows began to open; and the day came up with the first morning sounds, as early voices called, doors were unbolted, and the hoofs rang smartly on provincial *pavés* down the long French roads.

There was a sharper note beyond the misty valleys of the Pyrenees, where startled villagers woke to the roll of musketry on Catalan hillsides and heard the Carlists feel their way from the bare uplands of Aragon towards the sea. Spain, stormy Spain began to stir that morning, as dawn came to the little green at Kensington asleep beneath its elms. The sun was up; all Europe would be waking soon; and the light swept westwards on its way across the Atlantic.

It was still night beyond the Western Ocean. A few lights glimmered on the coast of Maine; the little streets of Boston were discreetly lit; and there was quite a glare on the night sky above New York. Sparks poured from the congested smoke-stacks of steamboats on the Great Lakes and from eccentric locomotives panting along a few miles of abbreviated railroad tracks. Lights showed at little windows in New England and coastwise villages looked out to sea, where the *George Washington* packet, seven days out from New York with Prince Louis Napoleon homeward bound for Europe, sailed into the dawn. But behind them in America black waves were pounding empty beaches in the night. Mile after mile, the darkness stretched above a wilderness of empty fields except where the lights glimmered from a little township or a lonely farmhouse. Lights twinkled through the darkness above a narrow belt of close habitation between the mountains and the sea. There were lights in Albany and lights along the little sidewalks of Broadway and lights in the White House at Washington; and westward, where the road climbed from the decorous windows of Philadelphia through the dark woods of the Alleghenies, lights showed in the little towns of Ohio. But further west they died away into the darkness of an empty land, and the black waters of the Mississippi flowed through the night. Beyond the river unbroken darkness shut down on an empty continent; and the vast silence of America, two thousand miles from sea to sea, lay waiting for the dawn.

2. Kensington

THE DAWN came through the trees at Kensington, and the little green before the palace slept on beneath its elms. The sun rose higher, and the clock in its preposterous clock-tower above the gate was pointing to five, when a sound of wheels broke the cool silence of the morning. A dusty carriage rumbled up and halted at the gate; two anxious gentlemen alighted; but the sleeping palace was profoundly unaware of their arrival. They knocked, they pulled the bell, they thumped until a sleepy porter admitted them to the little courtyard, where their progress was arrested once again. For the front door was tightly shut; and when finally it opened, the visitors were turned adrift into an empty room on the ground floor and left to their own devices. The minutes passed; and as their presence seemed to have been quite forgotten in a sleeping household, they rang the bell. When it was answered, they desired explicitly that the attendant of the Princess Victoria might inform Her Royal Highness that the Archbishop of Canterbury and the Lord

[10]

Chamberlain requested an audience on important business. But this intimation failed to cause the slightest stir. The sleeping house resumed its silence; and after a decent interval they rang the bell again. This time their importunity produced a formidable German governess, who stated with authority that the Princess was at the moment in so sweet a sleep that she could not be disturbed. The visitors replied impressively that their business was with the Queen and that business of state must come even before her slumbers. The magic worked; the sleeping palace stirred; there was a sudden scurry overhead; and someone roused the Duchess, who woke her daughter (they slept in the same room) with the alarming news that the Archbishop and Lord Conyngham were both downstairs and wished to see her. It was six o'clock in the morning of June 20, 1837; and a new reign began.

She came into the room with her hair about her shoulders and a shawl thrown over her dressing-gown. One of the gentlemen knelt at her slippered feet to kiss her hand and tell her that the King had died and that she was Queen of England. The old Archbishop followed with some edifying details of her uncle's end and a little homily. His sermon at her confirmation had reduced the girl to floods of tears; and now her eyes were brimming. But she clasped her hands, sent a becoming message to her widowed aunt, and went upstairs to dress.

At breakfast she received a gentleman visitor from Belgium. For the old King was not her only uncle. Another uncle reigned in Brussels, and there was no sacrifice which her good uncle Leopold was not prepared to make for the instruction of a devoted niece. He had even spared his faithful Stockmar at the first news from England that the old King's health was failing; and that unobtrusive counsellor had been in London now for close on a month. She found his conversation most informing, since he was always full of good advice and often brought a letter from her sagacious uncle that was more helpful still. Life seemed a little less bewildering with her uncle's *most wholesome, prudent, sound,* and *excellent* advice administered at frequent intervals by the judicious Stockmar. She had assured his royal master of her complete confidence in their *good* and *invaluable honest* friend; and on that wild morning it was quite a comfort to have Stockmar talking to her while she was at breakfast.

For she began to feel her solitary state. Loneliness, it seemed, was the lot of Queens; she had so much to do that day, and nearly all of it had to be done alone. Had she not received her alarming visitors at dawn *alone,* as her emphatic diary recorded? And now a hasty scrawl from the Prime Minister informed her that Lord Melbourne would be calling early. She would have to receive him by herself; and the royal diarist reported afterwards with brave underlinings that she had seen him *quite* ALONE, as she should *always* do all her Ministers. But though unaccompanied, she was not quite alone in spirit. For when Melbourne came in Court dress to kiss her hand and she told him that it had long been her intention to retain him and his colleagues, that was precisely what her uncle Leopold had written to suggest that she should do. The Prime Minister struck her as straightforward, honest, good, and clever—as good and honest, it almost seemed, as the invaluable Stockmar—and, surrounded by so much virtue and sagacity, there were grounds for hope that she might be able to perform her task with fair success.

And what a task it was. First, there was her little speech to be recited to the Privy Council. Lord Melbourne had written it out for her himself, and it was a very fine one. Then she must write a letter to her poor aunt Adelaide at

Windsor Castle. And, above all, she must remember all the good advice that Uncle Leopold had given her—to be kind to everyone, to show a feeling for the Church without in any way encouraging persecution, to maintain conservative principles, and at the same time to keep the Whigs in office. It all sounded extremely difficult; but if her uncle Leopold was to be believed, the practice of these complicated arts was the right way for her to be Queen of England.

Yet there was so much about her kingdom that her sagacious relative had never told her. He was explicit upon the subject of Lord Melbourne and the Church of England; his views were definite about the proper attitude for her to take towards the poor Queen of Spain and the still poorer Queen of Portugal; nor was she left in any doubt of his opinions upon the state of parties. But England did not consist entirely of Lord Melbourne and Lord John Russell and Sir Robert Peel, although they sometimes talked as if it did; and her benevolent instructors had told the Queen extremely little about the country over which she was to reign. Her life had been a gentle alternation of Kensington and Windsor Castle, of quiet days with her mamma and visits to her slightly overwhelming uncle. True, there had been her little journeys every autumn; but these generally took her to pleasant places like Plymouth and Ramsgate and St. Leonards, though once on her way to Wales she had passed through Birmingham and seen a neighbourhood where the whole countryside—grass, houses, men, and women—all seemed to be quite black and fires glimmered ominously in distant engine-houses and little ragged children stood about near heaps of burning coal. On that occasion (it was just five years ago) she had visited the manufactories and found them "very curious." But there was no one in the royal entourage to tell her just how many of her future subjects were engulfed for twelve hours at a time in these curious resorts.

[13]

Her excursions to the north of England never encountered little droves of ragged children chanting,

We will have the Ten Hours Bill,
That we will—that we will.

They told her all about the properties of matter and the works of art at Eaton Hall; she developed marked preferences in the drama; and when she went to Portsmouth, she saw the place where Nelson fell. But how could she know how vastly different her country was from that for which he had died barely thirty years before?

England was changing round her; but the change was scarcely visible from Kensington. Somewhere out of sight a nation of countrymen was slowly turning into a nation of townsmen. Unsuccessful farmers were drifting into towns and setting up in business; their labourers were hewing coal or digging cuttings for the railways; and unnumbered children enjoyed the benefits of two hours' schooling in return for nine hours in a mill. But half England still lived in the country, and more than half was country-born. It was still a pink-cheeked population. For though the towns were growing fast, their growth was fed by a long stream of rustic immigrants. The countrymen were moving into town beneath a spreading pall from the blast-furnaces. It was an age of movement—of canals out-pacing waggons and of railways challenging canals. Long-necked locomotives puffed their way along five hundred miles of rails; excited speculators lent, promoted, borrowed, and intrigued for at least a thousand more; and burly men in corduroys swung pickaxes, as they bridged and tunnelled England into a new shape, or swaggered in their Sunday best of velveteens and red plush waistcoats and gulped their whisky, as a navvy should. The roads were emptier, as stage-coaches were taken off. The Tally-ho left for the last time, and the wheelers stamped no more outside the posting-houses. But the dwindling traffic moved faster, where the bagman in his gig dashed past on his way from town to stock his country customers, who would not have to wait for the slow recurrence of a country fair. All the world was moving faster now, when Irish butter came in steamboats and men began to talk of 'getting up the steam' and 'railway speed' and whole factories were operated by steam-power. It was an age of wheels—of wheels spinning at pit-heads as the winding-gear brought up the cages loaded heavily with coal and blackened colliers, wheels grinding into tunnels and along railway embankments, wheels humming endlessly above the bowed heads and the busy spindles of north-country mills.

The *tempo* of her country's life was quickening on every side, as the little Queen walked gravely through her ceremonial minuet that morning. Lord Melbourne paid a second visit, and the carriages began to arrive for the Privy Council. The Duke came from Apsley House, and it was a delicious thrill for young Disraeli to drive to the palace with an ex-Lord Chancellor. He got no further than the door, since he was not yet a member of Parliament, much less a Privy Councillor. But his eager fancy kindled at the scene— a summer day, 'a palace in a garden,' the aged peer's emotion, and so many eminent personages assembling to do homage to a girl. Inside the room her level voice was speaking the words that Melbourne had written out for her; and when she had done, they swore allegiance one by one. As her formidable uncles (for she had two more uncles) kissed hands as her subjects, she coloured to the eyes; and once or twice, when she was not quite sure what to do, her eye sought Melbourne's. The Duke said afterwards that if she had been his own daughter, he could not have wished for a better performance.

[15]

Her part concluded, she withdrew, received two or three Privy Councillors alone, wrote up her diary, saw Stockmar, and dined by herself. Then she went downstairs for another talk with Stockmar. Lord Melbourne called again that evening, and they had a very *comfortable* conversation which lasted more than an hour. A final word with Stockmar rounded off the day; and after that she said good-night to her mamma (for she would be sleeping by herself in future) and went to bed as Queen of England.

3. Washington, D. C.

WOULD THE DEPRESSION never end? It had all come so suddenly; but, to all appearances, there was no reason why it should ever go. A year before light-hearted operators were sailing gaily through one of those eras of prosperity with which the unparalleled expansion of the United States confounded sceptics. With population growing at the formidable rate of half a million souls a year and the tide of immigrants setting steadily towards the new lands west of the Alleghenies, there was a burst of trading in which values soared to unheard-of heights and investment became indistinguishable from speculation. New enterprises grew up overnight to dig canals, build railroads, and develop likely areas, to say nothing of unlikely areas as well. Mills, wheat lands, and cotton-fields were lavishly financed; and there were wild sales of lots in non-existent cities and hopeful flotations of gold-mines in Georgia. These operations were supported by a rickety substructure of unsound banking and an unsuspicious flow of eager money from abroad. The going, whilst it lasted through the happy days of Jacksonian prosperity, was good. The cotton crop doubled itself in volume and doubled itself again in value; town lots changed hands at fabulous levels; wages leapt up; and when prices rose in sympathy, nobody minded because everyone was making money and investing it again to make still more. The urban scene was gay with lavish spending of paper profits. Dance-music tinkled in a small New York that died away into the fields before its adolescent streets had got past their early Twenties and felt the Bronx to be half-way to Canada. It took horse exercise or sauntered round the wooden palings of Washington Square and strolled on the Battery to watch the spars of ocean packets come slowly up the Bay. A cheerful world left cards, bought shares, danced, bought more shares, and danced again; its infant city, faintly liquor-scented, with a deficiency of pavements and an abundance of politics, sustained the cheerful note; and far beyond the city limits the Harlem River flowed beneath its bluffs.

The pinch came that winter, when the cost of living became uncomfortably noticeable after a partial crop failure and a more than usually successful effort to corner wheat. A riotous assembly in New York denounced provision-dealers, landlords, and paper currency with fine impartiality and, passing from unsound economic theory to still unsounder practice, proceeded to destroy large quantities of flour in the apparent hope of bringing prices down by shortening supply. That was the first mutter of the storm. At the same time a readjustment of the public finances involved heavy withdrawals from the banks, who passed on the discomfort to their customers by calling in their overdrafts. And that was not the worst, since foreign lenders emphasised the situation (as foreign lenders always do) by pressing for repayment of their loans. This pressure rendered bankers still more apprehensive and less sympathetic to their customers; and as its credit suddenly contracted, it dawned on the community that it was gambling on a rise which had not come with overdrafts which it could not repay.

At this uncomfortable moment President Van Buren drove up the hill from the White House to his inauguration on a fine March day in 1837. His more fortunate predecessor drove with him in the phaeton, and Andrew Jackson listened while the little man read his Inaugural. It was a capable address in a marked tone of optimism; and a few days later the new President drove 'Old Hickory' to the railroad terminus and returned to the White House to face his problems. He was an accomplished politician; but perhaps the problems would be almost too exacting for his Parliamentary accomplishments. An able lawyer from the East, he had served a full apprenticeship in New York politics; and Albany had learnt to know the ingenious touch of 'Little Van.' Promoted to the Senate, he displayed considerable skill in party politics. His utterances wrapped a sharp intelligence in dignified circumlocution; and the clear-eyed New Yorker, as he moved among the jingling spurs and trailing scabbards of Southern eloquence, was promoted to be Andrew Jackson's campaign manager. For he had ideas that seemed to mark him as the heir—the deft and Parliamentary heir—of Jefferson; and, better still, he had a touch, which led men to call him 'the little magician.' Bland, persuasive, and ingenious, he reappeared as Secretary of State. His knowledge of affairs had once inspired the first of those Talmudic reinterpretations of the Monroe Doctrine by which the career of that portentous aphorism has been marked; and his term of office was quietly distinguished. His decorous progress resumed, the trim figure mounted another step and served a full term as Vice-President. Then the last ascent was scaled; the swelling breezes of Jacksonian Democracy filled his sails; and he was safe at last in the White House to face the nation's problems with his political accomplishments.

But would they suffice? It was extremely gratifying to be regarded as a wizard; but the grim situation of his fellow-countrymen in the spring of 1837 seemed likely to give him every opportunity to be one. The whole fabric of commercial life was creaking ominously, as he informed a crowded audience from the east portico at Washington that their happy polity embraced "an aggregate of human prosperity surely not elsewhere to be found." His statement, if it was intended to portray the facts, was bold; and if it was designed to manufacture public confidence by official optimism, it was singularly unsuccessful. For the words of his Inaugural were spoken in the first week of March, and within a month the bankruptcies began. New York, as usual, led the way with close on a hundred failures in the first week of April, followed in the next three days by thirty more. Then the pace quickened, and the deluge closed above their heads. Defaulting borrowers plunged into bankruptcy throughout the country, and a panic-stricken deputation found the magician at the White House almost irritatingly composed. The banks stood out above the flood for a few weeks; but as the waters rose, they vanished one by one. For Liverpool and Manchester were calling in their loans; and when the harassed bankers pressed their own customers for repayment in their turn, they were confronted with a row of bankrupts. It was a depressing outlook. Their own resources consisted largely of bad debts and shares in worthless undertakings; such of their customers as were still in credit began to clamour for their money; and the grim logic of the situation forced the banks to close their doors. New York led the way once more; Philadelphia, Baltimore, and Boston followed suit; and within a week the dismal sound of closing doors was echoed from Charleston and New Orleans. It was not ten weeks since the new President's announcement of unparalleled prosperity. Credit had vanished from the face of the United States; and even the Administration, whose resources had disappeared in the explosion, was reduced to printing currency with which to pay its clerks.

Distress was universal. There were wholesale dismissals; wages fell to vanishing point, since no one could afford to pay for the production of commodities which nobody could buy; and the whole machine, which had spun so merrily a year before, came to a dismal standstill. Depression reigned; and it was not much consolation that Congress would assemble in September. Until then the little wizard obstinately declined to wave his wand; but even if he did, it was more than doubtful whether the waves would subside at his command; and, in any case, sixteen million Americans would have to get through 1837 somehow. That harsh syllogism was more powerful than anything that President Van Buren was likely to do, and its consequences spread more widely in the United States than the last ripple of his policies. For, almost unperceived by wiseacres at Washington, the United States were changing; and the crash of 1837 was a fresh chapter in the change.

The seaboard colonies that George III had lost were still the nucleus. The Revolution, after all, was only sixty years away; and Van Buren had rejoiced sedately in his Inaugural that he was the first President who had not been born a British subject. Two generations of activity had advanced the frontier of development beyond the coastal region, beyond the mountains in pursuit of the receding backs of Indians. But the United States were still a territory whose main directions lay north and south. Beyond the Atlantic slope a vast expanse invited immigrants. The tide of population set irresistibly towards the West, as the bright prospect of a new start in life in a new country gleamed alluringly before Europeans and Americans alike; and a new start was never more attractive than after a disaster. One critic had described the West unkindly as "the *el Dorado* of all bad managers"; and in 1837 most Americans had been bad managers. So the westward tide flowed on and the new lands filled with the debris of disaster in the East, as the survivors picked up the pieces and 'cleared out' (in current idiom) 'for the New Purchase' or 'broke for the high timber.' A clearing in the woods was infinitely preferable to unemployment in a city street; and while depression brooded over bankrupt stores and unresponsive banks, the casualties filed steadily towards the West to begin life again.

That tendency was of vast significance. It tilted the whole country in a new direction and gave its territories a new depth. One day, perhaps, the lines of the United States would be redrawn. Their main direction was still north and south along the Atlantic slope. But if the westward tendency grew more pronounced, the old direction of the country might lose its meaning and the lines of the United States would run east and west across the continent. The road towards the West was clear for a good distance into the Indian lands beyond the Mississippi. But behind the Indians the way was barred by the long Mexican frontier slanting across the continent from the Great Plains to the Gulf. For the ultimate West—California, Nevada, Utah, New Mexico, Arizona, and Colorado—was owned by Mexico, and a foreign country lay between the United States and the Pacific. A breach in the long barrier appeared in the southwest, where Texas had declared its independence and petitioned for incorporation in the United States. A delegation appeared in Washington that summer; but President Van Buren, who had no desire to add a war with Mexico to his current problems, primly declared the strict neutrality of the United States.

Nor was he greatly interested by an eccentric correspondent who wrote to him that summer from a New York hotel, expressing his profound regret that he had been unavoidably prevented from calling on him at the White House. Indeed, to casual observers there did not seem to be much reason why he should have called, as his own government had been at some pains to deport him from France for a promising attempt to alter the succession to the throne one snowy morning at Strasburg. But Prince Louis Napoleon was nothing if not punctilious. True, his punctilio had not prevented him from putting on a uniform to which he was not entitled, appearing in a barrack square, and indicating to the assembled troops that his claims to their allegiance were vastly preferable to those of their present sovereign. In consequence of these impulsive acts he had been deported without trial and appeared in the United States. Neither was much impressed. His private tone was patronising; a minor poet found him dull; and the young man's belief that he would one day be Emperor of the French filled Mr. Gallatin with grave misgivings on the subject of his mental balance. Shortly afterwards he was recalled to Europe by his mother's health and passed through London in time to see Queen Victoria driving to her first Parliament.

But President Van Buren had graver things to think about than stray pretenders to the throne of France. The summer waned; grave colloquies discussed the terms on which the banks might be reopened; and the shortage of currency reduced some parts of the country to the simple processes of barter. The President's reflections, when they were presented to Congress, were not particularly comforting. Government, he said, was not intended to confer special favours on individuals or to create systems of agriculture, trade, or manufacture, much less to engage in them itself. The less it interfered, the better; for it was no part of its duty to make men rich or to repair private losses with public money. His economics were severely orthodox; his Deal was anything but New; and his countrymen were bleakly left to their own powers of recovery without a single wave of the magician's wand from Washington. It was all most discouraging; and irritated men began to whisper that their President had marred the republican simplicity of the White House by purchasing gold spoons in the intervals of driving round in an English carriage. The irritation ultimately drummed him out of office to the air of

> *Farewell, dear Van,*
> *You're not our man;*

and the more devastating chorus,

> *Van is a used-up man.*

But that was still three years away. Meanwhile, the crisis dragged its dismal length across the United States. There was no confidence; finance was dead; trade flickered fitfully; and unemployment shadowed half the country. It had all come so suddenly; and, to all appearances, there was no reason why it should ever go. Would the depression never end?

EIGHTEEN
FORTY–EIGHT

1. Windsor Castle

CHRISTMAS HAD BEEN a family affair with trees and presents for the children. The scene had changed; and now there was a royal nursery, to say nothing of a royal consort. Mamma was a dim figure in the Queen's background; the formidable governess had gone home to Hanover; her uncles had receded; even her uncle Leopold, true to the habits of a lifetime and still disseminating good advice from somewhere on the Continent, was heard faintlier now. But good advice, when she required it, was close at hand in ample quantities, since Albert was prepared (after some hesitation) to be the father of her country as well as of her children. For the Queen had somebody to lean on now.

That had always been her need. Of course it had been quite an adventure for her to ride out with her gentlemen and gallop about Windsor Park, or to review the Guards and know the sudden thrill of feeling just like a man—as though she could have led her troops to fight her enemies. And it had been delicious to monopolise the attention of so many wise and clever persons, to have good Lord Mel-

[27]

bourne explaining everything to her as they rode up and down the front at Brighton and to hear Lord Palmerston say the most diverting things about everybody, although he was sometimes a shade unkind. She was her own mistress now; and people had to wait until she spoke to them and then to answer all her questions. But there were so many things that she needed to know, especially when the boxes came with her official papers. She felt a little helpless then, and the old loneliness returned. True, she had mitigated it with Melbourne's company, as the Prime Minister sat bolt upright for hours beside her explaining everything in his easy manner. But that was different, because Lord Melbourne was a subject. Besides, he would not always be Prime Minister. That had been distressingly apparent when he was beaten in the House of Commons and she had to send for Peel. The "cold, odd man" alarmed her; and the royal pen dashed off a quivering confession that "the Queen don't like his manner after—oh! how different, how dreadfully different, to that frank, open, natural and most kind, warm manner of Lord Melbourne." A royal tantrum had staved off the danger. But the reprieve was only temporary. No Government could last for ever; and one day the Queen would find herself surrounded with uncongenial strangers. It was a most unpleasant prospect, and she began to feel her solitude again. It ended on her wedding day, when the trumpets sounded and the organ played and Lord Melbourne (who had kept them all in fits of laughter about the splendour of his new Court uniform) was much affected, and her diary closed for the day with "I and Albert alone." For henceforth her solitude would be a solitude of two.

Now she had somebody to lean on; and since she rarely did anything by halves, the Queen leaned hard. The pressure had transformed her consort from an amateur of mildly cultivated tastes into a collaborator whose equipment grew more formidable every day. Not that the transformation was entirely painless, since his own inclinations lay in the more innocuous direction of a passion for geology and organ solos in the twilight. But a rash invitation uttered in the first embarrassment of his engagement to a Queen involved him in more serious affairs. For he had begged Stockmar to come over and sacrifice his time to a young husband's guidance, "at least for the first year." What could be more suitable, since Stockmar had advised their uncle Leopold during his brief and tragic term as consort of a future Queen of England? The invitation was accepted, and Stockmar settled down with gusto to the formation of a Prince. His pupil was soon deep in private tuition with an authority on *Nisi Prius* and reading aloud from Hallam's *Constitutional History of England*. Now the comparative frivolity of fossils was kept for holiday occasions, and Albert settled down to learn his new profession. As the head of his wife's household he presently began to assert himself administratively as the head of her Household, which was quite a different thing; and the amiable Prime Minister was often favoured with his views on foreign policy, to which he rarely troubled to reply. But, whatever ministers might think, the Prince was gradually coming to regard himself as a many-sided functionary. One day his duties were enumerated in a long letter to the Duke of Wellington, who had thought Prince Albert might properly succeed him as Commander-in-Chief of the British Army. The Prince thought otherwise, however, since he already viewed himself "as the natural head of her family, superintendent of her household, sole *confidential* adviser in politics, and only assistant in her communications with the officers of the Government . . . the husband of the Queen, the tutor of the royal children, the private secretary of the sovereign, and her permanent minister."

[29]

The modest catalogue contained some disputable items, since the Crown was amply provided with constitutional advisers already, and the earnest student was unlikely to find much authority in Hallam for a permanent minister in her own family. But the Queen was even more unlikely to challenge them, as her devotion knew no limits and the happy partnership supplied exactly what she needed. For the two writing-tables side by side, his reassuring presence at her audiences with argumentative public men had robbed her work of half its terrors. His pen was always ready with a draft; his lucid mind reduced the most involved discussion to a clear minute; and whilst his charms had won her love, his memoranda earned her gratitude.

This dyarchy, which was entirely without precedent, failed to command the unqualified enthusiasm of her subjects. In the first years of the reign opinion had been favourably engaged by the appealing spectacle of a young girl in occupation of a seat which had been monopolised for half a century by ageing and not particularly pleasant men. Indeed, her tenancy was rendered yet more popular in its appeal by the happy circumstance that the sole visible alternatives were still more ageing and unpleasant men; and her subjects' heads were nodded in approval over 'little Vic.' Old Creevey, who had surveyed her uncles with grim distaste for years, chuckled delightedly over the rumour that she was "a resolute little tit"; and the reign opened on the happiest of notes. But such felicity could hardly last for ever. Youth—even royal youth—is perishable. The girl-Queen soon became a young woman and, what was worse, a young married woman with a nursery. Whilst it was highly reassuring to observe that the succession was abundantly secured, the spectacle was not romantic. For the prevailing canons of romance confined their sympathy to unprotected females; and the Queen was anything but unprotected.

Indeed, it had almost to be confessed that her protector's shadow began to fall between her and the eyes of her admiring subjects. The presence of a husband in a happy marriage was, of course, inevitable; but was it necessary for an inevitable presence to be felt quite so much? True, the prevailing marital philosophy required a male to loom considerably in his domestic circle. But must he really cast quite so long a shadow? The encyclopædic Stockmar had presided with incomparable judgment over his princely education. But it was almost to be feared that there were gifts which it was not within the power of that good fairy to bestow. For tact has rarely figured in the Teutonic repertory; and to critical observers there appeared to be a slight deficiency of tact in the growing zeal with which Prince Albert now discharged his mission. There was not, there could not be, the slightest room for doubt that he had a mission. Reluctantly persuaded of the fact by Stockmar, he had formed himself for its discharge by patient self-instruction; and his acceptance of it left nothing to be desired. That is was wholly for his country's good was undeniable. But countries do not always know what is good for them; and there were moments when Prince Albert's ubiquitous benevolence was slightly oppressive. His domination of the royal home, perhaps, was just what might have been expected of any contemporary pater-familias. But his pervasion of the Queen's official life was less acceptable, and her more disrespectful subjects sometimes called her 'Albertine.'

Their close collaboration had a further consequence, which ministers occasionally found embarrassing. In earlier days a smothered sentence from Lord Melbourne as he ate his apple or a facetious note from Palmerston had been enough to get the Crown's concurrence in a state paper or an act of policy. But now the case was sadly altered. All the old informality had vanished; the Crown was stiffer in its movements now; and the submission, which had once been little more than a casual and friendly form, became a grave administrative process of which the conclusion was anything but foregone. For the Teutonic view of monarchy accorded badly with Whig laxity. Besides, the Crown had got opinions of its own. Now the monarchy was more self-conscious than it used to be; its sense of duty had expanded; and if its duty was to be properly discharged, the Crown could not concur until it was convinced. That was not always easy, since it retained its own opinions for reasons which were lucidly expressed in memoranda from the Prince's hand. These models of reasoning and information were often of high value, as they frequently embodied the ripe fruit of Stockmar's wisdom, or as much of it as the Prince felt that ministers would understand. Those harassed functionaries were not disposed to underrate their unseen colleague; for Lord Palmerston confessed that Stockmar was "one of the best political heads he had ever met with," and Melbourne estimated him more casually as "an excellent man . . . a bad digestion." But it was a new complication of official life for men, who already had the Cabinet and Parliament on their hands, to have to struggle with the close reasoning of Stockmar's brightest pupil; and in the process the Queen's ministers observed without undue elation that they were not her sole advisers.

Such things, of course, were not unknown. Monarchs were only human, and their friendships were bound to count, as politicians under George IV discovered in the 'Cottage Coterie.' But this was something more substantial, which operated almost like a miniature department of state. It filed, it minuted, it wrote extensive memoranda; its views were carefully recorded; and, what was worse, its views had a slight but inevitable bias in the direction of Saxe-Coburg-Gotha. For Stockmar was the mainspring; and though his head rode clear above the European scene, his heart was never far from Rosenau. When Albert needed him in an extremity, the Prince begged him to "come, as you love *me*, as you love *Victoria*, as you love *uncle Leopold*, as you love your German Fatherland." The catalogue of all that Stockmar cared for was significant. Not that a Coburger's loyalty was narrow. If anything, it was a shade too wide, since the ducal house had ramified extensively, and devotion to its spreading branches involved attachments far beyond the insular requirements of British policy. Its foremost member reigned in Belgium; his daughter was a French princess; two nephews had married queens in Portugal and England; and he was, besides, the son-in-law of King Louis Philippe. At least four countries were united by these silken strands, to say nothing of the German loyalty which kept Prince Albert busy writing memoranda on the *Zollverein*. Their unity was touching; their point of view was nearly always right and uniformly directed to the preservation of European peace; but it was, to say the least, a complication.

The Queen smiled on the new apparatus for the despatch of royal business. Her need had always been for somebody to lean on, and it was richly satisfied. Besides, she had her children now. The passing years, a loving husband, and the royal nursery were changing her. The small, determined person of her early days was vanishing in a more domesticated figure. Her tastes had altered; she no longer wished to dance all night long; and it might be doubted whether she would still feel quite at home on horseback between Lord Melbourne and Lord Palmerston. That was not the kind of company that she was keeping now. Her taste for gay old gentlemen had left her. Indeed, the old gentlemen themselves were not so gay. Lord Melbourne, a shadow of himself, sat waiting for the end at Brocket. He was quite broken down, and the stream of politics had passed him by completely, although the patient could still keep up his melancholy make-believe by telling them how he had been lying awake half the night thinking how he should advise the Queen the next time that she sent for him. As for Lord Palmerston, his private cheerfulness was unimpaired; but his official life was anything but cloudless now. For they had travelled a long way since a girlish pen confided to the royal diary that he was "the one with whom I communicate oftenest after Lord Melbourne." True, their communications were still frequent, since Lord Palmerston was still her Foreign Secretary. But the old intimacy had vanished; for the Queen had other intimates. Their correspondence was conducted on a recurring note of royal disapproval of his lamentable tendency to send off important despatches before the Crown concurred; and Palmerston in leading-strings grew slightly fretful. He was unused to supervision; but the Crown knew its duty, and the royal mind was quite made up to put the Foreign Secretary in his place.

The Queen had grown more serious. In her present phase the loving wife shared all her husband's interests; and Albert's interests were the reverse of frivolous. Her operatic tastes had been reformed; now she sang Mendelssohn instead of Donizetti and discovered a new taste for oratorio; even her private orchestra had been reorganised to play those graver melodies of which the brass band had been incapable. Her travels were instructive now; a trip to Scotland put the Prince in mind of so many other places that it had almost the value of a Continental tour. For Perth reminded him of Bâle, Glasgow of Paris, and the Highland landscape alternately recalled Thuringia and Switzerland; few places could escape the net of his comparisons, though he confessed that Edinburgh was unlike anything that he had seen before. His gravity pervaded her; for though gay in company and capable of sustained merriment which visitors occasionally found exhausting, he was *au fond* profoundly serious. A vein of melancholy, which sought refuge at the organ in the dusk, had been transmuted by his education into a grave interest in lofty subjects; and the little Queen, who had once giggled at Lord Melbourne, followed her husband with admiring eyes as he journeyed upwards towards the silent peaks. Her tone was more subdued; she had improving interests; the palace lights were not so bright; and it was noticed that they went out earlier. Her first year on the throne had been a sort of girlish Regency, an innocent prolongation of the Eighteenth Century; but now the Queen was unmistakably Victorian.

The change was to her subjects' taste. For England had been passing gradually out of the Eighteenth Century. Twenty years before it would have been quite unthinkable for any member of the royal house to accept an invitation to preside at meetings of the Society for the Improvement of the Condition of the Labouring Classes or the Servants' Provident and Benevolent Society. The dynasty had been expected to preside (in uniform) over the fighting services or (in the height of fashion) over the social pageant. But it was not required to set the royal seal upon its subjects' good intentions. Indeed, few of its subjects who were privileged to come in contact with the Crown had any. For the Eighteenth Century was nothing if not realistic. The beneficiaries of privilege saw with the clear vision of their age upon which side their own advantage lay; and as they entrenched themselves, their view of the *terrain* was unimpeded by any haze of sentiment. With the exception of a few eccentrics, good impulses were left to humbler persons, who rarely reached the House of Commons; and in the main they were confined to Nonconformists in the provinces. But the Reform Act opened the flood-gates, and the middle class began to signify. The Duke of Wellington surveyed its Parliamentary conse-

quences with the bleak aphorism, "I never saw so many
shocking bad hats in my life." For the provinces had come
to town; and in the years that followed the middle classes
found their voice. Its note was heard with growing clarity
for the next thirty years; and as it sounded, the bland harmonies of the Eighteenth Century were drowned beneath a
swelling symphony of good intentions.

Circumstances had combined to lend it power, since the
new forces which were now admitted to participation in
affairs acquired at the same moment a vast increase of
weight from their growing wealth. Industrial development,
which blossomed rankly on the devastated moorlands of the
north of England, transferred the British middle class from
retail into wholesale trade; and this promotion had vast
consequences in the field of public morals. For impulses,
which had been quite ineffective so long as they were confined to shop-keepers, acquired fresh meaning when the
shop-keepers had grown into manufacturers and politicians.
The country was no longer ruled by a committee of well-
connected land-owners; and it soon became apparent that
the provinces had come to town. New questions of trade
policy first claimed and then absorbed attention; and as
three-fifths of British exports were in the form of textiles,
the voice of Manchester was decisive in their solution. Mr.
Bright and Mr. Cobden thundered at packed meetings of
the Anti-Corn-Law League; the land-owners manned the
threatened walls of their citadel; and as it crumbled, the
Corn Laws were repealed. That choice was vital to the
whole course of English life. For England had decided to
recognise the *fait accompli*, to leave agriculture to its fate,
and to be what it had inadvertently become—a manufacturing country. There was a new hierarchy now in place of the
old landed dignitaries. The middle class assumed the sceptre;
manufacturers and shippers were the new masters of the

state; and by a happy chance the state was crowned by a Court in which they saw their own domestic ideals soberly reflected.

The congruity went deeper still, since the moral tone of England was rising fast; and the polite scepticism of the Eighteenth Century was presently submerged, as Evangelicals and Nonconformists brought virtue into fashion and, at the opposite extreme of spiritual thought, a new austerity breathed from the towers of Oxford. The fellow-countrymen of Dr. Pusey and Lord Shaftesbury were not light-minded. It was an age of church-building and systematic piety, of religious controversy and private struggles with unruly consciences. Strict belief became a duty; and morality, which had once been treated as a private foible, became the indispensable condition of respectable existence. A bold schoolmaster had announced the aims of education in an order that was most significant: "1st, religious and moral principles; 2ndly, gentlemanly conduct; 3rdly, intellectual ability"; and as Thomas Arnold applied his noble formula for the production of Christian gentlemen, he went far to provide England with a new governing class.

The need for one was evident, since the new direction of the nation's economic life had plainly superseded the old aristocracy of rank dependent on the ownership of land. The great decision of 1846 had deposed land from its position of supremacy; and even if the Corn Laws had not been repealed, the claims of rank had been profoundly shaken by the challenge of the French Revolution. Besides, it hardly satisfied the moral temper of the nation; and the eager Doctor under the elms at Rugby was creating a new aristocracy of character, a class of Englishmen whom their contemporaries recognised as 'thoughtful, manly-minded, conscious of duty and obligation.' He did not live to see the full results; he did not even live to see his school's example widely followed. That came afterwards. For his influence endured and widened; but its place of origin was not without significance, since Rugby was in the Midlands, almost within sight of the pit-heads and factory gates, where the new forces of the middle class began to train for leadership. The training was profoundly moral; its limitations, with strict taboos of thought and conduct, were obvious; but it produced a type of Englishman that was a total innovation and completely modified the nation's standards. That product was, perhaps, the noblest of the Queen's reign, since it replaced a slightly supercilious aristocracy with the ideals of gentlemen.

Such tendencies were in close harmony with the Court's increasing gravity. If Christmas had been a family affair at Windsor Castle, it had been the same in ten thousand English homes. The New Year resolutions of the royal children, which a proud father eagerly retailed to Stockmar, were echoed by his wife's youthful subjects; and the forbidding work, which Stockmar recommended for the Queen's perusal as having been specially written for ladies and prescribing an amiable and gentle disposition and the avoidance of frivolity, was just the volume that her subjects would have considered suitable for female reading. For if the Queen was unmistakably Victorian, so was the age.

2. Mexico City

ON THE LAST DAY of the month a mounted messenger left Querétaro for the south. Riding fast, he covered eighty miles a day and, to everyone's profound relief, was in the capital by the next evening. The whole of January had been filled with agitated comings and goings between United States headquarters in Mexico City and the temporary seat of government. General Scott, an enterprising gentleman from the State Department, the *de facto* government of Mexico, and an obliging intermediary from the British Legation danced an apparently interminable saraband round the problem. One armistice had expired already and been followed by the storm of Chapultepec and the last street-fighting in the capital, which ended with United States marines in the Palacio Nacional and the Stars and Stripes floating lazily on the great *plaza* opposite the Cathedral. And that, one might have thought, settled the matter. But this was reckoning without the national aptitude for delay and the real difficulties of the situation. Few governments whose command of popular support is precarious welcome

[39]

with any promptitude large cessions of their territory, even
when those cessions are to be made for cash and to an undefeated enemy who is in occupation of their capital. So
the *pourparlers* pursued a dignified and rotatory course,
until the conqueror let it be known that he was prepared for
further conquests unless something could be settled. There-
upon the *tempo* of their correspondence quickened; the last
scruples vanished; and when the messenger arrived, his
saddle-bags were found to contain authority to sign a treaty
with the United States.

They signed it the next afternoon at Guadalupe-Hidalgo
just outside the city; and when the signatures were dry, they
trooped across the street into the dim Colegiata and gave
thanks under the great dome. And all of them had much
to be thankful for. The Mexicans could celebrate the end
of a remarkably disastrous war, in which the ingenuities of
patriotic dialectic might manage to detect a victory or so.
But these were of the most technical description, since they
had invariably been followed by retreats which left the
invading forces in undisputed occupation of all their objectives; and the main thing to be thankful for was that the
war was over. True, they had parted with the whole of
Texas and a strip of the adjacent province of Tamaulipas
north of the Rio Grande. But that was not much loss, as
they had not exercised the least authority in Texas for the
last twelve years. A more extensive amputation, for which
they were compensated by the noble sum of $15,000,000,
simultaneously removed the provinces of Upper California,
New Mexico, and Santa Fé. This was more serious, as the
lost provinces stretched more than a thousand miles from
east to west; and by their surrender the northern frontier
of Mexico was instantly withdrawn six hundred miles,
slipping from the mountain-sides that look into Oregon to
the parched lands of Arizona. But New Mexico consisted

mainly of deserts and a few unromantic *pueblo* Indians; and the Mexicans were not greatly interested in California, where a long seaboard backed uncomfortably on to the coast range and a vast, unprofitable *hinterland*. Its little ports, where a few soldiers yawned in a *presidio* or a Jesuit mission crumbled in the sun, might have a slight value. But as there were barely six thousand Mexicans in the whole attenuated province, it meant little more to them, with its long coast and unexplored interior, than a few seaports scattered along a sort of Chile. It might mean more, of course, to enterprising neighbours. That was another drawback about California. For it already seemed to exercise a fatal attraction on the most undesirable immigrants. There were only a few hundred of them; but they tended to coagulate in lawless little nuclei, which concentrated on the more vigorous forms of money-making without regard to the less active standards of their Mexican *milieu*. Indeed, they harmonised with it so slightly that local aspirations had begun to turn in the direction of independence; and there could be little doubt that California would ultimately go the way of Texas. These uneasy stirrings in a distant province, which lay eccentric to the main areas of Mexican existence, reconciled them to its loss; and the removal of its northern prolongation made Mexico far more compact. But the transfer of California had a larger significance, since it gave free play to the westward thrust of the United States; and as the organ muttered in the great basilica, it was quite evident that the Protestant worshippers had the more substantial grounds for thanksgiving—more, indeed, than any of them realised that afternoon at Guadalupe, since someone had discovered gold in a mill-race eighty miles behind San Francisco just a week before.

That news, which brought Marshall riding in to Sutter's Fort in the last week of January 1848, was quite unknown to Washington and to the plenipotentiaries in Mexico; and their prayers were mingled in sober thanksgiving that the war was over. It had been a strange affair of slightly doubtful origins, which left each side convinced that it was profoundly in the right. For when President Polk nerved himself at last to admit Texas to the Union, he had sent an army to protect it whose operations seemed to Mexicans to constitute a plain violation of their northern frontier. The first shots rang out on the Rio Grande, and a nation of twenty millions went to war with eight million Mexicans. But the contest was less unequal than might have been expected, since the United States in 1846 were singularly innocent of military organisation, while the Mexicans had a rare aptitude for the more athletic forms of war. On the invading side, indeed, the main qualification for high command appeared to be distinguished service in the War of 1812. Besides, it was anything but simple to penetrate a territory fringed with a variety of deserts. Brown deserts, grey deserts, green deserts, deserts of all colours and uniformly unpleasant texture barred the road all the way across the country from Chihuahua to San Luis Potosí; and the watching mountains on the sky looked down at the perspiring *gringos,* as they plodded through the chaparral. A year of desultory fighting found the invaders from the north less than half-way to the capital and left Lieutenant Grant and Captain Braxton Bragg with disrespectful views of their superiors, which were not altogether shared by Colonel Jefferson Davis of the Mississippi Rifles. In the next phase a more enterprising strategy directed a descent by sea on Vera Cruz and a thrust up the steep road to Mexico City. This operation, watched by the sharp eyes of Captain Robert E. Lee and Lieutenant Beauregard, was more successful; and the first days of 1848 saw them in occupation of the capital. Indeed, they had been there for some weeks; but the big-hatted Mexicans still stood to stare at the *gringos* mounting guard outside the palace in the dusty square, whilst at Chapultepec the Stars and Stripes fluttered above the citadel that Spanish viceroys had built on Montezuma's hunting-lodge.

This naked exercise of military force was rich in civil consequences. For the resulting peace-treaty destroyed the last formal barrier which stood between the westward march of the United States and the Pacific. After the signatures that day at Guadalupe-Hidalgo the Mexican frontier no longer slanted from the Platte River to the Gulf, but stretched trimly almost due east and west across the narrowing waist of the continent from San Diego to the Rio Grande; and the United States ran clear from sea to sea. That fact was the direct and simple consequence of President Polk's slightly equivocal diplomacy; and in their results the scrambling victories of the Mexican War were more fruitful than any battle fought on American soil since Yorktown. The West was open; the United States had ceased to be a territory whose main directions ran north and south. Its government controlled the entire width of the continent; and after the new acquisitions of 1848 the whole country turned as on a pivot to face the West.

This pivoting of the United States, which followed an apparently trivial dispute with an unimpressive neighbour, was an event of vast implications. For it implied that the United States had changed direction. The lines of the whole nation had been redrawn; and now the main directions of its life ran east and west. The fact was plain, and its decisive impact diverted the main stream of the nation's history. The old lines were not yet effaced. Indeed, they lasted long enough to necessitate a tragic readjustment. For the North was still the swarming, energetic North where smart New Yorkers looked for openings in business and New England nursed its conscience; and the South, the languid South, dreamed comfortably of its own superiority and sipped its drinks and grew more cotton, as it reflected on the shaded porches of plantation houses that slave labour had been ordained by Providence and was quite inexhaustible, or looked out between white pillars at the dim magnolias and the long vista of the cotton-fields. But North and South had ceased to form the whole of the United States; and the addition of the West shifted the whole balance of the country.

The old divisions began to lose a little of their meaning, as the new proportions of the country emerged. For the United States were no longer the mere *hinterland* of an Atlantic seaboard and had become trans-continental. New lands and the discovery of gold in California were an irresistible incentive to the westward drive; and the nation's life flowed into the new channels of the trans-continental routes. That was the key to the next transformation of the country. For the true history of the United States is the history of its communications. Hitherto the river steamers of the Mississippi had served to penetrate the *hinterland,* as the flat-boats of an earlier age had served on the Ohio and the Erie Canal to the air of

> *Hi-O,*
> *Away we go,*
> *Floating down the river on the O-hi-O!*

or the more convivial measure,

> *You'll always know your neighbour,*
> *You'll always know your pal,*
> *If you've ever navigated on the Erie Canal.*

All the way from New Orleans to St. Paul the tall funnels of the old stern-wheelers glided up the endless reaches of the river; the bayous of the South receded and the interminable levées slid past, as a congested company of fellow-travellers smoked, gambled, played, and sang their way slowly into the Northwest. Starting from New Orleans and alive with steamboat characters and Southern colour, that had been the main thoroughfare of the United States. But the line of the great river ran almost due north and south; and when the country pivoted to face the West, the Mississippi steamboat ceased to satisfy more than a local need. The nation's need was now for the trans-continental routes into the further West; and this devastating change in its direction left the South in a back-water, its trade diminished, its wharves emptier, and its steamboats superseded.

The march into the West continued. But now it went by the Overland trails under the tall prairie skies. Due west from the raw farm-lands of Iowa the great ox-waggons jolted slowly forward, as the axles whined and the 'bull-whackers' cracked their whips over the straining backs. The men tramped alongside, and the women in the prairie-schooners looked out beneath the tilts to watch the unchanging Plains go by. Ten miles a day the march went on, with an occasional alarm of Indians or a stampede of cattle and the teamsters frying bacon in the dawn with unmusical accompaniments to wake the waggon-train for another day and ten more miles over the never-ending prairie. Along the trail a scattered line of graves, foundered waggons, oxen bones, broken bottles, and discarded household gods lay under the wide sky to show that other folk had passed that way; and the slow march went on into the West.

Now there was no impediment except the endless distances between them and the fabulous valleys of California. The earth, the sky, the roaming herds of buffalo, the slow lift of the prairie as it rose and fell beneath the white-topped waggons like an ocean swell were all American; and they were free to move across it, as the waggon-trains wound slowly forward over the green immensity. For it was all their country now. That circumstance was not without its consequences for one contingent that was on the move that year. The followers of Joseph Smith, who had been favoured with extensive revelations in a fair reproduction of the prose mannerisms of the Authorised Version, were a compact organisation known to themselves as the Church of Jesus Christ of Latter-day Saints and more briefly to their neighbours, from the title of their sacred book, as Mormons. A close community, secretive habits, strange religious terminology, and an annoying tendency to work extremely hard gave rise to misunderstandings, which soon turned to persecution; and their settlements drifted slowly westwards, impelled by local unpopularity and their own taste for independence. They had reached Illinois in their *hegira*, when it was decided after a martyrdom or so that the Saints could not do better than shake off the dust of the United States and seek a fuller freedom further to the west in the vague territories of Mexico. Somewhere beyond the sunset, it was hoped, the Mormons would be free from prying neighbours to plough and sow and reap and live according to their tenets; and a migration of Biblical proportions was planned for a community of fifteen thousand souls under the firm leadership of Brigham Young. Illinois was left behind, as the Saints crossed the frozen river into Iowa and headed for the last outpost of the United States. But while the Mormon waggons creaked across the Plains, war opened in the south. It was past midsummer and General Scott was circling the last Mexican positions outside their capital, when Brigham Young rose in a jolting carriage on the last slope of the Wahsatch Mountains, stared out across the gleaming levels of the Great Salt Lake, and exclaimed, "This is the place: drive on." For the Saints had found their kingdom. This was to be the State of Deseret, named from the honey-bee in the strange nomenclature revealed to Joseph Smith. But six months later a treaty signed fifteen hundred miles to the south of them in Mexico had incorporated their territory in the United States.

The march went on through the first weeks of 1848; and an interminable line of waggons wound through Emigration Canyon to the broad valley and the forty-acre lot where they were to build their Temple. The streets were planned; the crops were planted; and when their first wheat was attacked that summer by a pest of crickets, wave after wave of white seagulls came sweeping from the islands in the lake to circle the little fields and save the first crop of the Mormon settlers by an intervention that seemed miraculous. The settlement struck root, although an accident of war retained the Territory of Utah for the United States; and when the news of gold in California sent the 'Forty-niners' surging westward on the Mormon Trail, the eager travellers halted in the new City of the Great Salt Lake to trade their spare possessions in the little Mormon stores and to renew their teams for the last struggle up the Rocky Mountains. For the United States was entering upon its new possessions, and the world was on the move.

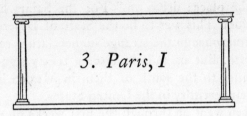

3. Paris, I

THE CROWDS in the streets were quite good-humoured.
Indeed, if they knew anything of politics, they had good
reason to be cheerful. For it was known in Paris on that
Wednesday evening in the last week of February, 1848,
that the King had taken fright and thrown M. Guizot over-
board—the unbending Guizot, who was so tightly buttoned
in his coat and had prohibited a harmless function, at which
deep-chested Opposition orators proposed to fortify their
friends with light refreshments somewhere beyond the
Champs Elysées and make long speeches on the blameless
subject of Reform. The week had opened in a pleasing
flutter of uncertainty as to the Government's intentions.
Would it allow the demonstration? And if it did not, would
the demonstration still take place? As so often happens,
the event proved to be a blend of both alternatives. For the
entertainment was prohibited; but something happened all
the same. Not very much, indeed; but quite enough to bring
the troops out round the Palais Bourbon and to keep
mounted police busy all the afternoon clearing the Place de

la Concorde. It had been raining, and their horses slipped about the road to an accompaniment of stones from small boys and rude remarks from the crowd sitting round the fountains. The old King was watching from the Tuileries; and as his subjects scattered across the great square outside, he turned to someone in the palace with the comfortable reflection that, when he chose, the crowds would disperse as easily as the sand with which he was sprinkling a royal signature on the sheet in front of him. After all, a little rioting was no novelty. The monarchy had survived a good many years of intermittent street-fighting in Paris, and the disorders hardly seemed more formidable than usual. There were a few scuffles in the Champs Elysées; and that afternoon somebody pulled up some railings, which came in extremely useful for levering the paving-stones to build a barricade or so. The short February day was ending, as the soldiers cleared the streets. A few shots were fired, and after dark some cheerful spirits made an immense bonfire of all the park chairs. But the old King was confident, and by midnight his troops were back in barracks. On Wednesday morning the situation was less healthy. There were more barricades; and the rioters developed a distracting tendency to cheer the troops and offer them refreshments, which did not facilitate their mission of restoring order. Besides, an injudicious inspiration of the Government had called out the National Guard. These middle-class Prætorians were an embarrassing addition to its forces, since they were not untouched by Liberal opinions and somewhat officiously assumed the more exacting *rôle* of intervening between the army and the crowds. It was quite hard enough to clear the streets without this added complication; but when the voluntary force took to cheering for Reform and obstructing the embarrassed regulars in the discharge of their distasteful duty, it became almost impossible. The King was

[49]

graver now. For the monarchy reposed almost exclusively on middle-class support; and if the National Guard deserted him, it was uncomfortably evident that something must be done. So M. Guizot was dismissed, and a cheering Chamber was informed that M. Molé had been invited to form a Government instead. The news was gratifying; and although the soldiers were still busy in the streets, the crowds were quite good-humoured.

They had every reason to be cheerful, as there was to be a change of government with a good prospect of Reform, whatever that might mean. For M. Odilon Barrot the future held a pleasant prospect of Parliamentary triumphs on the English model, with M. Odilon Barrot controlling the nation's destinies in the majestic *rôle* of a more eloquent Sir Robert Peel; for little M. Thiers a cognate vision danced before his fancy, with M. Thiers as an improvement on M. Odilon Barrot; and a cheerful crowd paraded up and down the boulevards, shouting for lights in every window and cheering impartially for Reform and for the King. When they had got as far as the Place de la Bastille, they marched round the July Column and sent up a great roar of *"Vive la Réforme!"* adding a respectful cheer for the massed soldiers in the square. Then they headed for the mean streets, emerging later in still larger numbers with torches and tricolour lanterns, singing songs and waving banners as they tramped along. The passers-by watched comfortably from the pavements, and it occurred to somebody that it would be a good idea to call on M. Guizot and break his windows. It was about half-past nine as they marched off in the best of spirits on this cheerful errand. When they arrived, the house was guarded by a battalion of infantry. The head of the procession halted, and they cheered the soldiers. But one of the rioters, who was carrying a torch, kept waving it in the face of the commanding officer. It was an awkward moment; and his challenging behaviour exasperated or alarmed an irritable sergeant, who shot him dead. (The shot was fired by a Corsican named Giacomoni, whose impulsive trigger-finger changed the course of history.) The shot broke the strained nerves of the unhappy soldiers, who fired a ragged volley into the crowd in front of them. The crowd stampeded, and the terror-stricken soldiers bolted in the opposite direction. The street emptied, as the echoes died away. But it was not quite empty. For at that range their volley had been deadly, and the dark road was littered with bodies. When the crowd crept back to the street-corner and saw its dead, a great moan went up. By some chance a van was driving past on its way to a railway station. They loaded it with bodies, and the van rumbled off between lines of raging men with torches in their hands. A single shot had done its work; and Paris had grown dangerous.

From that instant events marched with terrifying rapidity. Molé refused to form a Government that night, and Thiers was sent for; Marshal Bugeaud took command of the troops; and in the dawn Paris heard the tocsin clashing wildly from its steeples. The tide was rising fast. By Thursday morning the crowds that had been quite content on Wednesday to shout *"Vive la Réforme!"* had found another cry; and the more ominous refrain of *"A bas Louis-Philippe!"* was heard in the packed streets. By eight o'clock the troops were hopelessly entangled in a network of barricades and argumentative Parisians. By half-past ten they had fallen back dispiritedly on the palace, leaving their guns and a good deal of their ammunition in the doubtful custody of the crowd. Inside the palace a confused committee of scared politicians and dejected royalties surveyed the unpleasing situation. The resourceful Thiers favoured a prompt withdrawal to St. Cloud until the hurricane had spent itself. But even that retreat was hardly practicable unless the King could count upon his troops. So the old man, watched from the palace windows by his womenfolk, rode slowly out to review them with M. Thiers walking by his horse's head. There was an uncomfortable silence, broken by a few cries of *"Vive le Roi!"* and then the National Guard, his faithful bourgeoisie, was cheering wildly for Reform. His Praetorians had failed him, and the old King sharply turned his horse's head towards the palace. There was a hurried argument inside; and as the sound of firing drifted into the room, he signed his abdication.

The reign was over. Paris was a sea of roaring faces, shots, songs, distracted politicians, and gesticulating workmen. Presently an old man in a hat and coat hurried out of the palace with a lady on his arm and a big portfolio of papers. As they went down the palace garden, the sound of shots still followed them. On the great square outside the palace between the river and the Obelisk they found three dishevelled cabs and bundled into them. The cabdrivers whipped up their horses; a faithful valet ran behind; and with a meagre escort trotting alongside the last French king turned his back on the Tuileries and drove up the hill towards the Arc de Triomphe.

The old King had started on his travels. Behind him, in the uproar of the Chamber, a brave woman pleaded for his grandson and a Regency. But the mood of Paris had already travelled far beyond kings and regents. The rising tide had swept the monarchy away; and they were faced with a Provisional Government of M. de Lamartine, three politicians, and a working man. Far down the road to the seacoast a tired old man, unshaved and wholly unrecognisable, had taken off his wig. For the reign was over. Almost inadvertently the Second Republic had arrived; and 1848 was quite unmistakably 1848.

4. Continental

THE GALE was rising fast, and all the windows of the
world began to rattle. Shutters were bolted hastily, as
Ministers of Police pulled longer and still longer faces; and
as the hurricane roared overhead, European royalties like
anxious householders exchanged agonised reflections on the
prospects of a precarious and changing world. Public men
were torn between the uncomfortable alternatives of making
good (if they were Liberals) their own liberal professions
or conserving (if they were Conservatives) by active measures of defence a *status quo* which in many countries had
grown obviously indefensible. As on an earlier occasion
when the Paris streets had led the dance and challenged an
existing order, irresponsible observers might feel a sympathetic thrill—

> *Bliss was it in that dawn to be alive,*
> *But to be young was very heaven!*

Quite the reverse, however, to be a reigning sovereign in
1848. Queen Victoria, almost overwhelmed by "these *awful,*

[53]

sad, heartbreaking times," surveyed the Continent with frank bewilderment and wrote with melancholy emphasis to Brussels, " '*Je ne sais plus où je suis,*' and I fancy really that we have gone back into the *old* century." For the drums of '93 began to throb once more in nervous ears. The catastrophe in Paris almost staunched her uncle's flow of good advice; the King of Prussia threw himself (by correspondence) at her feet, alluding freely to his Maker and inviting Palmerston to make a public declaration in the slightly unexpected character of St. George; her Prince was feverishly busy with his papers; and Baron Stockmar's memoranda reverberated with the mournful regularity of minute-guns.

The Revolution had swept France; there could not be the slightest doubt of that. But would it break the dams and flood the waiting levels of the Continent beyond the French frontier? That was the problem which filled all their dreams and strained their waking hours. The poor French princess at Claremont was still haunted by a nightmare recollection of the yells of Paris and "those *fiend-like faces*"; and the same apocalyptic vision disturbed her royal relatives on every throne in Europe. For the grinning mask of revolution had appeared once more above the sky-line of a comfortable world; and thoughts began to turn to '93, to the red glare over Paris and the mounting horror of the *Marseillaise,* the pounding drums and marching columns of a new Republic and the dreadful contagion of the 'fool-fury of the Seine,' and the impending flood which Europe had dammed up so carefully in the peace-treaties of Vienna. Some horrified observers could see it all quite clearly, when the first news of the French explosion reached St. Petersburg at a Court ball in the Winter Palace and the tall figure of the Czar strode into the centre of the floor, holding a paper in his hand and shouting, "Gentlemen, saddle your horses: France is a Republic!" For it was plain to that robust intelligence that, if the French had challenged monarchy, the Cossacks must ride again to save it.

But the situation was not quite so simple. The uproar, indeed, was universal; in those spring weeks of 1848 a simultaneous impulse swept Rome, South Germany, Milan, Vienna, Venice, and Berlin. There was a sound of breaking glass in every Continental capital west of the Russian frontier; all the streets were full of scared police and shouting, singing mobs; and the output of individual eloquence reached terrifying proportions. But there was very little unity about the general uproar. For the voices which composed this stupendous aggregate of sound were all pitched in different keys and called vociferously for the most diverse improvements of their lot. Italians demanded to be governed by themselves rather than by Austrians, whilst Austrians in turn demanded to be governed by anybody rather than by Metternich; Czechs, Hungarians, and Croats collided in an ill-directed passion for self-government; and Germans were divided between a comprehensible determination to be governed better and a vaguer aspiration to be governed in a larger, more impressive unit than those provided by the thirty-eight constituents of the Germanic Confederation. Flags of every colour fluttered in all directions; there was a riot of new constitutions; and disappearing ministers eluded the unfriendly attentions of their fellow-countrymen with the agility of trap-door artistes. Competing voices clamoured the attractions of the most diverse beliefs on every side; and rival European prophets, each more inspired than his competitors, emitted their divergent teachings in a carnival of contradiction. While Mazzini and Manin insisted with sublime reiteration on the importance of being Italian, Teutonic voices emphasised the higher duty of being German. Parliamentarians praised parliaments, and patriots of every race—Poles, Magyars, and Slavs—exalted their own nationalities without the least regard to other people's. Not that the prophetic voices were exclusively optimistic in their tone or national in their objectives. For while bright-eyed reformers hymned the march of progress and Kossuth and Palacký intoned their national anthems, Carlyle retained the gravest doubts as to the utility of things in general and King Leopold's police removed a sage from Brussels, whose beliefs (in the convenient form of the *Communist Manifesto*) came dangerously near to a denial of the whole existing order. Karl Marx, an irritable person whose acute intelligence mistook his own continuous irritability for a critical analysis of other people's views, enlarged the field of controversy; and the harsh voice of economics was added on the general uproar to the more simple-minded cries of politicians and the clash of races. His influence, since he possessed in a unique degree a genius for disagreement, had hitherto been slight; and a *Weltanschauung,* which bore a distressing resemblance to a protracted bilious attack, made strikingly few converts in an age which obstinately believed that a new day was dawning on the world and that the whole tide of history had turned in the spring days of 1848. But though their author was deported and his readers were extremely few, it was significant of a confusing prospect that the words of his appeal stood in the peroration of his latest pamphlet: "Workers of the world, unite!"

So economics, politics, and racial aspirations combined in one enormous aggregate of discontents; and the winds blew from every quarter of the European sky upon the edifice of the existing order. Startled heads were thrust from windows and, according to their owners' temperament, were hastily withdrawn or stayed in fascinated contemplation of the catastrophe. Kings abdicated or appeared on balconies before cheering crowds in the most progressive attitudes. The King of Prussia, after a tentative attempt to shoot his subjects down, rode through his capital in the new colours and an uninterrupted series of alfresco speeches designed to satisfy them that he was the insurrection's latest and most voluble recruit; the King of Bavaria, with more restraint, followed Lola Montez into private life; the Kings of Hanover and Saxony indulged their subjects with becoming shades of Liberal concession; the King of Sardinia granted a constitution and, succumbing to the prevailing atmosphere, went to war with Austria for love of Italy; and the Pope himself pronounced the fashionable formulæ with creditable gusto.

As the gale rose, ministers came crashing down like trees. The wind was highest in Vienna, where the old order at its most decorative exposed the largest surface and the least resistance to the gale; and its rich ornament was devastated when a sudden gust of insurrection sent Metternich crashing from his pinnacle. That was the most significant event of the whole European year. For Metternich was more than a man. He was a principle; and when the Prince sat quietly receiving London visitors at the Brunswick Hotel in Hanover Square, it was the end of an age. His Emperor might hang precariously on the edge of abdication, and the Pope might flit about the Romagna in disguise; but these were casual events compared with the eclipse of Metternich. For his momentary disappearance broke the historic continuity of an epoch. That name had been the emblem of a whole system of international relations and domestic government that centred in Vienna. It was the repartee of Continental Europe to the unpleasant stir of French ideas and Napoleonic imperialism; and the system seemed durable enough, embodied in the post-war reconstruction of the Continent by the peace-treaties of Vienna and the impressive edifice of the Hapsburg *Polizeistaat*. The Metternich tradition had endured in Europe and the Austro-Hungarian monarchy since 1815; and for more than thirty years the ears of his police and the heavy tread of his white-coated infantry had followed the least whisper of departure from its strict injunctions. He was the guardian *par excellence* of the existing order; and when he fell, it was a lucid warning that his contemporaries had outgrown it. For if Metternich could be unceremoniously hunted out of Austria, it was a challenge to every axiom of the old order—to the right of ministers to govern as they pleased, the right of Austrians to govern other races than their own, and the most sacred right of all by which anointed persons could dispose absolutely of crowded populations on the green tables of diplomacy. These things had been the frame within which the Continent had lived since 1815; and as it reeled before the gale, the world began to breathe a freer air. Some of them might be recovered by desperate measures of police or by the dull swing of reaction. Obliging Cossacks could help to hold the Magyars down, and the Italians might be flung back with violence to mutter and conspire for a few years longer. After an abdication a younger Hapsburg still reigned in Vienna; and French bayonets, by a strange paradox, restored the Pope to Rome. But continuity was never re-established, and the gale that swept the Continent in 1848 ended the age of Metternich.

5. Kennington Common

WHAT THE SPECIAL CONSTABLE said to the American gentleman was that the peace of London must be preserved. As constables, even special constables, are rarely capable of an impressive aphorism, it was not surprising that he said it in French, being (as the American gentleman was comfortably aware) a nephew of Napoleon. For Prince Louis had begun to see himself as a guardian of public order. True, his extremely unobtrusive dash to Paris in the first week of the Revolution had not led to much. A muffler had been modestly drawn up to hide the big moustache. But the vague eyes could see over it; and he observed the stir and throb of a great city whose pulses were still feverish. Indeed, when some people who were tidying the streets after the riots had called on him to lend a hand in lifting paving-stones down from the barricades, the Prince achieved an oracular reply. "My good woman," he had said, "that is precisely what I have come to Paris for." The French Government, however, took another view. Reluctant to accept Prince Louis as a collaborator, it requested him to leave

[59]

France in twenty-four hours; and the Prince withdrew sedately to the security of King Street, St. James's, and the contemplation of his destiny. But when the calmer air of London was disturbed by the distant tramp of Chartists, it was quite natural for him to attest as a special constable at the police office in Marlborough Street, since the Bonapartes inherited a marked distaste for indiscipline and, as he remarked that day in April to the American gentleman whom he encountered on his beat, the peace of London must be preserved.

That could not be doubted, even if the Chartists proposed to hold a monster meeting south of the river and to march on Westminster with a Gargantuan petition of five million signatures; and there was not much more uncertainty as to who must preserve it. For the old Duke was still at Apsley House. In all national emergencies the regular procedure was to send for the Duke; and the Duke was duly sent for. As usual, the old man was obstinately calm—as calm as he had been that Sunday morning when Alava rode up to him on the ridge at Waterloo and Wellington asked blandly if he had been at Lady Charlotte Greville's on the night before. As the fatal date approached, the town was in a flutter. The royal family had been packed off to Osborne, and Lady Palmerston had entered "Revolution" in her diary for two days running. But the Duke beckoned a member of the Government across the House of Lords in order to inform him that "we shall be as quiet on Monday as we are at this hour." That, however, was not quite so certain, if half a million Chartists really met at Kennington and marched across the bridges.

On the next day (it was a Saturday) he met the Cabinet. They were Whig ministers, to be sure; but Whigs and Tories were much the same to Wellington, when there was duty to be done. For, as he said to someone forty years before, he was *nimmukwallah*—he had eaten the King's salt and knew it was his place to serve willingly wherever the King's government might see fit to make use of him. So the Duke met Lord John Russell and his anxious colleagues to consider the defence of London. They deliberated gravely in a military atmosphere of maps and intelligence reports, and the old man impressed them all immensely with his alertness and decision. His mood inspired the civilians; and Macaulay told someone afterwards that, as became an *amateur* of great events, he should recall the memorable scene to his dying day. The problem was to keep an adversary of uncertain strength away from central London with a force consisting of the Metropolitan Police, the special constables, some guns, the Guards, three regiments of foot, and a few cavalry. The enemy proposed to concentrate at Kennington, and it was essential to keep them beyond the river. So the bridges must be held at all costs. But it was never the Duke's habit to show his forces prematurely. That had not been his way in Spain or on the ridge above La Haye Sainte. So the military were to be kept out of sight, while the police were left in charge of the approaches. As he informed the Prussian Minister at Lady Palmerston's, "Not a soldier or piece of artillery shall you *see,* unless in actual need. Should the force of law, the mounted or unmounted police, be overpowered or in danger, then the troops shall advance—then is their time! But it is not fair on either side to call them in to do the work of police; the military must not be confounded with the police, nor merged in the police." He had always been opposed to "placing extensive civil powers in the hands of soldiers merely because they are of the military profession"; and his judicious principles were still maintained. So there was at least one place in Europe where the level voice of commonsense persisted above the uproar of 1848.

The day arrived; and on that Monday morning (it was April 10) a small crowd cheered the old man as he rode up to his headquarters at the Horse Guards. Lord Palmerston, who had packed off his lady to her daughter's for the day, took charge of the defences at the Foreign Office, where there had been a meagre issue of muskets and cutlasses and a brisk departmental controversy was already in progress as to the command. The special constables were much in evidence; and Mr. Carlyle, who had passed a wretched night, went out to see the revolution. But the spectacle was not enlivening; and as he tramped from Chelsea in the teeth of an unpleasant wind, it began to spit with rain and it dawned upon him that he had come out without an umbrella. At Hyde Park Corner he discovered that the Duke's iron shutters were all down. The Park was shut, a few chilly Lifeguards were sheltering under the arch on Constitution Hill, and there was hardly anyone about. This was not in the least what revolutions looked like in his professional experience. There were no traces of disorder on the gleaming pavements, and there was hardly any traffic in the road. The rain was getting worse, as the student of revolutions made his discouraged way down Piccadilly. A few cabs, a dust-cart or so, and two doctors' broughams were almost all that he encountered in its whole depressing length; and after an interminable lecture from a loquacious fellow-countryman, who kept him in the rain to tell him in response to a rash enquiry all that had been going on at Kennington, he resolved to shelter in the Burlington Arcade. When he emerged, it had come on to pour, and there was nothing for it but a swift retreat to Chelsea. The omnibuses were still running, and the thwarted eye-witness of revolutionary scenes rumbled slowly home.

But the disappointments of that rainy day were not confined to the author of the *French Revolution*. For the great demonstration never came within hail of anybody's expectations. In the first place, the threatened half-million Chartists whose revolutionary tread had reverberated in the ears of Londoners for weeks failed to materialise, being represented on the day by an assembly numbering somewhere between ten and twenty thousand people. Besides, their deportment as an armed insurrection fell miserably short of the expected standard of ferocity. Even the mild Prime Minister anticipated that they might "fire and draw their swords and use their daggers," while the more combative Lord Palmerston, whose distaste for foreigners found congenial employment at the Foreign Office, had looked forward to a cheerful bout of fisticuffs in which the Queen's constabulary were to administer resounding punishment to the Chartists' questionable foreign friends. For broadminded on the subject of revolutions on the Continent, the Foreign Secretary was less sympathetic when they came nearer home; and he was sadly disappointed when "the foreigners did not show," thus depriving loyal pugilists of their opportunity to "make an example of any whiskered and bearded rioter whom they might meet with," as to whom he was patriotically convinced that British fists "would have mashed them to jelly." But there was no affray, even of the mildest order, at Kennington. When a Commissioner of Police requested the Chartist leader to come and speak to him, the chastened Boanerges came quite meekly and received with signs of gratitude the formal intimation that no procession would be allowed to cross the bridges. He even offered to shake hands with his oppressor and, returning to the crowd, advised them to disperse. Then he drove off to the Home Office in a cab, where he repeated his assurances to the Home Secretary, while the great petition was unobtrusively conveyed to Parliament in three four-wheelers. So the spring day that opened with a threat of revolution ended with an apologetic

Irishman in a London cab, while the crowd at Kennington melted away. Lady Palmerston drove home to Carlton Gardens after dinner, and Carlyle reported to his Jane "the No Revolution we have just sustained."

That was its epitaph, though Palmerston in a more expansive mood described it as "the Waterloo of peace and order." In one sense, indeed, it had been a Waterloo, since Wellington had won it; but his defeated adversary was scarcely up to the Duke's standard. The forces of disorder were incompetently led by a half-hearted imbecile, whose progressive dementia became medically noticeable shortly aftrwards. O'Connor had received the announcement of official intervention with evident relief; and there was a striking lack of fire about his followers, whom the Prime Minister described almost pityingly as "those wicked but not brave men." The Duke's judicious strategy had counted for a good deal. The rain, perhaps, counted for more, since even blood will hardly boil on a wet day; and England owes more to her uncertain climate than it is customary for students of her institutions to admit. But the result was ultimately due to the plain fact that the Chartist cock would not fight. Even the five million signatures of the great petition melted under careful scrutiny to less than two millions, of which a fair proportion were light-hearted forgeries purporting to attest the Chartist proclivities of the royal family, the Duke of Wellington, Sir Robert Peel, several members of the Government, and an imaginary personage with the imperishable name of "Cheeks the Marine."

The plain truth of the matter was that the subjects of Queen Victoria were not greatly interested in revolutions on the large scale that was so popular abroad. These noble conflagrations, with which the night sky of Europe was pleasantly diversified in 1848, had each resulted from the sudden application of a simple general idea. For the crude machinery of revolution was invariably started by some broad conception of society, which could be easily memorised and looked well on a banner. But such notions were less readily acclimatised in the British Isles. A happy inability to apprehend general ideas appeared to stand between the people of England and their disturbing impact. At their approach the public mind almost invariably ceased to function or, conscious of its limitations, turned eagerly in other directions. In Great Britain the pursuit of theory was left to professed theorists, whilst an obstinately practical community eschewed the primrose path of general ideas and confined itself austerely to the solution of particular problems.

That was the key to the vast difference between British and Continental politics in 1848. Mazzini, Lamartine, and Kossuth were each the standard-bearer of an idea, which was adopted by their nation in a moment of revolutionary impulse. The events of 1848 abroad consisted in the sudden elevation of a number of embarrassed thinkers to political power, and in particular German politics suffered from a rush of professors to the head. But such phenomena were highly improbable in England, where a wise division of labour allotted the arduous business of thinking to a select and highly specialised caste of thinkers, while practical affairs were left to public men whose minds were almost wholly innocent of the loftier processes of thought. Indeed, the two operations seemed to proceed in watertight compartments. For Carlyle and Mill might theorise at large without much visible effect upon the course of public life; but when the nation needed guidance, it enquired what measures Lord John Russell or Sir Robert Peel or Mr. Cobden had to suggest. There was good reason for this apparent disregard of sages in favour of mere politicians, since the public appetite was less for general ideas than for policies. That was the British method—to concentrate on the particular, on the solution of specific problems by practical reforms. The balance of the constitution had been readjusted in 1832 by the enfranchisement of ten-pound householders rather than by pikes and tricolours; and the economic problem had been momentarily solved in 1846 by the repeal of the Corn Laws rather than by a social revolution, because the public mind shrewdly preferred the retail precision of specific policies to the wholesale experiments of revolutionary ideology. It was significant that there was no hope of rendering a revolution acceptable to this supremely cautious people except by calling it Reform; and in a country where the public mind was almost wholly interested in the Parliamentary proposals of public men upon specific problems capable of prompt solution the Chartist effort was doomed to failure by its frankly revolutionary appeal.

Its predestined futility was aggravated by the inadequacy of its leadership and by the practised skill of Wellington's defence. But it may be doubted whether Chartism could have triumphed in 1848 under the best of leaders, even if a rash Government had precipitated a Peterloo. For its appeal was worse than uncongenial: it was stale. Ten years earlier, perhaps, it might have led to something. But if the attainment of reforms by physical violence had ever any attractions for Englishmen, it had none left in 1848. The black years of post-war confusion were far behind, and ministers no longer carried pocket-pistols or bolted their carriage doors on the inside against possible assassins. Two years earlier a fiscal revolution, achieved by mere persuasion, had secured cheap bread; and it was not surprising that the triumph of the Anti-Corn-Law League diverted men's attention to Parliamentary methods.

Besides, it was an age of swiftly growing enterprise.

The railways had begun to pay; steam-power mills flooded a receptive world with their amazing stream of cotton goods; iron manufactures were pouring overseas; coal began to be exported; and the exciting innovation of steamships promised a vast expansion of demand. The air was full of orders, of expanding business and new development; even a crisis in the money market had been weathered without undue dislocation; and the times were far too brisk for a miasma of universal discontent to hang upon the air. Stagnation is the chosen soil from which revolutions can be raised; and England in 1848 was anything but stagnant. That, perhaps, was the prime reason why Carlyle could write almost ruefully of "the No Revolution we have just sustained," while Prince Albert reported happily to Stockmar that "we had our revolution yesterday, and it ended in smoke."

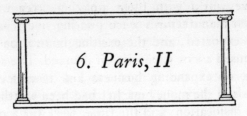

6. Paris, II

As the year mounted towards midsummer, Paris was still feverish. But the symptoms were quite different now from those which had preceded the February convulsion. That had been a wholly political affair, a swift paroxysm of public irritation with the form of government, which had jerked a monarchy out of the saddle and replaced it with a republic. Its objectives had all been thoroughly attained; the old King was a refugee somewhere in England, and his succession was shared between a talkative Provisional Government and a still more talkative Assembly. Unfortunately changes of regime, however heartening, are powerless to solve all problems, since economic troubles rarely yield to political treatment. A transfer of allegiance, new designs for postage stamps, a change of uniforms, and a fresh coinage will hardly exorcise the spectre of starvation; and so long as that was present, the economic problem was unsolved. Purely political reforms are quite irrelevant to economic problems, since it is no more enjoyable to starve under a republic than under a monarchy; and a dull mass of discontent remained wholly untouched by the successes of the February Revolution. For while the sky was bright with promise above the white sails of the young Republic, a long groundswell of misery ran strongly and the new ship began to creak.

Starvation was the danger; and a strange economic aberration had done its best to concentrate starvation in the capital. Well-meaning politicians, faced with the miseries of unemployment, succumbed at once to the temptations of a rash policy of public works without the customary pretence that any of the works were of the slightest public utility. The *Ateliers Nationaux,* a group of ill-conceived establishments where unskilled labour found useless employment at the general expense, were an erratic gesture by which the Republic sought to indicate its kindly feelings towards the working class. For there was a growing danger that their paths might diverge, since it was manifest that the mere proclamation of a new form of government had failed to satisfy material demands. True, it had fully met the aspirations of the middle class, which were wholly political; but it had no power to feed hungry men, and their unsatisfied demands might open a new phase of revolution. That was the worst of revolutions: they were so easy to begin, but it was always difficult to say precisely when they would end. The middle class had struck its blow, deposed the King, installed its favourite politicians, and was prepared to intimate that the revolution was over. Not so the hungry workmen, for whom the revolution was only just beginning. That sad divergence ranged the Republic on one side with those dashing young republicans in yellow gloves, whose views on property were strictly orthodox, and the grim disciples of the *République sociale* on the other. The contrast was pointed by the indignant Engels; and Marx, perhaps, was right when he reviled the "radical bourgeois" as the worst enemies of Socialism, since their opposition deprived it of the undivided support of the masses and set the stage for a disastrous conflict between pure democrats, who were prepared to peg the revolution at its present level, and still purer Socialists, who were resolved to carry it one glorious step farther. A half-hearted effort to postpone the issue, to provide employment within the limits of the existing economic order, had inspired the institution of the *Ateliers Nationaux*. But the sole result was to draw starving men to Paris, where 117,000 unemployed performed useless tasks at a cost of 170,000 francs a day, an expensive means of concentrating half the discontent of France in the mean streets of a single city. This *Danegeld* might procure a breathing-space for the new Republic. But it could not go on; and at the first attempt to end it, the economic revolution flamed out.

It was past midsummer when the drums began to beat again and the mean streets of Paris went out to battle. A scared Assembly made over the supreme authority to Cavaignac, dictatorship succeeding momentarily to democracy; and the lean General, who had learnt his business in the brown distances of Algeria, went to work with grim effectiveness. Four blazing summer days ended the civil war and stabilised the revolution; but whilst it lasted, it had been a dreadful business. For in its essence the June rising was a servile war; and the barricades fought grimly, shooting in a sullen silence without leaders, without cheers, and almost without hope. The killing was quite ruthless; and one ghastly day a general was murdered and the Archbishop of Paris, who had bravely intervened, was shot. The troops fought pitilessly; there were women among the casualties; guns were freely used against the barricades; and as the smoke drifted across the racked city into the June sky, Frenchmen in uniform shot down Frenchmen in blue blouses. After a sanguinary interval the firing died away: there was to be no social revolution in 1848.

Indeed, to all appearances it was extremely doubtful if there would be much revolution left of any kind. For though the General had laid down his supreme powers with a gesture composed in equal parts of Cincinnatus and George Washington, a grateful legislature duly reappointed him as Chief Executive. True, the appointment was strictly temporary and terminable in due course by the election of a President. But the agony of June had taught a fair proportion of his fellow-countrymen the fascinations of dictatorship. After a breathless interlude of adventure on the high seas there was a good deal to be said for an uneventful anchorage; and if the ship was not to drag its anchors at the next threat of disturbance, it would be just as well to select heavy ones. A craving for authority grew on them, as the summer faded. There was a President to be elected; and the leading question in the public mind was whether authority would find its best representative in the spare figure of Cavaignac or in the name of Bonaparte which, as its bearer had remarked, was "a symbol of order, nationality, and glory." Considering the bright beginnings of their revolution, it was an odd choice to confront the electors of the Second Republic. They ultimately chose the latter, and France slipped imperceptibly towards the Second Empire.

But their descent from the windy heights of democracy to the morass of absolutism was determined by the weary mood of 1848, by the jaded temper of disillusion and alarm by which the first exaltations of that splendid springtime had been followed. On every side that autumn Europe was under authority. Cavaignac ruled France; Windischgrätz held down Vienna; Jellačić had the Magyars by the throat; and Radetzky's guns boomed across Italy. It was a time of swift and pitiless dictatorship triumphant almost everywhere in Europe; and it would seem more natural to remember 1848 for its dictators than for its revolutions. For all its revolutions seemed to fail, leaving a formidable row of dictators installed in more or less comfort and apparent permanence. Yet their names are strangely faded, since their work left hardly any trace. In spite of all contemporary appearances there are few names more shadowy than Cavaignac and Windischgrätz for the simple reason that dictatorship is only a device by which an air of permanence is lent to temporary retrogressions; and nations rarely take pleasure in recalling those by whom their retreats have been conducted. For dictatorship is oddly mortal; but the revolution lived.

7. *Chicago, Ill.*

ONE DAY that winter something happened which did more to change the world than all the Continental drama of 1848. Three thousand miles from Europe and seven hundred from the stir and flutter of New York the city of Chicago watched Lake Michigan. It was a city, because a population of four thousand souls had entitled it to call itself one in 1837; and it watched the lake, because (to tell the truth) there was not very much for it to watch on shore. There were six times as many people now, a gas-works, seven hotels, six newspapers, and a factory of agricultural implements; and the population had a reasonable hope of touching thirty thousand by the year 1850. The little Fort had vanished with the Indians; and more innocent excitement was provided by a new theatre, where the township was regaled with Shakespeare in the intervals of *Black-Eyed Susan* and *The Lady of Lyons* and the rare sensation of a real horse performing in *Mazeppa*. It was a thriving little place; but if it was to thrive to any purpose, something must be done about communications. For it was a lonely little

[73]

place as well, lying between the windy lake and the interminable prairie. The distances were vast on every side; and it was manifest once more that the true history of the United States is the history of transportation.

Since Chicago was a port, where hogs and wheat were loaded into steamboats for shipment to the East by way of the Great Lakes, the public mind ran upon waterways. But other enterprising men were dazzled by a vision of plank roads, on which a horse might draw a waggon at the steady rate of ten miles an hour in far greater safety than that permitted by the explosive and uncertain progress of railroads, with the added blessing that a horse-waggon could oblige its customers by stopping anywhere they liked. Besides, the cost of railroads was immense, and Illinois had not much money. Railroad enterprise had pullulated in the bright days of Jacksonian prosperity; but the depression withered its speculative promise, and most stockholders were left with shares in lines that no one had begun to build. One project of this order had proposed to connect Chicago with the lead mines one hundred and sixty miles away at Galena, Ill. Surveying was begun before the crash, and a few piles had been driven within the city limits before it was abandoned. Revived when better times returned, the Galena and Chicago Union Railroad had positively built ten miles of track out of Chicago. Some rolling-stock consisting of six second-hand box cars and a locomotive named *Pioneer* was purchased in the East and shipped by water to Chicago; and on November 20, 1848, the directors and stockholders of the line entrained for an experimental trip over their system. The ten-mile journey passed off without misadventure; and on the way home to the city they overtook on the road a farmer hauling a load of wheat. The train was stopped; the enterprising railroad secured the business; its obliging stockholders made room; and that afternoon in 1848 they handled the first car-load of grain to come by rail into Chicago.

That was the beginning of the Middle West, of the vast exploitation of the endless distances evacuated by the Indians. Without the railroads they were little more than an immense impediment, an undulating ocean of green distances to be navigated in prairie-schooners on the way to California. For though the red man and his buffalo were leaving the Great Plains, the territory was of no use to white men until the magic touch of rails transformed it. But the black locomotives performed that miracle, as they rolled uncertainly across the endless vista behind their cow-catchers with the sparks pouring from their unlikely smoke-stacks above the melancholy clangour of their bells. Those unattractive fairies worked a magic transformation; and as their wood-smoke defaced the wide prairie skies, the Plains became an empire, a vast reservoir of sober wealth whose weight was added to the North, a formidable counterpoise to Southern cotton. For the West marketed in the great cities of the East, and it was quite indifferent to the discontents of Charleston and New Orleans. That increment of power might be vital to the Northern States within the Union, as it would one day lend incalculable weight to the United States in the great world beyond the ocean; and it had its unobtrusive opening in the first freight carried by the Galena and Chicago Union Railroad that winter afternoon in 1848.

EIGHTEEN
SIXTY–ONE

1. St. Petersburg

THE RUSSIAN WINTER was half over; and the rust-red palace by the Neva still faced the yellow amphitheatre of the General Staff across the square. The rank classicism of a bronze quadriga in sharp outline on the pale February sky crowned their building and celebrated Czar Alexander's victories over Napoleon, whilst in the rooms downstairs his successor's officers considered the best method of repairing the less satisfactory operations of the Crimean War. The last indignities endured by Sebastopol were five years behind them now. The gorges of the Caucasus, where their advancing Cossacks slowly shepherded the last defenders towards the south, fixed their attention; and they considered the reports of columns operating far to the south-east in Turkestan towards Tashkent, as Russia developed her slow southward thrust into the sun. The ministry next door, where the spectacled Prince Gortchakoff peered at draft protocols, was busy with the last finesse of diplomacy. But behind the rich rococo of the Winter Palace their imperial master's mind was less occupied with diplomatic fencing or the un-

[79]

hurrying advance of Russian armies into Central Asia than with the haunting problems of his own dominions. They had haunted him since boyhood, when he learnt that there was nothing in the Bible that could be held to justify the institution of slavery as it was practised by his father's subjects. This conclusion was not displaced by anything that he had seen of them upon his early travels; and when he succeeded to the vast, discouraged empire while British guns were thundering outside Sebastopol, he faced the problem with a deep conviction that Emancipation must be conceded freely from above, unless it was to come chaotically from below. For it was equally repugnant to his conscience and to the march of history that a contemporary of Queen Victoria should reign over forty-seven million white slaves. He showed the way by the prompt liberation of all human beings owned by the Crown. But Russia still remained a nation of slave-owners, no less than the enlightened citizens beyond the Atlantic in those Southern States of which (to their dismay) Mr. Lincoln had just been elected President. For private property in human beings persisted on the everlasting Russian plain no less than in Virginia; and in 1861, by an odd chance, the destiny of both slave-states was settled.

There is an unchanging rhythm in Russian history, which compels an alternation of unsuccessful wars abroad with uncomfortable jerks at home. For Russian wars are mostly unsuccessful; and they are usually followed by an acceleration of internal politics that leads to grave events. A military empire can scarcely thrive upon an unsustaining diet of defeat; and as Russian armies were generally beaten except when they were used against their fellow-subjects or a backward race, their operations rarely added to the glory of the imperial regime. For nothing is more undeserved than the respectful apprehension with which the world has long consented to regard the Russians as a military menace, since their operations normally exhibit a devastating incompetence. At intervals in the last hundred years the Russian state embarked upon a war; and since it was quite unsupported by the requisite efficiency in arms, the war almost invariably ended in disaster. This recurrent accident was followed in each case by an unpleasant quickening of its domestic discontents; and to each military defeat succeeded an uncomfortable period of civil strain, until the final shock was so severe as to destroy the whole fabric of the nation's life. In spite of a delusive air of massive strength, that rhythm of alternating defeat and disorder was invariable. The tread of Russian armies seemed to shake the ground of Europe, and neighbours muttered nervously about 'the Colossus of the North.' But each war ended in defeat; and each defeat brought revolution nearer.

In 1861 a kindly ruler had anticipated the unrest that was bound to follow the discouragements of the Crimean War by launching an immense reform; and whilst officials struggled with the endless detail of Emancipation, the Czar plodded up and down his territories to stimulate the better impulses of his slave-holding subjects. They stood in ample need of such encouragement, since the impending loss of all their human capital formed anything but an attractive prospect for those cheerful *boyars,* whose fantastic opulence had made them the *rastas* of the first years of the Nineteenth Century; and their enthusiasm for the emancipation of their serfs was scarcely equal to their royal master's. But he persisted bravely, making speeches, reading memoranda, travelling, arguing with unenthusiastic ministers, until Emancipation gradually emerged from the uncertain hands of drafting committees on to the table of the Council of State. Its form was not ideal, since the new freedom of the Russian peasant was unaccompanied by any corresponding distribution of the Russian land, and the vast land-hunger of forty

million rustics remained unsatisfied. But as his pen traced
Alexander's signature beneath the Rescript of Emancipation on a winter day in 1861, the Russian Empire moved
slowly forward towards freedom. Their liberation was not
yet complete; and the inadequacy of the step may have been
detected by the curl of a class-conscious lip, since abject poverty persisted in the place from which slavery had been removed. But when the Czar's hand lifted from the paper,
there were no more serfs in Russia, though there were not
yet free men. For beyond the palace windows the Fortress
of St. Peter and St. Paul still lifted a slim, gilded finger skywards in its eternal warning.

2. Charleston, S. C.

A LOW OUTLINE lay off the shore. Beyond the city spires and warehouses, beyond the watching houses on the Battery where all Charleston strolled on cool evenings it lay like a dismasted ship across the harbour mouth. Inland the little balconies behind their blinds surveyed the shaded alleys of the town, and tall, pillared porches beneath the empty grace of a white pediment withdrew with dignity behind the rusted tracery of iron gates to dream of a lost age among the flowers or to look bravely out across the water, as the Ashley River crept past Charleston to the sea. The spring tides set the palmetto swamps whispering up-river; and shrouded trees along the country roads were veiled in a dim fog of hanging moss or shadowed an unlikely blaze of flowers, where a gentle angle of the river elbowed an incomparable garden. The bright flowers burned in the Carolina spring; grey moss hung dimly from the live-oaks; and at Charleston, where the hours struck slowly from St. Philip's and St. Michael's, the unpleasant outline of the fort hung midway between sea and sky.

[83]

It hung there shadowing their world, an angular reminder, as the Stars and Stripes ran up each morning on Fort Sumter's flagstaff, that the United States continued to exist, whatever Southern eloquence might say; and all the lightnings of that fatal gift played round the uneasy question. It was an awkward problem, since there were other forts in Charleston Harbour and they flew another flag. For South Carolina in solemn session at St. Andrew's Hall upon the velvet chairs sacred at other times to Charleston chaperons had seceded from the Union. Their reasons were a shade obscure. A growing feeling that the South was challenged in its age-long mastery of the United States disturbed them. It was unthinkable that regions which had provided Presidents and ministers in such profusion should be outnumbered in the nation. Their sons had been its leaders for so long; the Senate was their private forum and West Point their training school; they officered its army, made its laws, and commanded its ships. Their self-esteem was pardonable, since the country was beyond a doubt their United States. But would it always be? That was the disturbing question; and an uncomfortable feeling stole through the South that the United States were not so safe as they had been for Southern elements. The Union grew less congenial, as its balance was disturbed by immigration and the thrust of its new populations towards the West. Industrial expansion in the North imposed new fiscal policies, in which the needs of Southern cotton-growers were not the sole consideration. For the United States were changing fast; and it was highly doubtful to the Southern mind how long the country would continue to be their United States.

Besides, an irritating tendency of Northern thought and speech had dared to question the sole basis of the South's existence. They were a community of cotton-growers living by slave labour; and the noisy challenge of the North was

too threatening to be ignored, since slavery was the foundation of their economics, and the whole life of the South hung
by a thread of cotton. The Northern challenge was anything but academic, as it took the form of Abolitionist cor-
roborees, at which philanthropists of either sex, discarding
all restraints of courtesy or fact, lashed one another into
paroxysms of denunciation that left the South, never defi-
cient in repartee, under the dangerous impression that a fair
proportion of its fellow-citizens were "hot as the hellish
passions of their own black hearts, foul as streams from the
sewers of Pandemonium." This duel of abuse, unpromising
for the prospects of national harmony, passed from the platform into politics; and a long struggle opened on the thorny
topics of escaping slaves, State jurisdiction, and the future
of slavery in the new Territories, culminating in the demented heroism of John Brown's half-witted foray at Har-
per's Ferry.

But the gravest consequence of the protracted controversy
was a growing sense of isolation in the South. Its apologists
were conscientiously instructed that "the rest of Christen-
dom stands united against us, and are almost unanimous in
pronouncing a verdict of condemnation"; its bread-winners
believed that they were bound to live by means of which
their fellow-countrymen could not approve; and, human perversity being what it was, the Southern mind sought compensation for this disparagement in a vast expansion of
Southern self-esteem. For if they had been proud before,
they were ten times prouder now. Always romantic, the
Southern mind had long been subject to illusions as to the
aristocratic nature of its origins and way of life. Watering
a tenacious Cavalier tradition with a minimum of Cavalier
blood, it was always prone to see a belle in every woman and
a gallant gentleman in every man. An allied hallucination
implied that the ownership of land was in some occult way a

patent of nobility; and this, once predicated, entitled land-owners to contemn the base commercial classes of the North in favour of *"independent* South Carolina *country gentle-men,* the nearest to *noblemen* of any possible class in America." Their reading served to add fuel to this fire, since it was said that they absorbed vast quantities of fiction from the chivalrous pen of Walter Scott, imported to the South in car-load lots; and gentlemen in pleasant houses on the Ashley River began to see themselves as belted knights who might be called upon at any moment to defend the Holy Sepulchre against the paynim hosts.

Few moods are more unfriendly to clear thinking than a crusading temper; and as the South grew more self-conscious, it was fortified by the last absurdity of all, race-theory. For, exasperated by Yankee self-righteousness and the facile caricature of *Uncle Tom's Cabin,* it was not content to tell the North that its "priesthood prostitutes itself to a level with the blackguard, and enters the field of secular politics, in the spirit of a beer-house bully," adding without unnecessary chivalry that Northern womanhood, "deserting their nurseries, stroll over the country as politico-moral reformers, delivering lewd lectures upon the beauties of free-love or spiritualism, or writing yellow-back literature, so degraded in taste, so prurient in passion, so false in fact, so wretched in execution, and so vitiating to the morals of mothers in the land, as almost to force them to bring up daughters without virtue and sons without bravery." But Southern vanity found a more convincing explanation of its fatal disagreement with the North, since it began to be convinced that "the Cavaliers, Jacobites, and Huguenots, who settled the South, naturally hate, condemn, and despise the Puritans who settled the North. The former are master races; the latter a slave race, descendants of the Saxon serfs." Pursuing their researches, Southern genealogists detected a monopoly of Norman blood among themselves; and where Norman blood was present, it was pardonable to expect a Norman Conquest, which might take the form either of regenerated United States or of "a vast, opulent, happy and glorious slave-holding Republic throughout tropical America." Such were the unhealthy dreams engendered in the South by Northern disapproval and an unpleasant sense of isolation.

These tendencies were deepened and accelerated by the Presidential election of 1860, which emphasised the shrinkage of their influence by sending Lincoln to the White House. The South was horrified; and the wild diagnosis of a Richmond journal informed thoughtful Virginians that "with Lincoln comes something worse than slang, rowdyism, brutality, and all moral filth; something worse than the rag and tag of Western grog-shops and Yankee factories. . . . With all those comes the daring and reckless leader of Abolitionists." Before that prospect the last thread of Southern self-restraint snapped, and South Carolina seceded from the Union. Its life had always been a little isolated, and now the isolation was past bearing. So the Palmetto flag was substituted for the Stars and Stripes; and up-country gentlemen came riding into town, prepared for knightly deeds. They drilled with gusto, though most Southerners believed that there would be no fighting. For Southern honour had been satisfied by secession; and if Southern honour had been satisfied, there was no more to be said. The North was far away, and Northern honour was less susceptible. Indeed, it had already survived a shot fired upon its flag by eager Southerners, as a Federal supply ship came steaming into Charleston Harbour with stores for the little garrison. But it was always possible that the North might entertain a preference for the continuance of the United States, though the Palmetto flag waved gaily over Charleston; and the unpleasant

[87]

outline of Fort Sumter, vaguely seen across three miles of water, hung midway between sea and sky.

It shadowed Charleston; and it shadowed Washington as well, since the national situation was full of explosive possibilities so long as an isolated harbour fort was held by Union troops, while the surrounding forces marched behind the flag of a seceding State. The Northern mind was anything but clear as to the immediate problem. But few governments are so long-suffering as to submit indefinitely to armed rebellion within their territories; and whatever resolutions might be passed by the representatives of South Carolina, there could not be the slightest doubt that until recently they had formed part of the United States. That was an essential point in Northern eyes, as Northern loyalty was growing capable of something larger than allegiance to a single State. To traders with interests in a dozen States the Union was something more than a constitutional formality, since it created the territorial unit within which they were at liberty to operate. It was impossible for Northerners to trade with the expanding West without developing a national conception of the Union transcending their municipal attachment to the State in which they lived. Commerce, in fine, enlarged their loyalties and, finding them New Yorkers, made them Americans. Besides, a fair proportion of their population had escaped from Europe with the simple objective of a fresh start in a new country and without local predilections on the subject of States, however admirable, with whose names they were largely unfamiliar; and to recent immigrants the United States meant infinitely more than any of their components.

Upon this background of Union sentiment bewildered gentlemen at Washington surveyed the awkward problem of the South in the winter days of 1861, as six more States followed the perilous example of South Carolina and Southern delegates trooped into the State House at Montgomery, Alabama, to make solemn speeches beneath its curving galleries and vote a new constitution for the Confederate States of America. Mr. Jefferson Davis walked across from the first White House of the Confederacy for his Inaugural beneath the grave, approving eyes of Southern gentlemen. His eyes were grave as well; for when the telegram had come announcing that he was to be their President, he could hardly bring himself to tell his wife and Mrs. Davis, when she saw the look that clouded his lean handsomeness, felt sure the telegram contained bad news. They cheered him as he spoke, since hardly one of them saw war as the inevitable end of their proceedings. The Southern *pundonor* demanded their secession, and it was widely assumed that they would be allowed to go in peace. This hopeful view prevailed among the delegates at Montgomery, and it was significant that the post offices of the new Confederacy were ordered to conform peacefully to official routine by accounting to Washington until the June half-year of 1861. But Mr. Davis was less cheerful; and beyond the cheers he "saw troubles and thorns innumerable. We are without machinery, without means, and are threatened by a powerful opposition." And as he spoke from the tall steps between the great fluted pillars of that Southern portico, he looked down the long avenue between the balconies and shaded porches of comfortable Alabama houses and the endless vista that led straight to Gettysburg, the 'Bloody Angle,' and the long agony in the winter trenches before Petersburg.

What was to happen next? Bewildered Washington, faced with an exodus of Southerners, balanced uneasily between the two alternatives of coercion and acquiescence. As the first meant civil war and heroics were less fashionable north of the Mason and Dixon Line, there was a considerable tendency to play for time, murmuring wistfully

to the seceded States, "Wayward Sisters, depart in peace."
But time might prove to be an awkward ally, so long as the
unpleasant riddle of Fort Sumter was unsolved. Nobody
seemed to know the answer; and it was anything but simple
to devise a satisfactory finale for the piece which had ma-
rooned Major Anderson and eighty-four fellow-creatures
in the Union service upon an island in a neighbourhood by
which the Union had been vociferously repudiated. Charleston's notion of a happy ending was an interlude of Southern
chivalry, in which the garrison was given free access to food
supplies while gallant planters toiled beside their slaves at
the revetments of the new Southern batteries, followed by
a spirited *dénouement* enabling everyone to display gallantry and ending with the Palmetto waving unchallenged over
South Carolina. Washington's requirements were less spirited, if something could be worked out that was reasonably
dignified and did not involve an inadmissible surrender. There
was no desire to turn the fortress guns on Charleston in a
wild effort to recall it to its late allegiance. Even the Abolitionists inclined to leave the South in a disgraceful solitude,
and the most vocal of them doubted whether the Union had
any "right to a soldier in Fort Sumter." No government,
however, can desert subordinates; and since withdrawal
would be tantamount to an admission that the Confederacy
was sovereign in South Carolina, Lincoln and his colleagues
resolved that the embarrassed fort must be revictualled. A
flotilla of supply ships loaded stores at the Brooklyn Navy
Yard and sailed for the South.

But the decision hardly lay with Washington, where Secretary Seward aired his evident superiority to the new
President. For a ring of Southern guns, controlled by the
Confederacy, was trained upon the lonely fort from every
angle of the harbour; and the decisive word in the imbroglio
must be spoken at Montgomery. Scarcely more inclined than

Washington to precipitate a civil war, the South found it less easy to avoid heroic attitudes. Mr. Davis in his White House on the Alabama River was no more belligerent than Mr. Lincoln in his other White House on the Potomac. But strong language and the use of arms came more easily in Southern latitudes; and there was something to be said for a decisive action which might stimulate Virginia, still hanging in the wind, to march with the Confederacy. So an official telegram from Montgomery ordered the dashing Beauregard, in command at Charleston, to reduce the fort if it would not surrender. Anderson refused, adding the welcome information that if he were let alone, he would be starved out in three days. Southern punctilio required the date and hour of his evacuation; but when he gave both with a further undertaking that his guns would not be used in the interval unless fresh supplies or orders came from his government, his answer was found insufficient and he was duly warned that the shore batteries would open fire. Nothing more unreal could be imagined than the situation of Fort Sumter, where three days of starvation, if Anderson could be believed, would solve the problem. But Southern etiquette, enamoured of the duel, imposed a meaningless exchange; and if it was to be avoided, Beauregard was unhappy in his choice of intermediaries, since at least one of them was spoiling for a fight which would "put Virginia in the Southern Confederacy in less than an hour by Shrewsbury clock." (The language of Falstaff was not inappropriate on those martial lips.) The cartel was carried to the reluctant Anderson; and Charleston waited for the duel to begin at dawn. The little pillared houses waited in the night; still gardens by the silent river, where tall trees stood listening in their long draperies of smoky moss, lay waiting for the dawn, whilst all the watchers on the waterfront strained through the darkness and the lonely fort, hull-down across the harbour-mouth, hung midway between the night sky and the black waters of the bay.

It hung there as the darkness turned to dawn; and as the fort hung between night and day, the United States—mile after mile across the continent from silent beaches in New England to the last promontory that looked down on the Pacific—hung midway between peace and war. Fourscore years of growth had made them the most hopeful fact in the world of 1861, where the Emperor Napoleon III aired his slightly reminiscent splendours, Czar Alexander II his good intentions, and Lord Palmerston his firm conviction that the not too recent past was good enough for him, as well as for the subjects of Queen Victoria. It was, to some extent, a retrospective age in which men took their last glance at the receding outlines of the Eighteenth Century. Some took it, like Lord Palmerston, with unconcealed regret, while more progressive figures like Garibaldi or Cavour drew inspiration from those principles of nationality and secularism which were the last bequest of the departed century. Dedicated to the proposition that all men were created equal (and no less eighteenth-century in their initial inspiration), the United States had seemed to point to a more modern future in which trade would rule the peaceful scene and states vie only in prosperity. Trade, indeed, was not confined to the United States; but elsewhere it conducted itself a shade apologetically beneath the borrowed grandeur of a Second Empire title or discreetly ranged in its appointed place in the Victorian hierarchy, halfway between the upper levels of the landed gentry or the cathedral close and the last indignity of manual work. Beyond the Atlantic it was more unashamed. Society was simpler, and there were less categories to embarrass the pursuit of happiness. Achievement was the only test in a new country, success the sole nobility; and even government, preserved elsewhere as a hereditary mystery, was there a simple exercise by the people of the people's right. Small wonder that a fair proportion of the world looked enviously at the United States, at the vast opportunity and the consoling featurelessness of the social scene. Repellent to romantics—did not Disraeli titter that American society was like "the best society in Manchester"?—it was a standing inspiration to Radicals with its hopeful indication of a future in which a man could call his soul (and a fair amount of property) his own. That was the commonplace sublimity of the American experiment, which had dedicated half a continent to peaceful work; and on that spring night in 1861 the whole experiment hung midway between peace and war.

This interruption of its ordered growth seemed so uncalled for. Faced with the cruel fact, subsequent attempts to rationalise the haphazard course of events have represented the conflict between North and South as irrepressible. For there is always a temptation to assign ineluctable causes to chance happenings, since history is infinitely more impressive when it is inevitable. One cannot draw lessons from pure accidents. Besides, it would be too bitter to attribute all the misery that followed to an unhappy chance. Yet there was no compelling reason in economics or sociology for the war between the States, and the tragic outcome was almost completely lacking in Marxian inevitability. The North had no quarrel with the South for mastery of a disputed country, since the true lines of the United States ran east and west across the continent. Their duel, if there had ever been one, ended when the South was outflanked by the march of time, the westward march that sent the waggons creaking overland across the Plains; and as the tide of population set westward towards California and the steel ribbon of the railroads crept behind the advancing fringe, the South was relegated past recall to a secondary place in the United

States. That was a process of history which could not be revised by force of arms; and the unhappy outcome of the war did little more than emphasise it.

Yet there was one incalculable consequence that outweighed all the suffering, since the ensuing agony ensured for all time the unchallenged unity of the United States. That was a fact of deep significance for America and later, as their influence began to radiate, for the world beyond the ocean. For the cruel price exacted from the war-time generation purchased the continuance of that immense community. Its unity could not be challenged now without sacrilege; and so long as its growing millions lived and worked in peace from the Great Lakes to the Rio Grande, something more precious to mankind than comfort was preserved, since government of the people, by the people, for the people, could not perish from the earth.

A tragic generation paid the price in four years of gunfire and fratricide; and what a price it was. It paid it marching through the midsummer dust along the unshaded roads that ended in the little wooded hills along the Bull Run where Beauregard sent the startled Federals streaming back to Washington in the first flurry of the war, or beside the Rappahannock flowing tidily between its ridges whilst Lee parried the Northern thrust at Fredericksburg, or under the wide skies that looked down on the sloping fields in front of Richmond where the South turned to bay behind its shallow breastworks, scooped in the thirsty, sandy soil along the vast, untidy water-line of the Chickahominy. It paid where the small rounded hills of Tennessee climb steeply to the Ridge, the straight-backed Pyrenean Ridge above the gleaming levels of a river of blue steel that runs beneath the cliffs at Chattanooga, and beside the great angle of the river where Vicksburg peers across the broad and gleaming shield of the Mississippi and the tall shoulder of the river-fortress

stands in a sort of tangled Devonshire, a moist green country of amazing verdure and tall trees growing out of their
own reflections in still swamps that echoed with the dull
discharges of Grant's batteries until the fortress guns fell
silent and the Northern gunboats could run clear from
Memphis to New Orleans and an incomparable tongue at
Washington announced that "the Father of Waters goes
again unvexed to the sea." It paid in heat and cold, by night
and day, for four bitter years as the slow struggle swayed
across the country and the South writhed in an unyielding
grip. The red earth of Georgia saw them go by, as the
Northern thrust went deeper into the South and Sherman,
a little wild-eyed, told them grimly to prepare the people for
his coming; and the black waters of the Yorktown peninsula, that invite the noiseless onset of canoes between the silent pine-poles, reflected their marching columns. The open
country beyond Gettysburg, where men spent their lives with
reckless prodigality, had felt the furthest ripple of the
Southern wave; and later as the angry tide receded, it drew
slowly nearer to the green hollows and bare uplands of the
last Southern stronghold, where Richmond watched from
its brown escarpments and the news, the last unbelievable
news, came to Mr. Davis in his pew at St. Paul's, and Lee
trailed westward towards Lynchburg under the wide skies,
watched by the friendly slopes of the Blue Ridge through
which Jackson had so often slipped out of the Valley to
startle Washington or to scare unsuspecting Federals by a
sudden apparition on their unguarded flank. But now there
was no Jackson, and no Stuart to go riding round the Northern rear and cut the telegraphs; only a road winding before
him past the little Court House and down the slope towards
the Appomattox. Grant came towards him up the road, and
the two men walked together to a house. Finding no table
there, they strolled up a brick path into another small

dwelling-house that stood a little back from the highway. So the two soldiers sat talking; and all round them the easy slopes lay under the clear April light. The woods were full of halted men, and on the distant sky the Blue Ridge looked down in pity at the South's surrender.

But that was still four years away, as Charleston waited for the dawn and the black muzzles of the Southern guns tilted towards the silent fort. Grant was a dusty salesman somewhere in the West, and Sherman had come north from the superintendent's desk of an academy in Louisiana, and Lee in a dim room at Arlington was facing the harsh syllogism of his conflicting duties as a Virginian and a commissioned officer of the United States. Even the President was still a shadowy, almost an unknown figure with a distressing tendency to damp excited callers with homely answers in a Western drawl that struck them sometimes as a little clownish. For the incomparable voice at Washington had not yet found the full compass of its utterance that still hangs on the air with the clear purity of a struck bell, from its deep note of consecration in a new birth of freedom to the dying fall of his last purpose to proceed with malice toward none, with charity for all, with firmness in the right, as God gives us to see the right. . . . That was still hidden in the night, as the sky began to pale behind Fort Sumter. A gun thudded; a shell whined across a mile of water; and the war began. It was about half-past four in the morning of April 12, 1861.

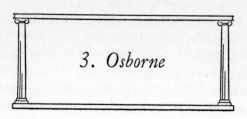

3. Osborne

THE SHORT DECEMBER DAY was over, and beyond the
lighted windows the Solent swung drearily in the night.
Inside the house a royal figure swathed in crêpe dragged
wretchedly about the silent rooms and "felt as if living in a
dreadful dream." The children were all there (she had one
of them to sleep with her) ; and her uncle Leopold from
Brussels had proposed himself, which was an immense comfort to her, as he could do so much in telling people what
they ought to do. But, in justice to them, it was only fair to
say that they were all doing it in the most exemplary manner. Lord Palmerston himself seemed quite heart-broken;
nothing could be more attentive than her other ministers;
the faithful Household far surpassed all standards of devoted sympathy; and though she had not strength to read
them yet, the tributes of a wider circle enshrined her dar-
ling in the grateful memory of an afflicted people, who
"might perhaps" (as she wrote a little ruefully) "have
shown this *more* during his lifetime." But that could not be
mended now; and as Bertie and the children tiptoed about
the silent house, she felt utterly alone.

It had always been a lonely business to be Queen of England. The royal solitude, perhaps, had thrilled her just a little on that first morning twenty-four years ago at Kensington. But she had soon mitigated it with the alleviation of an incomparable partnership, and the royal solitude became a solitude of two. For the Queen needed somebody to lean on; and through twenty happy years of married life she leaned increasingly upon her husband. A clinging nature taught her to play ivy to his oak; and his grave affection had impelled the deliberate creation in himself of a sense of public duty which enabled him to bear the burden. For twenty years of perfect harmony the weight of monarchy was carried on two pairs of shoulders, its heavy correspondence despatched from two royal writing-tables standing side by side, and its grave decisions taken by two minds that worked as one. A rare felicity for once enabled two persons to lead a single life and, sharing opinions and pastimes, to perform one royal functionary's work with the united energies of two. But that was over now. A dragging chill that turned suddenly to typhoid fever had ended it; and the Queen, shattered by three dreadful weeks at Windsor Castle, was utterly alone. Indeed, bereavement left her in something worse than solitude. For she had lost a portion of herself; and the Prince Consort's death, which widowed her, came almost with the shock of amputation.

The broken woman looked hopefully towards a highly personal Nirvana of reunion with her lost husband. Meanwhile there was the cheerless prospect of her remaining days on earth. She hoped sincerely that they would be few, quite overlooking the unhappy circumstance that she would be forty-three next birthday and was exceptionally robust; and she could hardly doubt that they would be uniformly wretched, now that the sun round which her life revolved had been withdrawn. But even in the first abandonment of her self-pity there were indications of a programme that was highly creditable to her strength of character. For in an age when widowhood was frequently accompanied by the deliberate collapse of a sort of spiritual suttee, the Queen preferred a more courageous attitude. As she must live— and she announced her firm resolve that nothing should be done by her to make her any worse than she already was— her life should be his monument, her actions a reflection of his mind, her reign a prolongation of his influence upon the country in whose service he had worn himself to death. That became the burden of her grief—"to *follow* in *everything all* HIS *wishes, great and small."* His views were now her law, his plans the programme of her life; and it was some consolation, since in the daily effort to divine his mind upon each problem she could feel him near her still.

This spectral dyarchy was now to govern England; and if England only knew what was good for it, all would be for the best. Lord Palmerston was most obliging now, and he had highly sympathetic colleagues. Lord Russell had been more than kind; the amiable Granville had enjoyed her confidence for years; and Mr. Gladstone had always been a favourite with the Prince, since he was by far the ablest pupil of Sir Robert Peel, who was Prince Albert's *beau idéal* of a British statesman. Built upon somewhat less forbidding lines, the old Prime Minister exhaled an air of comfort, as

Agricultural meetings he holds by the ears,
Through their pacings puts Hampshire Volunteers,
Or with Rowcliffe takes up the gloves for fun,
This elderly evergreen, Palmerston.
    Sing hey, my brisk John Palmerston!
    Sing ho, my blithe John Palmerston!
    Let Tory and Radical own they've none
    To compare with my jaunty John Palmerston.

[99]

He'll resist the gale, or he'll bow to the storm—
He'll patronise Bright, or he'll chaff Reform—
Make a Shafts'bury Bishop, or poke his fun
At original sin, will John Palmerston . . .

This amiable veteran appeared to hold domestic politics in a cheerful equilibrium that was unfriendly to disturbances in either sense. It was years now since Russell had introduced a Reform Bill; and progressive persons muttered darkly in corners, echoing the unfriendly sentiments of Mr. Bright, who came nearer to blasphemy on the subject of Lord Palmerston than upon any other topic. But, after all, the Government had sent that paladin of progress, Mr. Cobden, to negotiate a Commercial Treaty with the French; the harvest of Free Trade was gathered steadily in growing manufactures and expanding shipping; and Mr. Gladstone's Budgets were a treatise in annual instalments upon the last word in modern finance. This homage to the future amply satisfied the exigencies of a sense of progress, while more stable elements felt few misgivings on the subject of a Cabinet adorned by the controlling presence of Lord Palmerston, whose long career was reassuring in its mere chronology. Had he not presided in the War Department when Lord Wellington was in the Peninsula and drafted protocols for Talleyrand to read when Metternich was in his heyday? There was small risk of unexpected innovation from such a quarter; and though Palmerston moved with the times, there was no fear that he would ever find himself in advance of them.

That dangerous prerogative belonged to impatient Radicals and to their eloquent recruit, the Chancellor of the Exchequer. For Mr. Gladstone's fatal logic impelled him to erect economy into an idol, whose worship interfered with the customary financial sacrifices on the altar of national defence, and to explore the possibilities of a wider franchise without the nervous inhibitions of an older generation. Small wonder that his leader murmured that there would be strange doings when Gladstone had his place. But until then his fellow-countrymen reposed in Palmerstonian security. In twenty years the national income assessed to tax had risen from one hundred and fifty-six millions to two hundred and twenty-one; in six years the export trade climbed from a volume of one hundred and thirty millions to one hundred and eighty-eight; and a thrifty cornucopia distributed the fruits of this expansion in such judicious benefits as cheap books, cheap claret, and cheap railway-fares. It was an age of high profits and high principles; and every year the tide of comfort mounted higher. As the Prime Minister wrote proudly, "Gentlemen's Houses are better and more extensively provided than was formerly the Case. Tenant Farmers are not disposed to live in the Houses which were held good enough for their Predecessors; and the Labourers have had provided for them Habitations which would have satisfied the Smock Frock Farmer of former Times." Life was less picturesque; but it was infinitely more enjoyable under a new commercial class soberly resolved to keep what it had got and to get as much more as the unfolding opportunities of business would permit. It was the culmination of bourgeois ethics in a paradise of orderly self-seeking. Less material ideals were safely relegated to art and letters, which soared (with Mr. Tennyson) towards the stars without the sobering necessity of making both ends meet. But beyond Farringford and the less airy dwellings where young Pre-Raphaelites adored the wan perfection of Miss Siddal England was severely practical, a nation happily absorbed in the excitements of Palmerstonian prosperity, as new factories with taller chimneys spread a wider pall of smoke and the countryside contracted before the advancing tide of brick and the new stucco palaces of recent wealth exhibited the strange profusion of their ornament and the Victorian age stood at its most Victorian.

But though there was small cause for worry in the state of things at home, the scene in 1861 was more disquieting abroad. The Continent had lived for forty years under the dispensation of the peace-treaties of Vienna. Those powerful incantations averted war for upwards of a generation; but the settlement was not immortal, and its authority had gradually evaporated before the rise of forces which the treaty system had not taken into account. The omission was deliberate. For it was not to be expected that Prince Metternich and Lord Castlereagh would respect the right of populations to choose their own allegiance, since in their view the principle of nationality had (like the Rights of Man) been one of the flamboyant pretexts behind which the late French aggression had marched across Europe; and what loyal Austrian could doubt that Hapsburgs were no less entitled to rule over Czechs, Italians, and Magyars than over Viennese? This misapprehension was corrected by a few decades of old-fashioned government, in which paternalism verged upon domestic tyranny. Under this stimulus the vogue of romance, with its accompanying taste for the revival of long-vanished national glories, acquired the urgency of current politics and combined with the deferred explosion of ideas upon the risky topic of self-government, which the receding tide of French revolutionary influence had left in the subsoil of European consciousness. The results were most unsettling for a treaty system founded upon anything rather than the principle of nationality, and the settlement was promptly challenged at a dozen points across the Continent. Poles, Italians, Hungarians, and Czechs questioned the dictates of Vienna; and though their effort to reverse the settlement was crushed in 1848, their questions were unanswered. The challenge still persisted; and the fitful light of freedom burned in Italy, until the guarded flame of a few secret societies became a noble blaze of national resurgence in the strong hands of Garibaldi and Cavour. The French successfully asserted a still more categorical denial of the treaty system, when a nephew of the Emperor whom the treaties had deposed became their ruler; and the enigmatic presence of Napoleon III was now the main focus of unsettlement in Europe. His restless diplomacy—Palmerston wrote to a colleague that "the Emperor's mind seems as full of schemes as a warren is full of rabbits"—broke the long peace and violated the traditional alignment of the ex-Allied Powers hallowed by the Holy Alliance, when he ranged England on his side against the Czar in the strange imbroglio of the Crimean War. In 1859 his revolutionary sympathies made French armies, by which Austrian resistance was broken at Magenta and Solferino, the main instruments of Italian liberation; and he was perpetually hoping for a European conference to bring the treaties of 1815 up to date, a proposal which elicited from Palmerston the bland response that "those who hold their estates under a good title, now nearly half a century old, might not be particularly desirous of having it brought under discussion with all the alterations which good-natured neighbours might wish to suggest in their boundaries." But the Continental equilibrium was no longer balanced on the faded formulæ of those forgotten instruments. For though Poland was still a hope, Italy was a reality; and the Continent appeared to be controlled by a more fluid element, constituted by the slow-moving impulses of Napoleon III.

His dictatorship wore the accustomed air of permanence, since all dictatorships invariably look as if they would last for ever. France, skilfully alarmed by the imaginary imminence of the *Spectre rouge* in 1851, had fled to the shelter

[103]

of his name; and one more Bonaparte ensured the continuity of national life at the modest price of a complete suspension of all political activity. After the wild uproar of 1848 a welcome silence settled on French politics, and public business was transacted by his nominees. Refreshed by this repose, the national intelligence began to interest itself once more in its own affairs; and the Imperial dictatorship endeavoured to respond by a slight relaxation of its political authority approximating roughly to the Parliamentary liberties conceded to her subjects by Queen Elizabeth. This stage in a dictator's life is always the most precarious, since the steep ladder of dictatorship, often so easy to ascend, is infinitely harder to come down; and the descent is often faster and leads further than the climber meant. The Second Empire was gently launched upon this incline which, its director hoped, might bring it to the safe levels of Parliamentary government. But in the event the slope proved too severe for the brittle fabric of his authority; and when it ultimately reached the bottom, there was no Emperor.

Some touch of the uncertainty involved in that delicate transition already blurred the sharp outline of the Empire and of the long shadow which it cast across the Continent. France was still paramount in 1861, and its slow-spoken Emperor behind his big moustache was still the leading figure in the world. But would they always be? The flaring lights of Paris were still turned up as high as they had ever been; but, by the mournful destiny of all dictators, they must either burn still higher or go out.

That was the difficulty. He could not force the note of French supremacy for ever. It had been comparatively simple for a man of more intelligence than was usual among monarchs to dominate the Continental scene. His policies bore more relation to the modern world; his armies jingled spurs and trailed their scabbards more gallantly, and their proud Imperial emblems—the great N's on their sabre-taches, the tall bearskins of his grenadiers, and the dull gleam of the *Cuirassiers* in their big helmets—were a sober-ing reminder of the long columns which had once marched across the world to victory behind their eagles; even his fleet alarmed Lord Palmerston into a paroxysm of coast-defence and set the Poet Laureate writing lyrics for the Volunteers. But the Emperor could hardly force the note for ever; and there were other voices on the Continent which might break in upon his solo. A warning murmur sounded, as he held the centre of the stage after the Austrian defeat at Sol-ferino. For the Prussians began massing troops behind the Rhine, since (in a shrewd diagnosis) they would "regard any serious defeat of Austria in Italy, or anything that should seriously endanger her position in the Quadrilateral, as a danger to the left flank of the German position." True their mobilisation was extremely faulty; the Prussian army of 1859 was still the army of von Bonin and an exceedingly imperfect instrument of war. But that would soon be reme-died, if von Moltke and von Roon could have their way; and it was an unpleasing revelation that there was a German point of view, since hitherto the Continent had got on pleas-antly enough without one.

The Hapsburg mosaic had formed the highly decorative centre of a still richer tessellation, in which assorted German states were loosely assembled in the vague pattern of a Germanic Confederation. It was little more than a diplo-matic convenience, which bore faint traces of its feudal origins; and there were few facilities for the application of a German point of view to the formation of a German policy. The German soul, if it existed, was unsatisfied in the field of politics. As one of them had written, he "could not say abroad, 'I am a German,' could not pride himself that the German flag was flying from his vessel, could have no

German consul in time of need, but had to explain, 'I am a Hessian, a Darmstädter, a Buckebürger: my Fatherland was once a great and powerful country, now it is shattered into eight and thirty splinters.' " The lively transformation-scenes of 1848 had included among the less satisfactory exhibits of that year of sudden impulses and swift retreats a sketch of German unity. But it was almost equally defective in time, *personnel,* and place, since no amount of well-intentioned eloquence could turn a Frankfort Parliament into the operative centre of a new Germany or convert the unstable personality of King Frederick William IV into its champion against the forces of reaction. Besides, the forces of reaction had an awkward way of triumphing in 1848; and as the dawn faded, Germany relapsed once more into its aboriginal multiplicity. But even that might be remedied, if the Germans followed the heartening example of Italy; and in December, 1861, King William intimated that Prussia might appear in the part played in Italy by Piedmont. His rehearsals for the *rôle* took the form of an elaborate reorganisation and rearmament of the Prussian army. But the chief performer was still a diplomat abroad with a capacity for pointed sayings and an amazing taste in liquor. For Count von Bismarck had the unclouded vision and the simple ruthlessness by which the Frederician tradition might be continued. The Prussian kingdom had originally been raised from feudal unimportance by one thin-lipped monarch, who kept the flame of war burning through half the Eighteenth Century in order to maintain a naked theft of Austrian territory; and if his work was to be resumed, Europe would become a less pleasant place to live in than it had been. That was the worst (for Europe) of the emergence of a German point of view.

The masters of the Continent in 1861 were largely untroubled by these forebodings, since Napoleon was vaguely favourable to the creation of a Prussian counterpoise to Austria, and in spite of all that Prince Albert and Count Stockmar wrote Lord Palmerston could never be prevailed upon to take a German state altogether seriously. Indeed, his main preoccupations as the year went out were transatlantic. For the Civil War was on, and neutrality is never easy for maritime powers. A Northern cruiser had committed the inexcusable irregularity of stopping a British mail-steamer and removing four Southern passengers by force. The names of Captain Wilkes, the *Trent,* and Messrs. Slidell and Mason acquired a feverish notoriety, as a sharp argument proceeded between Washington and Downing Street. War-correspondents hopefully began to study the American campaign of 1812, and the Guards sailed for Canada. Lord Palmerston dropped in one evening at the Confederate offices in Suffolk Street, Pall Mall, and had a most exciting talk about the possibilities of armed Franco-British intervention to stop the war; and Lincoln in his yokel phase was slightly irritating to the Queen's minister at Washington with a vague assurance, when pressed about the burning question, "Oh, that'll be got along with." But the Cabinet was cautious; the law was on their side; a draft despatch of Russell's was discreetly modified, toned down still further by the Prince Consort's failing hand, and rendered even milder by a last revision in Cabinet; and as Secretary Seward intimated that his prisoners would be set free, the war-cloud passed. That anxious piece of drafting had been the Prince's last public work. Now the Queen was quite alone in the bewildering solitude of Palmerstonian England and the Europe of the Second Empire, alone among her crowding memories of his ideals that had been so noble and his opinions that had been so precise; and the short winter afternoon was over, as the tide ran mournfully through Spithead beneath the windows of the house that he had built.

EIGHTEEN
SEVENTY–ONE

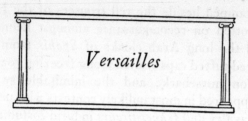

Versailles

THE SNOW lay thick on France that winter. Across the stillness of its white expanse the muddy network of the roads traced a black pattern, as they threaded an uncomfortable way between the snowy fields. Naked trees extended their eternal gesture beside frozen rivers; and from the chimneys of its little towns the smoke rose thinly into the pale January sky. A strange stillness seemed to pervade it, and that year the country's life was more than usually arrested in the midwinter hush. There were noticeably fewer trains to snort along embankments or go shrieking into tunnels, which was not surprising when it was observed that a good many tunnels ended in a heap of fallen masonry and railway bridges were apt to lack an arch or tilt uncomfortably into rivers. And there was less movement on the roads than might have been expected. In the towns a few muffled figures hurried along empty pavements; and even where a crowd assembled there was an air of desolation. But the countryside presented a still stranger scene. For a high proportion of the wayfarers were military; and though they wore French

[111]

uniform, the uniforms were strangely assorted. Blue-coated *moblots* tramped beside the red trousers of the Line; *gendarmes* trotted on reconnaissance amongst helmeted dragoons and the long Arab cloaks of *Spahis* from Algeria; sailors in red-tufted caps trailed along freezing roads behind admirals on horseback; and the inimitable swagger of Zouaves appeared in most unlikely contexts with units of dismounted cavalry and *francs-tireurs* in lurid costumes of their own invention. It was a fantastic blend, in which the military debris of the Empire was inextricably mixed with the improvisations of a new regime. But not all the uniforms were French that were to be seen on French roads that winter. Startled villages heard the sharp note of hoofs and saw the flutter of the pennons on the long lances, as the Uhlans trotted by with levelled carbines. A squeal of fifes and the dull rattle of the drums brought on marching columns of great-coated men wearing the sombre greens and blues of Germany. The marchers wore spiked helmets or the most unbecoming caps; and as the waggons jolted past behind their teams, bearded men looked out or sat pulling at their long pipes. For Germany was on the march; and as the Krupp guns clanked through French villages, the German thrust went deeper into the heart of France.

This oddity of the French scene that winter was nowhere more apparent than at Versailles. The steep angle of the chapel roof still shouldered high above the French king's palace, and his horse still pranced with circumspection on its pedestal in the great forecourt. But the scene beneath those royal windows was modified by more than time. For the sentries at the palace gates wore foreign uniform, and there were no French colours to be seen. True, French-women in shawls still hurried by to market in the little shops, and a few chilly Frenchmen went about the streets with a diminished air. But the strange thing about them was that they did not seem to be at home. Their homes were in Versailles; and yet the place, to all appearances, did not belong to them, and those hurrying civilians wore the sad but unmistakable air of exile. For by a tragic paradox of war they were exiles in their own country, since that winter an invading army had made itself at home in Versailles.

Each morning, as the stiff figures of the foreign sentries presented arms outside the *Préfecture,* a neat *calèche* went down the street behind the drawn swords of a Hussar escort and outriders in Prussian livery. Inside the carriage an old man with narrow eyes saluted gravely, as the bearded men along the pavements stiffened to attention and German hands were lifted smartly to spiked helmets. Sometimes he passed the riding figure of his son, as the Crown Prince of Prussia, with his big beard and his noble air, rode out to his command on the heights overlooking Paris; or the old man paused for a few words across the apron of his carriage with the lean visage of von Moltke. That wasted septuagenarian loved to sit behind the empty frame of a round window in the attic of an abandoned villa on the high ground between Sèvres and Meudon. He spent his mornings there; and as he leaned back in a broken chair, he could watch the shells bursting three miles away in Paris, a rewarding spectacle for its designer. In the evenings he presided at the long table in the Hôtel des Réservoirs, where the Staff dined. A hungry galaxy of German princes dined at a table of their own; and the big restaurant was full of food and wine and German voices. The cultivated Fritz was in a villa of his own, where they sometimes had a little music after dinner. There was no lack of pianists, and an aide-de-camp sang sentimental songs to their accompaniment; or when the painter who sometimes came to dinner had brought his 'cello, the Crown Prince could listen to his favourite *Meditations* of

Gounod, and the music drifted down the snowy garden into the freezing night.

Life was less elevated, if no less Germanic, at the suburban residence to which Count von Bismarck had transported the entire apparatus of Prussian foreign policy. All day long the little corps of his familiars—the bearded Abeken, von Delbrück, Lothar Bucher, and von Keudell—drafted and ciphered in the unpretentious house behind its railings in a quiet street. Sometimes the Chancellor worked late with candles on his table. But his conviviality was rarely checked. Perhaps there was less music than elsewhere, since Bismarck was not conspicuously sentimental. Yet he proved himself a faithful devotee of the Teutonic trinity, atoning for any lack of fiddlers by his vociferous attention to pipe and bowl. For the formidable Chancellor smoked, talked, and drank quite inexhaustibly after office hours. There was a terrifying *abandon* about his relaxation, which concealed the frigid processes of the most calculating mind in Europe behind a rough good-fellowship; and the big, bald man with the mastiff's eyes talked through the smoke at the head of the table in his unobtrusive little house in a side-street at Versailles. Tobacco, talk, and drink flowed with the fine profusion of a hunting breakfast. The hunt, indeed, was nearly over. The palace up the street was full of German wounded; long rows of patriotic canvases on which French armies triumphed with monotonous superiority looked down at the ranged cots; and the proud lettering of the façade, which dedicated it '*à toutes les gloires de la France,*' stared coldly at the German guns parked in the forecourt. The palace windows gazed blindly up the broad avenue that led to Paris; but the road to Paris ran no further than the last German outpost in the freezing trenches outside a starving city.

It was a strange reversal, by which Napoleon was sitting dismally in a provincial *château* somewhere in Germany and

[114]

his lovely Empress at a depressing house in Kent, while the King of Prussia took his tea after dinner in a French *Préfecture* and plain-clothes policemen from Berlin walked up and down outside. For France, or what remained of it, was a republic now. It is the melancholy fate of republics to inherit defeated empires; and MM. Thiers and Gambetta issued resounding manifestoes from a safe distance at Bordeaux, while German armies held Paris in an iron ring or lunged unmercifully about a conquered country, shepherding Chanzy's ragged columns towards Normandy or hunting Bourbaki across the snow into Switzerland. The tricolour still fluttered on the battered forts of Belfort; and the guns spoke slowly from Mont-Valérien, as Paris answered the last German challenge. But France was beaten to its knees. Foreign troops held the whole centre of the country; foreign bugle-calls rang clear across its sullen villages; and foreign guns rumbled along its roads in the midwinter hush, as the pale January sky looked down at the inverted world of 1871.

But the summit of the whole tragic paradox that winter was at Versailles; and one chilly Wednesday in the second week of January it reached its apex. The occasion, it was felt, would be historic. Something in the nature of a large oil-painting was plainly called for; and the prescient Crown Prince telegraphed to a Court painter, who had gone home on leave, that if he could be at Versailles by January 18, he would witness something worthy of his brush. Such productions were not unfamiliar that winter at Versailles. Indeed, their manufacture was conducted on a considerable scale, since Great Headquarters were modestly aware that history had its eye upon them and did their best to help. So there was a good deal of promiscuous sketching; bearded amateurs explored the mysteries of perspective; and more systematic operations were carried on by professionals, who were installed in studios about the palace and maintained a steady output combining patriotic fervour with a fair degree of actuality. Professor Bleibtreu, whose *forte* was military scenes, painted industriously; and Anton von Werner, with "General von Moltke with his Staff before Paris" on his mind, sketched away at French scenery and German portrait-heads, only slightly handicapped as a truthful recorder by his romantic admiration of the "northern blond hair" of Moltke's invariable wig. The royal telegram found him at Karlsruhe with three days in which to get to Versailles and witness the historic scene. He travelled post-haste across France and got there just in time. It was still dark when he arrived on the historic morning; and it was a little disconcerting after a breathless journey through the war-zone to be asked by an immaculate Court-Marshal if he had brought his dress clothes with him. But this omission was soon remedied by the rapid purchase of a suit which was both French and ready-made; and, thus attired, the painter was prepared to watch his masters making history.

By eleven o'clock the great square before the palace was full of German troops, and interested Frenchmen paused to stare through the railings. Inside the Château German officers in their best uniforms were trooping up the stairs between two rigid lines of *Cuirassiers;* and when they reached the Galerie des Glaces, they saw that a long platform had been built across the end, where all the colours of the German armies were tastefully disposed against a background of red velvet. This pleasing scene was multiplied in the great mirrors, which were also privileged to reflect an altar and no less than seven German clergymen. At twelve o'clock the King of Prussia entered with a train of princes. Proceedings opened with divine worship and a sermon, followed by a hymn; and the old King walked down the long gallery to the platform at the end. There he read out a declaration that he accepted the new title of Emperor. The heavy figure of his Chancellor stepped forward; and Count von Bismarck in the blue tunic and great boots of a Prussian *Cuirassier,* holding his helmet by the spike, proclaimed the German Empire. A bearded Grand Duke called for cheers; and as the old man stood there before the German colours and between the drawn swords of two white-coated *Gardes-du-Corps* who flanked the dais with the gleam of their cuirasses, the cheers rang through the gallery and echoed in the ceiling painted for King Louis' victories two hundred years before. The noble mirrors on the French king's wall reflected a wild forest of German swords and German helmets lifted in honour of a German Emperor; and the cheering ran through the troops on the great square outside the palace. After the proclamation his officers filed past the Emperor; there was a round of presentations; and the first ceremony of the German Empire was over.

The big room emptied slowly in a cheerful hum of German talk; and the tall mirrors were alive with tight Prussian uniforms, bearded faces, epauletted shoulders, all varieties of unbecoming helmets, and the bright ribbons of every order in the rainbow of Teutonic honour. Bismarck's scowl and Moltke's fallen cheeks lived in them for an instant, as the scabbards trailed across the palace floor; and their bright surface, in which King Louis had once seen himself, obediently gave back Iron Cross and *pickelhaube.* The silhouette of Germany passed confidently across the glass, until the footsteps died away and the great mirrors were left waiting in an empty gallery.

That winter morning's work in the great gallery at Versailles was the dramatic ending of a complicated story. The principal performers, it is true, were far from satisfied. King William would have preferred to wait until the war was over; and a last-minute objection from Bavaria annoyed him by preventing his proclamation as Emperor of Germany and substituting the less authoritative style of German Emperor, which he regarded as an empty honorific. Bismarck had acquiesced. But the concession displeased his sovereign; and no greeting passed between them after the ceremony. Indeed, the royal irritation went so far that when a prince, whose military accomplishments included heraldry, showed him a blazon of the new Imperial coat of arms that evening after dinner, the old man sulkily declined to look at it. But what was not enough for him was quite enough for Bismarck, who had created a German Empire out of the most unpromising material.

The task had not been easy; but it had been astonishingly quick. Eight years before the pieces on the German board were scattered in their customary disarray—a multitude of pawns, some bishops, and a few castles casually disposed in deferential attitudes round Austria, which appeared to be the only royal piece upon the board. The Prussian kingdom was a piece of frankly secondary value, whose movements were restricted by the twin possessions of an army which was not particularly efficient and a parliament which effectually prevented anyone from making it much more so. Bismarck, imported from diplomacy into politics, defied the parliamentarians with easy insolence, enabling Roon and Moltke to reform the army at the indignant taxpayers' expense, whilst he deftly balanced Prussian policy between the indispensable support of Russia and the slightly patronising tolerance of France. Thus poised, it might be possible for Prussia to take the lead in Germany. The Russians would not interfere, since they had not forgiven Austrian indifference in the Crimean War. Besides, the Prussians had been most obliging when the Poles gave trouble of the usual kind and Bismarck was good enough to close the Prussian frontier against his neighbour's revolutionaries. For he was always most attentive to St. Petersburg. He had been there *en poste;* and a close study of the Prussian past convinced him that a repetition of the Frederician agony of war on two fronts must be avoided at all costs. It was his firm belief that, if his country wished to operate in Central Europe with an easy mind, its rear must be safeguarded by an amicable relation with the Czar. That was the leading gambit of his game, from which he never wavered in all the years that followed; and whatever Prussia might attempt in Germany, there was not the slightest danger that the Czar would interfere.

The French were equally obliging, as Napoleon III had been at war with Austria and felt vaguely that there was something to be said for Germans of another species, whom he had not antagonised by the extremely galling, if unselfish, amputation of their Italian possessions. Besides, the Emperor had an innate prejudice, which underlay the greater part of his political proceedings, in favour of nations struggling to be free; and Prussia was nothing if not nationalist in its aspirations. It was not easy to discern how they could constitute a menace to the French. Next to the dash and glitter of his own incomparable troops—the bronzed victors of Sebastopol and Solferino and the lean practitioners of colonial warfare in Algeria and Mexico—their soldiers were singularly unimpressive with their black helmets and a preposterous addiction to the goose-step; and the elegant *sabreurs* of the Second Empire watched with a condescending smile the slightly academic labours of von Moltke at his desk. Smart *képis* were titled at still more rakish angles in indulgent contemplation of the Prussian needle-gun, the new breech-loading field artillery, and other military toys with which the ingenuity of German *savants* entertained the German soldier. It was impossible to view these spectacled beginners at the art of war as any sort of danger to the dashing veterans who had planted tricolours on the Malakoff and were busy hunting stray republicans across the dusty distances of Mexico. For France was a world-power whose strong arm had lately made a King of Italy and was entering cheerfully upon the more exacting task of making an Emperor of Mexico, while Prussia went about her more domestic tasks in Germany.

Like most products of the German mind, they were extremely complicated. But when the Germanic Confederation got into an argument with the King of Denmark about Schleswig-Holstein, it did not seem to matter greatly. True, the Prince of Wales had lately married an extremely pretty Danish princess, and Lord Palmerston dropped an impressive hint that Germany would be well advised to refrain from tampering with Danish territory. But the French Emperor was indisposed to help, and the Queen was frankly unsympathetic, since her unseen oracle directed her to side with Germany. So the Confederation did its best to browbeat the Danes, and that questionable entity directed Hanover and Saxony to discipline the King of Denmark. But Bismarck shouldered them aside and claimed the privilege for Prussia, because if any territory was going to change hands, it would be just as well for Prussia to be there. This intervention impelled the Austrians to take a hand from a vague sense that any German action would be incomplete without their leadership. But the ensuing operations against Denmark were almost completely Prussian in their conduct and direction, and the campaign of 1864 was the first effort of the new Prussian army. It was not conspicuously brilliant, although the Danes were duly shepherded out of the Duchies and turned to bay in the redoubts of Düppel that barred the way to Copenhagen. The Continent resounded with half-hearted protests against a singularly brutal act of violence against a smaller nation. But Bismarck had his way, and Europe ratified the *fait accompli* with an unconvincing semblance of diplomatic decency. So everyone (except the Danes) was happy, and the stolen Duchies were for the moment in the joint occupation of Austria and Prussia.

That was the first movement of the new German composition; and if its military execution left something to be desired, its political intention was quite unmistakable. Henceforward Prussia would act for Germany; and if Austria was unwilling to recognise the claim, so much the worse for Austria. In this event it would be circumspect for Prussia to strike a friendly bargain with any enemies that Austria might have; and Bismarck developed a new, if not quite disinterested, sympathy for the Italians in their unsatisfied desire for Venice. The Italians, on their side, were not reluctant; but before consecrating a new friendship they desired to be assured that the French Emperor, who was their natural protector, would not disapprove, and Bismarck proceeded with redoubled gusto to cultivate the French. His king went to stay at Compiègne; the Prussian Minister of War attended autumn manœuvres at Châlons and was handed the Legion of Honour by a small Prince Imperial; and the resourceful man himself called on Napoleon at Biarritz for an interminable bout of inconclusive talk about the map of Europe. But though the Emperor was vaguer than ever, his perspicacious guest could see that Venice haunted him. His own recovery of Italy for the Italians had been broken off in 1859 before the restoration of Venice, and his busy mind played round the unfinished task. He had already sent an Austrian Archduke to Mexico in a vague hope that Austrian gratitude might somehow impel the Hapsburgs to part with Venice. But the news from Maximilian was hardly of a character that was likely to inspire anyone with gratitude; and Napoleon was not unwilling that the sacred task of reconstituting Italy should be completed with Prussian aid. That left the board clear for the next move; and with a reasonable hope that Italy would be his ally Bismarck set about to pick his quarrel with the Austrians.

He picked it with rare virtuosity, since it was based upon the alleged impropriety of the Austrian command in Holstein in tolerating the pretensions of a German claimant to the Duchies. True, his claim had been one of the foundations of their joint intervention in 1864. But since the war, it seemed, the conscientious Bismarck had been legally advised that the Duchies had belonged to the poor King of Denmark after all. This might appear regrettable in view of the unhappy circumstance that Austria and Prussia had now relieved him of them. But that could not be helped; and the one consolation was that, as the Duchies had belonged to Denmark, the Danes had been perfectly entitled to surrender them. It followed that their new tenants had a perfect title and that the Austrian command at Altona was quite out of order in tolerating any other claimant. Fortified by this Gilbertian jurisprudence, Bismarck with perfect gravity protested to Vienna against such shocking conduct; nor did their age-long tradition of ineptitude desert the Austrians, who obliged the challenger by showing indignation at the Prussian challenge. This suited him completely, as his option on the wayward affections of Italy only ran for ninety days. If he could force the Austrians to fight within that period, the wary Latins were prepared to risk another war against the Austrian oppressor; and in that event the Austrians would be caught between two fires, with every chance of losing Venice in the south and failing to resist the Prussians in the north. The trap was perfectly successful;

and the accomplished player won his highly complicated game with three weeks to spare. For the Austrians, who could always be relied upon for suicidal blunders, chose war with Prussia, which entitled Prussia to exercise its option on Italy as an ally. Italian blood boiled according to the time-table; and as von Moltke moved his armies into line, the chivalrous King Victor Emmanuel rode out to the delivery of Venice and (if necessary) to the death.

Bismarck's precipitation of the war had been a perfect piece of base manipulation. But the war of 1866 was not quite so simple in its course as a mere three-cornered fight between Prussia, Austria, and Italy. For it was complicated by the surviving tangle of the Germanic Confederation, which impelled South Germany and Hanover to side with Austria against the Prussians. The harsh Prussian utterance was not yet accepted as the voice of Germany; and the minor constellations of the Teutonic firmament made a last effort to escape the orbit of Berlin. It failed disastrously, since Austrians are rarely on the winning side. The Han-overians were rounded up at Langensalza, and the Austro-German defensive in Bohemia was no less disastrous. A campaign of seven weeks alarmed the world with the spectacle of an Austrian *débâcle* at Sadowa and the Prussians marching on Vienna. New methods and new weapons had made their army the most formidable military fact on the Continent; and the French Emperor, who might have intervened in a commanding pose, stood aside a little helplessly as Prussia marched to supremacy in Central Europe. It was exceedingly unpleasant to watch the supersession of the Austrians by an unscrupulous competitor. But what was he to do? He was not ready for a war, since the campaign in Mexico had inconveniently absorbed large quantities of military stores and given French taxpayers into the bargain a strong distaste for such activities. Besides, it was not altogether clear what he would fight for, even if he was prepared to fight. It had been simple to reward himself for the campaign of 1859 with Savoy and Nice. But what was he to claim from Germany? And would they pay the bill, if he presented it? He was unwell that summer; and his nerves were shaken by a dreadful interview with a half-crazed woman who had come all the way from Mexico to Paris in order to reproach him with desertion of her husband in that glaring wilderness, where Maximilian had turned to bay and the implacable republicans were gathering to take their last revenge on an unwanted emperor. Carlota dragged her shattered wits across the Continent for a last collapse into dementia under the sad eyes of the Pope; and the French Emperor was left with an increasing sense of failure and the unpleasant problem of the new military power which Bismarck had produced beyond the Rhine.

It grew no simpler as the years went by, the last embarrassed years of the decade that he had seemd to dominate so easily. He needed all his magic now. But his health was not so good as it had been; his public was distinctly less appreciative; and when he made his passes, none of them appeared to have the least effect upon the unimpressionable Germans. Some other wand than his had waved, and the political outlines of Germany were changing fast. For Prussia had absorbed Hanover and Schleswig-Holstein and was now the head of a North German Confederation, which someone impolitely termed "a congress of roaches presided over by a very big pike." It had alliances besides with the South German states; and German unity had practically been achieved with Prussia on the throne once occupied by Austria. This was alarming, since Austria had wanted little more than to be let alone, while Prussian appetites were more incalculable. Besides, the Prussian army was a new factor in the game; and French soldiers began to look apprehensively towards their eastern frontier, where the new Germany "looms out" (in the words of a British diplomat) "like some huge ironclad from which no sounds are heard but the tramp of men at drill, or the swinging upon their pivots of monster guns." It was a little ominous, although the French had a new rifle now and miracles were promised of the *mitrailleuse*. There was even a vague effort to draw Italy and Austria into alliance with the Second Empire. But Italy would never play so long as the French felt themselves bound by a misplaced religious sense to deny King Victor Emmanuel access to his inevitable capital by mounting guard over the Pope at Rome; and though the Austrians might be willing to align themselves against Berlin, it would require more than an exchange of royal courtesies and some inconclusive military conversations to shake off an age-long habit of inaction.

So the sick Emperor and his uneasy countrymen lay rather isolated in the path of Prussia. For Bismarck, having done his work in Germany, was turning to the west; and one quiet Sunday in June, 1870, they learnt that it had been proposed to make a Hohenzollern King of Spain. The strange proposal had a Prussian origin. Indeed, it would be highly gratifying for Berlin to place a German outpost in rear of France beyond the Pyrenees; and the effect of the suggestion on the French was bound to be explosive. This was too much; and while the Continent rang with French protests, the Minister of War in Paris was asked if he was ready. But the old King of Prussia, who was sipping water for his health at Ems, declined to press the offensive candidature; and everyone was much relieved. There would not have to be a war, and French diplomacy had scored a point at last. But a demented vanity impelled them to improve the victory by trying to extract an undertaking that the King of Prussia would never countenance a repetition of the outrage. The French ambassador, who tried to buttonhole the King one sunny morning on the promenade with this additional request, got no encouragement from the old gentleman; and his applications for a further audience were politely headed off. That might have ended the affair. But Bismarck was dining in Berlin that night with Roon and Moltke. Their evening opened rather gloomily, because it looked as though there was to be no war with France. But when the telegram arrived from Ems, a few happy touches by the Chancellor, who thoughtfully revised it for publication, transformed the news item, making it appear that the French ambassador had been finally dismissed that morning by the King of Prussia. There could not be much doubt of the result when this was read in Paris. If King William had not done very much that morning, his Chancellor did rather more at dinner, and French *amour propre* could be depended on to do the rest next day. After this contribution to international harmony the little party was resumed in a distinctly brighter mood, and the trio grew noticeably more convivial. Moltke was almost gay, and Roon vociferously intimated the renewal of his faith in God; for war was now within their grasp.

It came within forty-eight hours of the publication of the news in Paris. For the provocation was infallible; and as the tired Emperor discharged his thunderbolts reluctantly, the streets filled with excited patriots, yelling *"à Berlin!"* The supposed insult to Count Benedetti at Ems released a flow of French emotion. It had been unspeakably distasteful to observe the swift advance of Prussia to European eminence, and French feelings had been expressed in an increasing sensitiveness and a multiplicity of diplomatic moves that led them nowhere. But now the time for diplomacy was over, and France realised with an immense feeling of relief that it could reassert itself in action—the familiar action of

French armies springing forward to attack behind the lines of levelled bayonets, as French shells whined overhead and the *mitrailleuses* poured in a deadly stream of bullets. For if France had a dawning doubt about the Empire, it had none about the army; and the cheering crowds along the boulevards indicated its destination, *"à Berlin!"* The swift frenzy united the whole nation; and a pleasing symbol of its new-found unity was the official toleration of the seditious *Marseillaise* itself, rendered to tremendous applause by a bearded baritone inside the Opera. But French ministers were not so happy in their utterances, since the Premier, desiring to assure the Chamber that he and his colleagues assumed the grave responsibilities of war with a clear conscience, informed his hearers that they did so with a light heart, and the Minister of War announced that the completeness of the army's preparations extended to the last button of its gaiters. The phrases rang unpleasantly in later ears; and M. Emile Ollivier and Marshal Le Bœuf were followed down the corridors of history by the reproachful echoes of *'le cœur léger'* and *'le dernier bouton des guêtres.'* But there seemed nothing wrong about them in the roaring Paris streets of July, 1870. Someone had insulted France, and France sprang feverishly into war. The rift was no less thankfully received beyond the Rhine, where its resourceful author had contrived a German war for the consecration of the new Germany. Solemn crowds were chanting *"nach Paris!"* with an indignant sense that the Fatherland had been wantonly attacked by France. The Queen of England shared their conviction; and Mr. Gladstone was not quite certain that she was not right, although the Prince of Wales, who was invariably clear-sighted on the subject of the Prussians, held another view. Had he not seen them misappropriate the Duchies from his wife's countrymen and lure the Austrians over the precipice of war? It did not re-

[127]

quire much penetration to suspect the Prussians. But their latest enemy had more than the Prussians to reckon with, since all Germany marched with them. That was the master-stroke. The armies of South Germany, which had fired at Prussian helmets four years before, marched singing to the railway stations in a holy war against the French. No other war than that could have united them; and no other hand than Bismarck's could have produced the war.

The rest was a swift tragedy. Before the French offensive could develop, the Germans were across the frontier. The invasion flooded the green valleys of Alsace, as MacMahon fought among the trees at Wörth through a long August day. The bayonets lunged in the sunshine, as the blue and scarlet of the Zouaves came swinging into action and the *Turcos* plunged yelling forward through the vines, and a despairing charge of cavalry swept by with drumming hoofs. But as the shadows lengthened, the beaten columns trailed back into the dusty sunset, and the German flood crept nearer to the blue line of the Vosges. Then it was sweeping round the French armies, where they stood in front of Metz watched by the empty eyes of the sick Emperor. He left them, huddled in his carriage, before the trumpets sounded for the charge at Mars-la-Tour; and the bare ridge of Gravelotte saw the French turn to bay, as Moltke herded them under the guns of Metz.

August was nearly over now, and the last army of the Empire moved uncertainly into the north-east. Perhaps it would deliver Metz; perhaps it would encounter Moltke and break the spell of French defeats. It must be possible for France to win a victory; and if a victory did not come quickly, there would not be an Emperor in France much longer. That was the dictator's tragedy; for no dictator-ship survives defeat. His name had been a promise of French victory; but the promise was strangely unfulfilled, as his armies stumbled through the summer rain and the dark flood of the invasion crept across a startled country. He could not face the Paris streets without a victory; and Eugénie's indignant telegrams informed him daily that he must either win one or . . . But there was no alternative, and Napoleon continued to drift miserably on the long swell of his tragedy. He was alone with it, between the Germans and a capital he dared not enter; and the rain slanted down on the bowed shoulders of his marching men, as they headed for the north-east. His boy was taken off to safety now, as young children are led away before the end; and there was nothing in his ears except the rumble of gun-carriages on sodden roads and the tramp of his battalions through the driving rain. The dismal march across Champagne went on; and far behind them France waited for the news. His capital was dazed and angry; his Regent, a lonely woman in an empty palace, took chloral and nerved herself to face his ministers; and as his last army trailed into the north-east, the Emperor dragged after it, a tragic figure with dull eyes and ragged, greying hair that scared the loyal villagers who had come out to cheer, as the bright escort clattered by, and stood staring after a sick man in a jolting carriage.

His journey's end was in the dark streets of a silent little town, where they arrived late one night and told him that it was called Sedan. That was the final scene, with the guns thudding in the mist of a September dawn as the last army of the Empire felt the trap close round it. For they were caught between the Germans and the Belgian frontier, and there was nothing for it but a last despairing fight. Napoleon, far past despair, faced the unutterable torment of the saddle; and as his face was white, he had put false colour on his cheeks to ride along the reeling line under the German fire through a long morning of defeat, a painted emperor hoping to die among his soldiers on the bare hill-sides above Sedan. But the guns still thudded on, until the shaken man commanded them to hoist a white flag on the citadel and wrote offering his sword to his good brother, the King of Prussia. For there must be an end of all this killing. He had not managed to get killed himself, and there was nothing else for him to do. On the next morning he drove out between the trees along the misty road to Don-chéry. The guns were silent now; for the French army had capitulated. Outside a cottage by the road the Emperor talked quietly with Bismarck in the still September air, his *képi* seeming almost rakish next to the severity of the other's German uniform; and when he met King William at a little country-house, they told him that he would be sent to Wil-helmshöhe.

The news of that surrender ended the Second Empire. For two days later, as the Paris newsboys called *"Napoléon III prisonnier,"* a swift impulse swept the capital; and whilst his Empress crept away to England, the streets were roaring *"Vive la République!"* and MM. Thiers and Gambetta came into power. But the Germans still advanced; and as the leaves fell, the dark stain of the invasion spread across the country, until the autumn deepened into winter and the German guns were booming before Paris and the snow of 1871 lay thick on France.

At Versailles they trooped downstairs into the daylight after the great ceremony in the palace, and life resumed. The siege was nearly over; and there were longer intervals between the detonations, as the Paris forts answered the steady thunder of the German guns. The French reply was slower now. The forts were flagging, as the shells whined overhead to burst among the houses in the streets behind them. For they were shelling Paris now, and the starving city was quite systematically raked by German shells deliberately aimed at the civilian quarters. A dazed population huddled in cellars, where night was almost indistinguishable from day, to eat their disappearing rations as the shells crashed into the rooms overhead; and this improvement on the rules of warfare was admirably calculated to stamp out the last spark of resistance in the maddened capital. A final *sortie* came hopelessly to grief under the German guns at Buzenval; and in the winter dusk a dejected French politician drove through the Bois in an old *coupé* of the Emperor's to cross the freezing river in an open boat by the light of burning houses in St. Cloud on his way to Bismarck.

It would be indelicate to call their interviews a negotiation. Bismarck was not concerned even to make them look like one; for when they told him of his visitor's arrival at Versailles, the Chancellor whistled a huntsman's air and cheerfully remarked, "Gentlemen, the kill!" The hunt was over now, the long, ingenious hunt for Prussian dominance that began seven years before when Bismarck shouldered his way into the dispute about the Danish Duchies. It was only five years since he had imposed his will on Austria; and here was M. Jules Favre waiting in the next room to see him in the name of France. When he appeared, the Chancellor felt almost sorry for the gaunt politician with his lank hair and his beard. The sympathetic Bismarck told someone afterwards that Favre "had such large hands and feet that he was almost more like a German than a Frenchman." But his sympathy, founded upon this touching resemblance, was not permitted to impair his cold dexterity; and when the haggard man came out from their final interview, his face was wet with tears. Paris was to surrender; and there would be an armistice for the election of a National Assembly, which could negotiate a peace-treaty. But the dazed Frenchman was informed that unless he would surrender Belfort, where the little garrison persisted bravely in the last beleaguered fortress, the Army of the East must be excepted from the armistice. He could not know the consequences, as he was without precise intelligence as to the recent operations of Bourbaki's command; and this happy touch permitted Manteuffel to hunt them into Switzerland, eliminating a French army and simultaneously destroying the last chance of a relief of Belfort. That was the armistice dictated by a broad-shouldered figure in a white Prussian uniform to a dejected lawyer in an ill-fitting frock-coat. A further stipulation imposed on Paris a cash payment of £8,000,000 in order to avert an immediate occupation by the Germans, the modest Chancellor insisting gallantly that the city was too great a lady for them to consider a ransom that would not be worthy of her.

This mood of geniality persisted, when Favre returned to Versailles with Thiers to ascertain the terms of peace. The Chancellor was more than usually courteous to the old statesman; but once more his courtesy was not allowed to interfere with business, since the big man in uniform informed his small, black-coated visitor that the price of peace would be Alsace, a great part of Lorraine, and an indemnity of six milliards of francs. He was unmoved by the reflection that the inhabitants of the new German provinces would be almost wholly French, replying in terms worthy of Prince Metternich that such political arrangements were really no concern of the inhabitants and that they must share the fate of the territory in which they lived. For the principle of nationality, it seemed, was only applicable where it did not conflict with German requirements. Bismarck was no less indifferent to a grave warning that the annexations

would inevitably lead to another war, replying tartly that
the Germans were prepared to take the risk of that. Indeed,
French feelings did not greatly matter to him, since he insisted further that the German army must march into Paris;
and it was plain that a high importance was attached to this
degrading process, since Bismarck was not prepared to
waive it except upon impossible conditions.

After a struggle (and a doubtful episode in which two
German financiers did their best to get control of the defeated country) he reduced the amount of the indemnity by
one milliard francs, which left it at the unprecedented sum
of £200,000,000. (It was significant that the German bill
for a swift and victorious invasion of France was more than
seven times the total reparations asked by the Allies in 1815
after twenty years of war, in which the French had devastated half the Continent.) But there were no concessions
as to the parade of German troops through Paris, unless
the French could bring themselves to part with Belfort.
That was impossible; for, quite apart from its military
value, the one French fortress where the tricolour had been
kept flying throughout the war had acquired a patriotic
sanctity that placed any question of its surrender far beyond the bounds of possible discussion. It must be retained
at any sacrifice; and the French made the inevitable choice,
retaining Belfort at the cost of shaming Paris, since the
Germans were positively prepared to let them keep the
fortress and a strip of the lost province of Alsace for the
privilege of marching through the conquered streets of a
defeated capital. It might seem a high price to pay for a
mere ceremony; but to the German mind it seemed worth
paying for the public degradation of the French. Those
were the terms of peace dictated at Versailles by German
statesmanship—two French provinces to be annexed, an
indemnity of five milliards of francs secured by the occupa-

tion of sixteen French departments, and a German army to march down the Champs Elysées.

The last night of February, 1871, was mild and clear and more than usually still. The *cafés* emptied on to the Paris pavements, and the last scattered talkers from the open-air meetings along the *boulevards* went slowly home. The omnibuses were still running; but there was no other traffic. All the customary noises of the night had fallen silent. No street orators denounced their betters; no *fiacre* rattled across a square with a late passenger; no printing-presses thundered in the basements of newspaper offices, since there would not be any newspapers in Paris on the next morning. A few cavalry patrols moved silently about the empty streets; and as the moon looked down on Paris, the great place was almost motionless—a dead city where the long lines of houses lay waiting along empty pavements in the grey moonlight, waiting through the slow hours of a winter night with drawn blinds and shuttered windows for the dawn to break.

Early the next morning (it was Wednesday, March 1) a German officer came riding down the Champs Elysées with an escort of Uhlans. He rode as far as the great square, where the stone figures of French cities on their pedestals sat watching through their mourning veils. But all the windows in the Champs Elysées were shuttered, as the little cavalcade went by. Behind him they could hear the rattle of the German drums. The troops were on the move; and the old King of Prussia came from Versailles to watch them march past on the race-course at Longchamps, where he had taken the salute three years before from French battalions with a French Emperor beside him. It was a sunny afternoon, and after the review the bands went clanging up the long incline towards the Arc de Triomphe, where the great arch carved with French battle-honours came up against the sky. The marching lines swung round the monument, which had been barricaded and sand-bagged against the perils of the siege; and the watchers on the pavement heard their music die away down the long slope towards the square, as thirty thousand Germans marched beneath two lines of shuttered windows down the Champs Elysées and wheeled into the Place de la Concorde. That was the end of their parade. A line of empty limbers closed the square, where the masked goddesses of France still watched the visitors through mourning veils. Bismarck had driven in as far as the great arch; but someone recognised him, and his reconnaissance ended in an unpleasant scene.

That night the Germans bivouacked in Paris; and on the next day they could still be seen in the Place de la Concorde. Now they were posing to be photographed in easy attitudes or waltzing heavily with one another to the music of a military band, which was playing German dance music not far from the veiled effigy of Strasburg. Some of them, indeed, got even further into Paris, since those conscientious sight-seers penetrated to the Louvre in order to survey its art treasures. For their artistic appetites were undeterred by the unhappy circumstance that the antiquities were mostly elsewhere and those which had been left behind were quite invisible. But when a crowd of Frenchmen in the street below caught a glimpse of German uniforms at the upper windows, there was an angry roar and a hail of stray missiles, until someone had the bright idea of pelting them with coppers as the first instalment of the indemnity. This awkward episode closed suddenly with their withdrawal to the temporary German territory of the Place de la Concorde, where Paris was privileged to hear their music for another night. There was even a torch-light tattoo in the Champs Elysées. But in the morning they were gone; and as the shutters opened and the town came slowly back to life, Paris began to stir again after its nightmare.

And what a nightmare it had been—the feverish excitement of the hot nights before the war with everybody snatching newspapers along the boulevards and shouting *"à Berlin!"*, the brittle gaiety of the early days when false news of victories along the frontier sent a crowd surging into the Place de la Concorde and two standing figures in an open carriage had sung the *Marseillaise* across a sea of faces, the first incredulous reception of the truth, and then the bitter flavour of defeat. A hot fit of anger sent the Empire spinning and brought on the Third Republic with heroic gestures of an unconquerable people stripped to defend itself; but the dream faded, as the invasion crept slowly nearer and the German guns began to boom outside the city. The slow horror of the siege coiled round it; and defeat was flavoured with starvation. Patriotic frenzy died away into indiscipline; and the proud city lived unsteadily through days of insubordination after nights broken by German shelling, until the horror mounted to the last *crescendo* of the peace with the lost provinces and the five milliards and the Germans marching down the Champs Elysées behind their bands.

It was not easy for the city to shake off its nightmare with those sights dancing before its eyes and that melody still ringing in its ears. The strain was over now; but as the tension of the war relaxed, its nerve failed suddenly and Paris swerved towards dementia. The swift madness of the Commune gripped it, and for ten weeks the red flag fluttered uncomfortably over the city. The pertinacious Marx blessed it from Haverstock Hill. That seer, surveying Europe from the slopes of his suburban Pisgah, was gratified to notice that, although the Commune's grasp of *Das Kapital* was lacking in the finer shades, it seemed to follow something he had written twenty years before in a German pamphlet published in New York; and this slender evidence of his paternity moved him to write innumerable letters in his tiny handwriting to urge the workers of the world (or as many of them as he knew by name) to recognise it as a genuine attempt to destroy the machinery of bourgeois government. For, in the prophet's vision, that agreeable process was a necessary prelude to the dictatorship of the proletariat and the ultimate transition to a classless world. There could be little doubt that the Commune had a sound instinct for destruction. Its bare achievement in bringing down the *Colonne de la Grande Armée* full-length in the Place Vendôme was quite sufficient evidence of that; and Marx turned aside for a few moments from the interminable task of purging the International, which was his own creation, of any person whose opinions differed from his own in order to advise the Commune on military matters and, when his advice had been rejected, to write its epitaph in the most eloquent of all his pamphlets. But though the world loved to trace the hidden hand of international conspiracy in the explosion and a grateful government in later days has named the least seaworthy of its battleships *Parishkaia-Kommuna,* Marx in a cooler mood confessed that "apart from the fact that this was merely the rising of a town under exceptional conditions, the majority of the Commune was in no sense socialist, nor could it be." For it was less a manifestation of the organised Utopia of Socialism than a collective nervous breakdown, in which the underworld of politics welled up in a turbid flood upon whose surface elements of pure disorder whirled in company with imperfectly instructed enthusiasts and frank enemies of almost any form of organised society. A shattered country nerved itself to check the delirium of Paris; and as the *pétroleuses* ran crouching through the smoke of burning buildings and a wild-eyed garrison gesticulated upon barricades, the tricolour fought its way back into the city and France reconquered Paris.

That was the last vicissitude endured by Versailles in that year of mad inversions. For the French Republic brought its headquarters to Versailles, where Thiers presided grimly over the recapture of his capital and German soldiers watched with grounded arms, as French infantry stormed barricades with French defenders.

The nightmare faded slowly, and the life of France resumed. But that winter's work at Versailles had changed the world. There was a German Empire now; the German sentries paced a new frontier; Metz and Strasburg were German fortresses; and the gold that France had paid was soon safe in a German strong-room at Spandau. But though the peace dictated at Versailles by Bismarck took Alsace and Lorraine from France, it gave something to the French as well. For it left such memories of public shame as no war has ever left with any nation in the world. The consequence, written in the next six decades, was grave indeed. A dark resentment replaced the milder flavour of the old diplomatic rivalries, and a new bitterness was born of German inability to win a war with civilised restraint. But the great palace was still standing at Versailles; and in the Galerie des Glaces the mirrors waited on.

EIGHTEEN
EIGHTY–ONE

1. Winter Palace

THE GOLDEN SPIRE of the Admiralty still hung in the sky above St. Petersburg, and a rust-red palace stood beside the frozen Neva. Across the way staff officers still bent above their maps in the big rooms. But now the maps ran further to the south, since Khiva lay behind their marching columns and they were waiting for reports from Skobeleff, two thousand miles away among the Turkomans upon the edge of Persia. One Sunday afternoon a carriage swung out of the palace gates. Six Cossacks rode behind, and there was a Cossack with a carbine standing on the box. For now the Czar took no more unguarded walks along the quay since the unhappy morning when a scared young man had three shots at him and missed. The age of good intentions and reform had been succeeded by a sterner age of Cossack whips and hanging generals; and in the palace rooms, where kindly gentlemen had once discussed Emancipation and High Schools for girls, military governors debated questions of police. (The Cossacks of his escort trotted close behind the Czar, as he drove smartly through the snowy streets.) It was a sad decline from the reforming zeal of 1861. But what was to be done, if terrorists insisted blindly upon hunting the one man upon whose will reform depended? His nerve stiffened under the ordeal, and his escapes were legendary. Indeed, the national incompetence became his leading safeguard, since the mines intended to blow up his train either failed to explode or blew up the wrong train; and once, when thoughtful hands had mined his dining-room, an erratic time-table delayed his dinner and the dynamite wasted its sweetness on the desert air of empty chairs.

Yet it was anything but easy for Alexander to persist in well-doing with such encouragements; and the Czar's life became a guarded progress between palaces, while military governors hanged Nihilists and Nihilists murdered police officials in grim alternation. It was the tragedy of Alexander's reign that for once the Russian Government was more intelligent than the Russian people; and in consequence the bright morning of reform was clouded by a dismal afternoon. (The guard had been inspected safely now, and his carriage drew up at a palace door for a call on a Grand Duchess.) Besides, the fatal rhythm of Russian history made itself felt once again. A few years earlier he had embarked upon a war with Turkey, in which the customary insuccess of Russian armies seemed to lift after a dreadful interlude in front of Plevna. The Turkish dam broke suddenly, and the Russians came flooding through the Balkan valleys until their outposts saw the slim minarets and swelling domes of Constantinople come up against the sky. A shaken Sultan signed a peace-treaty that Russia could accept with pride. But Europe intervened officiously; and British pressure imposed a Congress, at which the glorious provisions of San Stefano shrank into the modest acquisitions of Berlin. Prince Bismarck had appeared in the quite unexpected *rôle* of 'honest broker,' while diplomacy abstracted half the fruits of Russian victory to an accompaniment of small witticisms from Prince Gortchakoff and abominable French from Beaconsfield; and Russia, which had won the war, was shocked to find that it had lost the peace.

A mood of disillusion followed this reverse. (The Czar stepped back into his carriage, and the horses' heads were turned once more towards the Winter Palace.) Once again a failure to secure advantages abroad was followed by an unpleasant quickening of discontent at home, and the *tempo* of insurrection accelerated sharply. Fresh outrages by the devotees of progress were met with new brutalities by the executive; and soldiers who had done well against the Turks found themselves doing better still against their fellow-countrymen. For Gourko, Todleben, and Melikoff approached the government of Russia as a military problem; and the Czar's movements resembled the uneasy progress of a convoy down a threatened line of communications. (As the coachman whipped up his horses, the Cossack erect upon the swaying box beside him fingered his carbine and stared down the snowy street in front of them.) Not that he had completely wearied in well-doing, since Melikoff proposed a sort of constitution still pointing vaguely in the direction of reform, to which the Czar assented. Indeed, the Rescript had been signed and was awaiting publication on that snowy afternoon, as his carriage turned into a street by a narrow canal among the endless pediments and pilasters of official architecture. They had outpaced the Cossack escort now, and the short winter afternoon was fading. A woman at a corner fluttered a handkerchief. A bomb crashed into the road; and as the following police came running from their sledges, the Czar stepped out of his shattered carriage. Once more he was quite unhurt. There was a flurry in the street; but as he stood there in the snow, a second bomb destroyed him. A shred of life remained, as he was lifted

[143]

gently into the rust-red palace that waited in the great square beside the frozen river; and when he died, the last hope of reform in Russia died with him.

Alexander's murder on that winter day in 1881 was a dreadful irony, since it condemned his subjects to a renewal of the tyranny which his unshaken courage had begun to lift. Reform was over now, and persecution took its place. The busy minds that had conceived Emancipation and the whole effort to create a modern state in Russia were promptly superseded by the simpler mental processes of the Holy Synod; and a guarded tyrant behind the narrow windows of low rooms in a mezzanine at Gatchina ruled in a silence broken by the busy whispers of police. The Prince of Wales came over for the Czar's funeral and was lodged behind the great façade of the Anitchkoff Palace. Nothing could be more depressing to a cheerful visitor than the pervasive presence of innumerable police; and he was shocked at the dimensions of the prison-yard in which the Czar of All the Russias took his guarded exercise. For Russia had become a tyranny once more, as Alexander II slept with his forefathers beneath the gilded finger of the Fortress of St. Peter and St. Paul pointing perpetually skywards.

2. Marlborough House

THE HOUSE stood well back from the corner of Pall Mall and overlooked St. James's Park. It had served many purposes since Wren built it for the great Duke and his incomparable Sarah. Prince Leopold's brief honeymoon with Princess Charlotte, Queen Adelaide's retirement, and a more recent dedication to the improving objects of the School of Design had scarcely impressed it on the mind of London. But when Londoners passed Marlborough House in 1881, they stared respectfully at the very pinnacle of the West End. This was the apex of Society, the crown and centre of that restricted circle where, as an old lady wickedly remarked, all the women were brave and all the men virtuous. Perhaps Society was rather larger than it used to be. Had not Lord Beaconsfield been writing wistfully in *Endymion* of the distant days when "the world, being limited, knew itself much better"? For his long memory reached almost back to the lost elegance of the Regency, and his susceptibilities were slightly jarred by "the huge society of the present period" and "the fierce competition of its inexhaustible private entertainments." But though it was enlarged, it had its limits still; and they were watched by the ceaseless vigilance of queenly hostesses and club committees. Behind those battlements Society performed its evolutions. They dined, they danced, they drooped at Grosvenor House receptions; their mantelpieces were adorned with cards for ducal parties; they paid calls; they braved the elements at garden-parties in the distant grounds of Holland House. It was an age of Private Views, "when first" (as its chosen chronicler has written) "society was inducted into the mysteries of art and, not losing yet its old and elegant *tenue,* babbled of blue china and white lilies, of the painter Rossetti and the poet Swinburne"; an age of the more public spectacle provided in the London season by the selfless labours of the Professional Beauties, as they swayed slowly through the Park for all the world to stand on chairs and see or hurry off and buy their photographs from that delicious shop-window in Regent Street; the age of Gaiety burlesques; the noon-time of Miss Nellie Farren; the magic epoch of Mr. Whistler's first and Lord Beaconsfield's last witticism; the golden age when it was always Lady Someone's afternoon, and all the racing tides of the advancing century hung for an instant at slack water. For the world stood almost still in 1881. Small wonder that an envious posterity cries that "it would be a splendid thing to have seen the *tableaux* at Cromwell House, or to have made my way through the Fancy Fair and bartered all for a cigarette from a shepherdess; to have walked in the Park, straining my eyes for a glimpse of the Jersey Lily; danced the livelong afternoon to the strains of the Manola Valse; clapped holes in my gloves for Connie Gilchrist." But the cynosure of the whole shifting scene stood foursquare at the corner of Pall Mall, where Marlborough House caught a faint murmur of the traffic as the horse omnibuses rumbled along Piccadilly and the hansom-cabs went smartly by.

The master of the house, a friendly presence with a pointed beard and pale, protruding eyes, surveyed the long procession of his variously assorted guests through the faint spirals of a large cigar held in a royal hand; and one day early in November he reflected that he was just forty and that forty "certainly sounds formidable, but (*unberufen*) I am feeling well and strong, as if I were twenty-five, and trust I may still have some years of usefulness before me." This was a modest birthday aspiration for the Prince of Wales. But forty years of filial respect had taught him that it would be just as well not to expect too much. Disraeli had once suggested that he might reside in Ireland and learn something about administration in the intervals of hunting; Gladstone, who rarely found himself in such agreement with his light-minded rival, renewed the same suggestion in a more specific form, proposing that the Prince should hold Courts at Dublin in the intervals of sitting at the Indian Council, following army manœuvres, and reading an appropriate selection of the Foreign Office despatches. A further hint (though hints were scarcely Mr. Gladstone's *forte*) suggested that it might be helpful if the Prince of Wales did something to assist his mother in "the visible duties of the Monarchy," since the young couple at Marlborough House were obviously qualified to share the public burdens of the Crown, which bore so heavily upon the widowed Queen.

Bereavement and the passing years inclined her to a close seclusion, in which the royal movements were prescribed by an unchanging ritual. Her summer in the Isle of Wight, her autumn in the Highlands became a habit from which it was impossible to deviate without grave consequences to her nervous system. Busy ministers were forced to acquiesce in the necessity of constant pilgrimages to distant health-resorts for the performance of official duties. But their inconvenience was the least consequence of her retirement, since Mr. Gladstone, a staunch monarchist, began to fear its ill-effects upon the Crown itself. It was a time when the acceptance of dynastic institutions was anything but unquestioning on the Continent. France was a republic now; Spain tried the same experiment; Russians indulged in every known form of sedition; and English Radicals occasionally salted their progressive principles with a bold infusion of republicanism. The Crown would be a little easier for loyal politicians to defend if British taxpayers were favoured with more opportunities of viewing its respected wearer; and Mr. Gladstone harped assiduously on "the social and visible functions of the Monarchy" and the Queen's "general withdrawal from visible and sensible contact with the people of your realms." For if grief and failing health impeded the performance of her public duties, there was an obvious alternative; and ministers began to write to one another about "putting forward the Prince of Wales" for the discharge of duties which his mother found beyond her strength. But though the Queen's sense of their magnitude, as well as of her own bereavement and infirmity, was undiminished, the scheme failed to attract her; and it had withered in an icy blast of royal disapproval. There was no further effort to instruct the Prince formally in the *arcana* of British government; and as the years went by, the Prince of Wales depended for his information on the stray confidences of public men.

This relegation to the social sphere defined his *rôle*. Since access to the higher regions of administration and royal ceremonial was still denied, he declined happily upon Society. Here was a region in which his titular pre-eminence was not dependent on his mother's will. State secrets circulated daily between his mother and the Cabinet in locked despatch-boxes; but as they were considered hardly suitable for him, he took

the hint and found with evident relief that he did not require a Cabinet key for admission to the West End. This
was his kingdom; and Society received its leader with unqualified delight. A morbid statistician calculated once that
in the course of nine months the Prince of Wales attended
thirty plays, twenty-eight race meetings, and more than forty
social fixtures, a figure which was unfavourably compared
with an aggregate score in the same period of forty-five
official functions and no more than eleven attendances on
the cross-benches of the House of Lords. But was the Prince
to blame? If he was not allowed a Foreign Office box, there
was still his box at Covent Garden; and in the enforced
vacuum of his existence it was a pleasant change to sup with
Mr. Irving and Miss Ellen Terry on the stage at the Lyceum
or to discover for himself that actors could sometimes be-
have uncommonly like gentlemen. Most forms of sport
amused him; and as he once confided in reply to the modish
importunities of a confession album, he was "happiest when
. . . I can, like plain Mr. Jones, go to a race meeting without it being chronicled in the papers next day that His
Royal Highness the Prince of Wales has taken to gambling
very seriously, and yesterday lost more money than ever he
can afford to pay." A little flutter on the turf or at cards
after dinner afforded him the pleasant feeling of uncertainty
that was so lamentably absent from his official life. That
was the worst of his routine. For, in the absence of any
public duty of real significance by which his mind might be
engaged, it was almost painfully trivial and of a devastating
regularity. The Prince was left without the slightest room
for doubt of what was going to occur, and his engagements
stalked by with an inexorable certainty.

The day would come, and on the day he would drive up to
the appointed place, lift a tall hat to the onlookers, and
alight. There would be presentations, and he would dispense

the right remarks to gratified recipients. The ceremony, of which he knew the smallest details in advance, would follow; he would make his speech; there would be polite applause and more presentations; and afterwards he would drive home to Marlborough House with the consoling knowledge that one more improving agency had been launched upon a sympathetic world. There was a ruthless regularity about it all, and never more so than in 1881. That summer he went all the way to Kensington to lay a foundation-stone for a school of art and science and make a speech about the march of progress and his father's interest in technical education; he dined in honour of the Colonial Institute with the Lord Mayor and made a speech about the Colonies; he drove to Notting Hill and made a speech about infirmaries; he went to Westminster and made a speech about the late Dean Stanley; he went to Norwich in order to oblige a country neighbour by opening a Fisheries Exhibition. He was further privileged to inaugurate an International Medical Congress and no less than three docks at three widely separated points of his mother's realm, proceedings at the third (in Wales) being diversified by a rendering of "Men of Harlech" by a choir of two thousand voices, in which the feminine performers were picturesquely attired in national costume. The smooth succession of events was quite unrelenting. He knew precisely what would happen; and it always happened precisely as he had foreseen. So it was scarcely to be wondered at that he escaped from the treadmill of triviality with a rare gusto. It was an unspeakable relief to find himself occasionally in momentary doubt as to which horse would be first past the post or how the cards had been dealt. In spite of all his mother's frowns Newmarket was an almost necessary escape from Benevolent Societies. The company was brighter; but, above all, the prospects were not so deadeningly sure; and the Prince happily installed himself as the leader of Society in its lighter moments.

Not that his interests were uniformly trivial. His public duties might be confined to the small change of royal benefaction; but his outlook was European. He had always had a taste for foreign politics since the days when her son's outspokenness about the Germans distressed an anxious parent. If he had to choose between France and Germany (and since 1870 those underlying alternatives confronted Europe), there could not be the slightest doubt about his choice. France, shattered by defeat and the annexation of Alsace-Lorraine, had been left to her own devices. It was not in the current fashion to devise consolation for defeated nations or to heal their wounded self-esteem with a sympathetic course of sick-room diplomacy; and the French, unlike the victims of subsequent defeats, had been left to work out their own cure. But the Prince always felt at home in Paris; and by a happy accident Dilke, who was his chief informant on international affairs, was intimate with Gambetta. An introduction was effected; and there were some pleasant evenings of informal talk, which left the Frenchman with a happy certainty that "the politics of Europe and the world interest him as much as they interest us. . . . He loves France at once *gaîment et sérieusement,* and his dream of the future is an *entente* with us." That year he took a hand in the negotiation of an Anglo-French Commercial Treaty; armed with instructions from the Foreign Office, he interviewed M. Jules Ferry and his Minister of Commerce in order to prepare the way for Dilke, who followed him to Paris later as the official negotiator. The Prince was always pleased to talk freely in the company of intelligent Frenchmen. But these practical activities were far removed from the mere interchange of amiable generalities after dinner at the Café Anglais; and his *penchant* for diplomacy inclined him plainly in directions from which actual results might be expected. The German atmosphere was less congenial. He was in Berlin that winter for Prince William's wedding and played his part in the festivities with avuncular geniality. But Bismarck parried all his questions, and he was not sorry to give a lift to the commercial negotiations on his way home through Paris.

It was a busy and instructive year for an active-minded Prince, resolved to supplement the empty trivialities of his routine by doing something for his country. There were his Paris contacts and the slightly thwarted mission to Berlin and his depressing visit to St. Petersburg. Granville and Dilke had managed to elude the official interdict and kept him tolerably well-informed about the Continent, whilst he found nothing to complain of in the posture of affairs at home. A year earlier his mother had been filled with wild alarms by the disturbing spectacle of Mr. Gladstone emerging from his study to perorate interminably through draughty schoolrooms in Midlothian and sweep the Conservatives out of office and relegate Lord Beaconsfield to his library at Hughenden, while grim plebians like Mr. Chamberlain brought a disturbing flavour of the masses—and almost of the tumbrils—into the Cabinet itself. But, however disconcerting to the Queen, the nation's verdict was distinctly less unpalatable to the Prince of Wales, who scarcely shared his mother's anguished certainty that she "never COULD have the slightest *particle* of confidence in Mr. Gladstone." That fatal prejudice was mainly due to Mr. Gladstone's awkward taste for public and protracted demonstrations of his cherished view that Lord Beaconsfield was often wrong, whereas his sovereign knew quite well that Lord Beaconsfield was always right. Her conviction was quite unshaken by the fact that the electorate had just accepted Mr. Gladstone's view with emphasis; and this

[152]

heartless verdict left the Queen hoping bravely that his Parliamentary majority "will separate into many parts very soon, and that the Conservatives will come in stronger than ever in a short time" and privately resolved that she would *"never* write except on formal *official* matters to the Prime Minister." But the Prince of Wales was less dismayed—or more constitutional. Immune from the compelling charms of Lord Beaconsfield, whose devotees were often feminine and always elderly, he failed to view the advent of a Liberal administration in 1880 as a harsh warning of the wrath to come. For he was something of a Liberal himself. He had a deep respect for Gladstone, and a good many of his friends had places in the new Government. There was one of them in particular, whose installation at the Foreign Office had filled his sovereign with dark misgivings and angry memories of unforgivable avowals of republican opinions; but the Prince was happy to accept Dilke's aid on the occasion of his own excursions into foreign policy.

The world was changing; and perhaps the Liberals might direct the change on lines of which he could approve. There was no cause for apprehension yet in the delegates of rather more than half a million workers assembling in a Trade Union Congress, no indication that the sober paces of Liberalism on the path of progress would be hopelessly distracted by the twin spectres of Ireland and Egypt. A second epoch of Gladstonian reform was opening in 1881; and the nation's hopes were shared by the Prince of Wales. So many of his friendships lay upon that side of politics; the Liberals might even be relied upon to help him to a modest share of real activity, to tell him what was going on, even to find employment for him. It was his mother's tragedy that spring, when Beaconsfield was taken ill. The old man was still unconquerably spiteful about Mr. Gladstone; and when they brought a royal letter of enquiry to his couch, he

[153]

insisted gravely with a supreme touch of courtly mummery that it should be read to him by a Privy Councillor. But the long fight with his accumulated ailments ended as it was bound to end; and the Queen was left to wear her mourning without her beloved counsellor, bereaved once more and sentenced to live on into a world that grew increasingly unsympathetic, where Mr. Gladstone aired his crotchets and the wildest innovations masqueraded as reforms and republicans appeared as Privy Councillors and no one seemed to put foreign nations in their place as Lord Beaconsfield would have done and everything grew harder for an ageing woman to understand.

But the Prince found it less bewildering. It was a cheerful time, since the age of Gladstone was also the age of Gilbert and Sullivan. *Patience* had mocked at the advance of culture, where Mr. Wilde's lily waved in the van beside the oriflamme of Mr. Whistler's lock. But other cohorts were on the move in 1881. For recent wealth impinged steadily upon Society in spite of all Du Maurier could find to say (and sketch) in derogation of Sir Gorgius Midas; and his incomparable duchesses drew together like tall galleons in mid-ocean, as the first American heiresses came brightly on the social scene. The world was mutable indeed; and the times, though still Victorian in allegiance, had become undubitably Edwardian in tone.

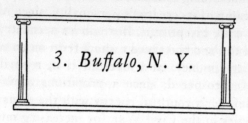

3. Buffalo, N. Y.

THE WIND from Canada came off Lake Erie, and twenty miles away a racing river dropped suddenly over a hundred-foot ledge into a boiling fog of shattered water. But the inhabitants of Buffalo, accustomed to their climate and the proximity of Niagara, were less habituated to the propinquity of another force of nature. For it had only come into the neighbourhood quite lately, when two gentlemen in Rochester sold a three-quarter interest in their refinery to the Standard Oil Company.

This promising concern, which had been born in a side-street in Cleveland less than a dozen years before, cast a considerable shadow on the oil business. Its name was mentioned without enthusiasm in Titusville and Oil City and the untidy Pennsylvania townships along the ragged banks of the Allegheny where petroleum was pumped out of the ground, because it had an awkward habit of securing lower freight-rates from obliging railroads that enabled it to undersell competitors and to keep prices at a lower level than oil producers liked to see. Its methods, varying be-

[155]

tween a commanding tone and unusual powers of persuasion, bore the stamp of its creator's personality, since Mr. Rockefeller was quite exceptional. Born on an upcountry farm, he gravitated to the city, served a short term on an office stool, saved a little money, and invested it in a small produce business. It prospered, since a propitious combination of Mr. Rockefeller's youthful energy with the demands of the Union armies in the Civil War for increasing quantities of produce maintained its profits. But the war could not go on for ever; and something in the air of Cleveland made it unlikely that Mr. Rockefeller would remain a produce-broker all his life. For nature, which could not be disobeyed, had made the place a centre for oil distribution, and Mr. Rockefeller was fitted by his natural equipment for the magnificent uncertainties of trade in that commodity. His first enterprise was a refinery, which somehow managed to secure the wayward affections of the railroads and owed much of its success to preferential freights. Such favours rendered competition arduous, and it was not surprising that the Standard Oil Company was shortly in possession of twenty out of the twenty-six refineries in Cleveland. But Mr. Rockefeller's horizon was not bounded by the city limits. He was already thought to have had some connection with a questionable attempt to organise the whole industry in a single corporation, which had provoked the individualists of the oil regions to summary (and apparently successful) resistance. But though the large conception failed to materialise, his sober appetite continued to absorb refineries. Pittsburgh and Philadelphia soon followed Cleveland into his control, and Standard Oil was reaching out for mastery in New York and Baltimore. Nor was Mr. Rockefeller satisfied with hegemony in the manufacture of his chosen commodity, since its transportation might constitute a menace if it was permitted to remain in independent hands.

So much of his control depended upon highly satisfactory arrangements with the railroads that he viewed without affection the new development of pipe-lines, by which oil producers might be rendered independent of his railroad friends. The miracle of science, by which oil could be pumped over the mountains, failed to number Mr. Rockefeller among its wellwishers. But as he could not prevent it, he elected to control the process; and oil producers were presently confronted with his ubiquitous domination of another field.

The results were terrifying, since it had grown to be almost impossible to handle oil at any stage in its long journey from the soil of Pennsylvania to the consumer's lamp without encountering Mr. Rockefeller at some point. The oil producer was faced on every hand with his refineries and his transportation. For Standard Oil was ready to acquire the natural product and direct it to the consuming centres; and when it reached them, Standard Oil was equally prepared to market it and to eliminate competing dealers by ruthless undercutting. The prospect for independent traders darkened progressively; and Buffalo in 1881 was favoured with an impressive demonstration of the risks attending independent enterprise in oil.

Two gentlemen in Rochester had recently disposed of their refinery to the Standard Oil Company. Unimpressed with the significance of this event, two former employees of the concern resolved to operate a small refinery at Buffalo in competition with their late employers; and their subsequent experiences were illuminating. The first time that the safety-valve blew off, it caused no comment, although the misadventure was directly due to an impulsive foreman who had insisted upon making up the fire to a temperature eloquently defined by someone as "inordinary hot." But no one in Buffalo knew that he had received a handsome

[157]

offer from a director of the Standard's latest subsidiary to break his contract with their competitors, together with some extremely practical advice as to the simplest way of terminating the connection by an act of negligence which would ensure his own dismissal. The negligence was slightly overdone, because he followed up the first explosion by an exact repetition of the accident and a prompt disappearance to New York, where he was seen in company with his insinuating friend from Rochester and a Standard Oil director. After a period of leisure on their pay-roll he was transferred at their expense to the more peaceful *rôle* of canning fruit in California, and the Lubricating Works of Buffalo had lost their best assistant. Their leading salesman went, when Standard Oil's subsidiary brought suit against him, although the action was considerately settled when he consented to leave Buffalo; and their manufacturing processes were threatened by a crop of actions, in which the indignant patentees in Rochester claimed that their rights had been infringed. The loss of two valuable employees and an endless vista of patent litigation afforded a depressing prospect for the new concern. But it had dawned upon their late foreman that he might be more profitably employed than raising fruit in California. So he returned to Buffalo with the interesting narrative of his dealing with Standard Oil's subsidiary, and his late employers were enabled to indict three Standard directors and their two associates from Rochester for criminal conspiracy. A crowded court explored the story, and Mr. Rockefeller was there to listen to the evidence. It is gratifying to record that his own colleagues were acquitted; but the gentlemen from Rochester were both found guilty. The sequel was unpleasing, since the Buffalo concern, whose energies had been transferred from the simple business of refining oil to an unending course of litigation, succumbed to its exertions and went into liquidation, when its assets were found to be just sufficient for the payment of the firm's debts and its own lawyers' costs.

Such were the penalties of independent enterprise in a former paradise of rugged individualism. There was an irony about the sequence of American events. The white settler had replaced the Indian, who was now a schoolboy legend in the East and an occasional anxiety to army posts in the Far West. But the slow drive of enterprise appeared to have deprived the solitary white man of his own usefulness, and he was expropriated in his turn by the vast economic units which the United States seemed to require for their exploitation. A lonely trapper could explore, a group of families in covered waggons following upon his heels could occupy the unfolding territories of the West with a thin population. But before these could yield more than a bare livelihood to a few scattered homesteads, large-scale enterprise must intervene with rails and grades and telegraphs and trestle bridges. Railroad construction was the true index of effective occupation; and by 1881 the transcontinental network was complete. That had been the history of the United States since the Civil War. For its true history was always the history of transportation, in which the names of railroad presidents are more significant than those of Presidents of the United States. Those names emerged—Gould, Vanderbilt, Hill, Huntington, and Harriman. Even in Canada trans-continental enterprise was summoning Van Horne to Winnipeg that year to take the railroad over the Kicking Horse Pass in preparation for the happy day when its completion was celebrated and an inspired conductor called "All aboard for the Pacific."

It was an age of vast collective enterprise, unfriendly to obstruction by individuals and prolific of huge economic organisms, of which Standard Oil was the most highly developed. The age of Lincoln had departed; and in the less heroic age of Hayes and Garfield national leadership in effective enterprise passed from the White House to Wall Street, to the offices of vast corporations and the boardrooms where Mr. Rockefeller and Mr. Huntington projected their campaigns. It was a development by which the New World found its economic strength and, by other means than those foreseen by Canning, might one day redress the balance of the Old.

EIGHTEEN
NINETY–SEVEN

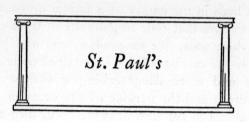

St. Paul's

... A<small>ND</small> C<small>APTAIN</small> A<small>MES</small>, who was the tallest man in
the whole British Army, would lead the Diamond Jubilee
procession. There would be Bengal Lancers and New South
Wales Mounted Rifles and Rhodesian Horse and Zaptiehs
from Cyprus and Dyaks from Borneo, who were breath-
lessly reputed to be careless about human heads. It was to
be a grand imperial occasion in honour of

> *the Widow at Windsor*
> *With a hairy gold crown on 'er 'ead.*
> *She 'as ships on the foam—she 'as millions at 'ome,*
> *An' she pays us poor beggars in red.*
> . . . . . .
>
> *There's 'er nick on the cavalry 'orses,*
> *There's 'er mark on the medical stores—*
> *An' 'er troopers you'll find with a fair wind be'ind*
> *That takes us to various wars.*

This would be quite different from her first Jubilee ten years
before, when the Queen drove to Westminster Abbey for

[163]

her thanksgiving behind an escort of her royal relatives. That had been in the nature of a family occasion. For the escort of Princes that rode so gallantly in front of her consisted of three sons, five sons-in-law, and nine junior relations, while the carriages behind contained no less than five daughters and three daughters-in-law with a galaxy of grandchildren; and the heroine of the occasion was subsequently painted in her own drawing-room with a group of fifty-four relations. Her mood in 1887 had been as personal as the procession. For she reflected sadly that she was "alone, though surrounded by many dear children"; and when the organ thundered softly in the Abbey, she was still *"alone* (oh! without my beloved husband, for whom this would have been such a proud day!)," although it was his *Te Deum* that they were playing. And when it was all over, she gave Jubilee brooches to all her daughters and granddaughters and Jubilee pins to each of her sons, grandsons, sons-in-law, grandsons-in-law, and the Duke of Cambridge. But they were not free from care, since Fritz, the most splendid of her sons-in-law, was slightly affected in his throat and stood there like a dumb giant in his white Prussian uniform. And through it all she was perpetually conscious of an empty place beside her, which nobody could fill. That aching certainty still coloured all her thoughts; and though the Jubilee of 1887 left the Queen "very tired, but very happy," her final entry for the day was a touching record of "how painfully do I miss the dear ones I have lost!"

This chastened mood was admirably suited to a celebration falling in the later years of a frustrated decade. For the Eighties were an age of high beginnings that almost uniformly died away in subsequent entanglements, a disappointing epoch, a time when hardly anything appeared to end as its designers had intended. Its politics were wholly typical of the prevailing air of thwarted effort. Opening among the ruins of Disraelian imperialism in Zululand and Afghanistan, it listened hopefully to the high music of Midlothian. Proud engine-drivers drew into stations all along the line from Edinburgh to Euston, while Mr. Gladstone at a carriage window entertained respectful audiences with eloquent reflections until the train drew out again and happy Liberals stood packed and cheering on the platform. That was the morning-star of a new day that somehow failed to dawn. For the bright hopes of 1880 soon died away into the sands of arid controversy about Mr. Bradlaugh's oath and Sir Bartle Frere's impetuosity. High principles at home were insufficient to avert defeats abroad; and it was anything but easy for the public mind to concentrate upon the march of progress and the blessings of reform with the melancholy names of Maiwand and Majuba ringing in its ears.

Besides, the symphony of politics was sadly marred by a discordant note which ruined all its careful harmonies, as Ireland raised her dismal and recurrent voice in an attack upon the imperfect hearing of Great Britain. That interruption became the leading *motif* of the whole decade. Its penetrating and lugubrious note wailed through the corridors of Westminster, as Parnell led a jangled chorus of agrarian outrage, Parliamentary obstruction, boycott, conspiracy, and murder which broke in upon the ordered march of Mr. Gladstone's melody, as the slow chant of Wagnerian pilgrims had been overwhelmed by the shrill onslaught of a diabolical *crescendo*. Once the voice of Ireland had been triumphantly obtruded, British politics proceeded lamely to the air of that depressing jig. A Parliament elected to improve conditions in Great Britain helplessly consumed hour after hour of legislative time in discussing whether and, if so, which Irish members should have been arrested or alternatively released, and if Chief Secretaries, who began to flicker in and out of

Dublin Castle like rabbits in a haunted shooting-gallery, had employed too little or too much force in the discharge of their administrative duties. A new bitterness crept into English politics from Ireland, as Liberals learned to detest Conservatives with Irish fervour and Conservatives returned their feelings with the cold fury of Belfast. The air of politics grew acrid with the new distemper; and party leaders laid aside their old urbanity, degenerating swiftly into bad-tempered duellists.

This dislocation interfered deplorably with Mr. Gladstone's second advent. The indomitable old man had returned to politics at seventy in order to eliminate Disraeli and resume the ordered march of progress. But, his first objective gained, he found his march towards the second hopelessly obstructed by the Irish interruption; and if that were not bad enough, an unforeseen succession of events in Egypt made him an empire-builder *malgré lui*. Nothing had been further from his thoughts than Dublin Castle and the Nile, as he first touched the deep drum of his moral indignation in Midlothian. But when he was in office once again, Ireland and Egypt rapidly became the alternating burden of his song; and there were times when Egypt was the more absorbing of the two. It was quite undeniably the more distasteful, since every fibre of his being recoiled from ordering the fleet to bombard Alexandria. This was a Palmerstonian performance; but if order was to be restored in Egypt, there was no alternative. Once launched upon the fatal slope of intervention, Mr. Gladstone slid with gathering momentum (though with no diminution of his original reluctance) the full length of that uncomfortable gradient. Order had been restored by a bombardment of the forts at Alexandria. But if order was to be maintained, someone would have to penetrate a little further inland and discipline the Egyptian rebels. Since the Khedive was quite unequal to the task, a British army did it for him at Kassassin and Tel-el-Kebir. And that was not the end, since the Khedive was scarcely equal to the next task with which Egyptian statesmanship was faced. Deep in the Sudan a lonely theologian of unusual histrionic gifts had proclaimed himself the Mahdi and was threatening the uncertain hold of Egypt on its southern territories. The tribes were on the move; and an attempt to check the insurrection ended in disaster to an Egyptian army in the burning scrub of Kordofan. The best advice that anyone could offer to the Khedive was palpably to cut his losses and evacuate the Sudan. But even that was quite beyond his powers, unless somebody would go and do it for him. So an unhappy chance detailed a noble eccentric "to go up and evacuate"; and 'Chinese Gordon' found himself once more in the big palace by the Nile at Khartoum, telegraphing twenty times a day to Cairo and doing everything in the world except evacuate. The slow skein of circumstance unwound; and Mr. Gladstone, who had bombarded Alexandria from the purest motives and sent the Guards to Egypt in a high-minded effort to preserve the wholly blameless fruits of his bombardment and lent Gordon to the Khedive in order to relieve an anxious ally from embarrassment, soon found himself despatching British troops halfway to the Equator in an inconsequent endeavour to extricate a lonely hero, whose strict obedience to orders was open to some question, from a sun-baked town to which the Queen and the Khedive had both renounced all claims.

The tragic paradox of Khartoum, by which the middle years of the decade were darkened, was typical of its frustrated course. For in the Eighties nothing ever seemed to end as it was meant to; and where non-intervention had already ended in an armed occupation, it need occasion no surprise that a military mission ended in a martyrdom. For there was no flag flying at Khartoum, when a battered steamer struggled round the bend of the river into sight of Gordon's headquarters. The Relief Expedition failed to relieve Gordon or anybody else and left the Queen telegraphing resentfully to ministers without bothering to have her resentment decently concealed in the obscurity of cipher. She had mistrusted Mr. Gladstone ever since his fervid onslaughts on Lord Beaconsfield; and now her mistrust was more unconcealed than ever. Events unfolded like a depressing transformation-scene, in which each change was for the worse. The face of English politics was overcast with Irish grievances; that problem was obscured by Egyptian complications; Egypt's sky was darkened in its turn by the tragedy of the Sudan; and one more transformation lent the scene its final gloom, as Mr. Gladstone turned Home Ruler. This was too much for the Queen, for most of the electorate, and for many Liberals. For whilst his sovereign's disapproval was almost shrill, his party split; and that unhappy fissure relegated Mr. Chamberlain, a born Radical, to live out the remainder of his life in unnatural alliance with Conservatives. It was indeed a decade of frustration. Mr. Gladstone's first effort to achieve Home Rule ended in defeat. A bitter interlude of broken friendships and unnatural alliances set in; and at the height of it, whilst angry politicians shook their fists in one another's faces and discovered the most discreditable motives for everything their colleagues did, her subjects were convened to celebrate the Queen's Jubilee. Small wonder that the celebration on its public side was a shade subdued, reduced by circumstances to a personal, almost a family occasion in honour of a feat of longevity performed by a respected relative.

That had been the air of 1887, in which Lord Tennyson wrote without much conviction of

Fifty years of ever-broadening Commerce!
Fifty years of ever-brightening Science!
Fifty years of ever-widening Empire!

The trade returns were not conspicuously gay; the nation's outlook on this world and the next had not been particularly enlivened by recent discoveries; and as for the Empire, it was impossible to derive much satisfaction from the evacuation of Suakin or to conceal the fact that a major portion of the second party in the state appeared to be engaged in what a fair proportion of their fellow-countrymen regarded as an attack on its integrity.

But the next decade changed the scene, and hearts beat high in 1897 at the news that Captain Ames, who was the tallest man in the whole British Army, would lead the Diamond Jubilee procession. The shadows of the Eighties had been left behind. Parnell was dead; the voice of Ireland had become an aimless wrangle between minor Irishmen and no longer broke in upon the stately monotone of English politics. A deeper voice was silenced, as Mr. Gladstone took his final leave after a last failure to persuade his countrymen that something must be done for Ireland. But the Conservatives and the Liberal-Unionists and the House of Lords and the Queen were too many for him; and they left the enemies of England a priceless legacy of Irish discontent. The old man with his failing sight and hearing went back to the unbroken stillness of his library; and the dull round of politics resumed without him. The Parliamentary scene was less heroic without that unequalled controversialist crouched on the Front Bench in his frock-coat with its invariable tea-rose or thundering across the table of the House of Commons with uplifted forefinger and blazing eyes in tones that had once exasperated Disraeli, amused Lord Palmerston, and encouraged Sir Robert Peel.

[169]

His long career was an epitome of sixty years of English politics. But all that was over now. The old man was peering at his books at Hawarden, and his succession was disputed by a smaller race. Diminished Liberals, whose growth had been retarded by his shadow, scurried about like startled rabbits round a fallen tree. They did not matter greatly, since they were out of office. Besides, they were committed to Home Rule, which had been emphatically repudiated for the second time, or at the very least to friendly association with persons of questionable loyalty.

For the age was nothing if not loyal, when an angry poet could strike his lyre in order to complain that

*The poor little street-bred people that vapour and fume and
    brag,*
*They are lifting their heads in the stillness to yelp at the
    English Flag!*
*Must we borrow a clout from the Boer—to plaster anew
    with dirt*
An Irish liar's bandage or an English coward's shirt?
*We may not speak of England; her Flag's to sell or to
    share.*
*What is the Flag of England? Winds of the World,
    declare!*

Nor was a declaration wanting in Mr. Kipling's full diapason with geographical embellishments drawn from the four quarters of the sky. A little tired of the unrewarding spectacle presented by affairs at home, the public mind had sought relief in the far places of the earth. Denied the luxury of distant travel, it revelled in the road to Mandalay at second-hand, whilst its fancy played agreeably round those Elysian regions somewhere east of Suez, where a comfortable laxity of conduct did not interfere with the respectable assumption of the White Man's Burden. Its favourite heroes uniformly shaded their eyes with a bronzed hand to stare across the quivering distances of the Bayuda Desert or the Khyber Pass or Matabeleland towards a skyline from which the Queen's enemies might be expected to appear at any moment. Its minor themes were the jammed Gatling and the broken square, sad echoes of old, unhappy operations in the far-off Eighties; and when it swept into the major key, it roared its acclamation to the Flag or warned the listening earth to

> *Walk wide o' the Widow at Windsor,*
> *For 'alf o' Creation she owns:*
> *We 'ave bought 'er the same with the sword an' the flame,*
> *An' we've salted it down with our bones.*
> *(Poor beggars!—it's blue with our bones!)*
> *Hands off o' the sons o' the Widow,*
> *Hands off o' the goods in 'er shop,*
> *For the Kings must come down an' the Emperors frown*
> *When the Widow at Windsor says 'Stop!'*

This was the elevated mood of 1897, of which the Diamond Jubilee procession was to be the proud embodiment. It was a strange development, contrasting oddly with the less assertive tone in which Napoleon had been defeated by the subjects of George III. The contemporaries of Lord Liverpool, by whom Nelson had been kept at sea and Wellington in the Peninsula, had never forced the note of conscious power to the same pitch of shrillness. But that, perhaps, was just because self-consciousness was not their *forte;* and if they thought at all, they thought a good deal more about their formidable enemy than about the ringing note of their own broadsides. Since their day, however, a good many things had happened. The rise of Prussia and the consequent predominance of heavily armed empires had gone a long way to reduce the range of England's voice on the Continent. Lord Palmerston had spoken to a respectful world. But when Lord Salisbury addressed it, he was less certain of a respectful hearing from nations comfortably conscious that the peace establishment of the British Army amounted to something less than a quarter of a million men. Bismarck, in fine, had elbowed England off the Continent. That had been obvious even in Lord Palmerston's last years, when British frowns were ineffectual to prevent the march of Prussian policy; and Lord Beaconsfield's endeavour to cry halt to Russia had owed more to stagecraft than to the reality of British power. The Continent was now the stamping-ground of conscript armies three million men strong; and that circumstance inevitably limited the European *rôle* of England so long as the Queen's ministers remained content with a force consisting of the Guards, some cavalry, and the County regiments supplemented in a *diminuendo* of military value by the Yeomanry, the Volunteers, and the Militia. One course remained in an unsympathetic world; and by a natural compensation British energy sought outlets in less crowded fields. For if Europe was uncomfortably full, there were other continents. The broad sea-ways were open; and it was consoling (as well as comparatively inexpensive) to assume control of the road to India or of the Cape to Cairo route. Besides, the vast industrial production of the machine age began to clamour for new markets among backward races and for fresh supplies of raw material from virgin soil. Undeveloped territories and chains of coaling stations gleamed alluringly in all parts of the world; and British enterprise, alternating between a brisk acquisitiveness and a genuine reluctance to acquire any more, wove these scattered elements into an Empire. The process, like most British processes, was largely unconscious. Frontiers advanced as inadvertently as a child grows. But the growth itself was undeniable; and in its later stages, when the entire African continent was deliberately partitioned by the European Powers, it became conscious of itself.

The Diamond Jubilee was the supreme expression of that self-consciousness. The Englishman of the Queen's middle years had not been particularly aware of the Colonies; and when their existence was recalled to him, his recognition of the fact was somehow lacking in enthusiasm. Even Disraeli, who was later to become the patron saint of the new imperialism on grounds that were not altogether clear, had once exhorted his fellow-countrymen to "leave the Canadians to defend themselves; recall the African squadron; give up the settlements on the west coast of Africa; and we shall make a saving which will, at the same time, enable us to build ships and have a good Budget." But this unheroic mood gave place to a more spirited phase, in which he made large, imperial gestures. The Queen was solemnly proclaimed Empress of India; and the British taxpayer woke up one morning to find himself the owner of a large block of shares in the Suez Canal Company. The fact that these impressive transformations were largely nominal (since the Queen had been the sovereign of India all the time, and real control of the Suez Canal resided rather in the British Navy than in its shareholders) in no way detracted from their significance. For the British Empire had begun to be self-conscious. Even its misadventures, when Cavagnari was murdered at Kabul or a Zulu *impi* wiped out the 24th at Isandhlwana, became milestones on a road that led towards a glorious objective. The old haphazard growth had ended in deliberate expansion. For the public mind began to realise in the later years of the Queen's reign that a proud nation could become something greater than a mere European

[173]

Power. That *rôle* might satisfy Frenchmen or Germans. But by a transfer of its effort to the far corners of the earth the island kingdom was elevated into a world-power of more than Roman magnitude; and on the moral side its consciousness of this achievement flowered in the rich blossom of Imperialism.

That exotic appeared in many forms. Its exuberance was an immense relief after the spiritual austerities of the preceding age; and it inspired innumerable careers, ambitions, and enterprises, to say nothing of short stories. But the new revelation was most aptly summarised in its psalmody, where complacency alternated with a slightly dubious humility.

Fair is our lot—O goodly is our heritage!
(Humble ye, my people, and be fearful in your mirth!)
    For the Lord our God Most High
    He hath made the deep as dry,
He hath smote for us a pathway to the ends of all the Earth!

A mysterious merit seemed to reside for its initiates in the mere fact of remoteness; and the most notable of all its utterances in the year of Jubilee appeared to use the epithet "far-flung" as a term of praise. *"Dominion over palm and pine"* was somehow felt to be superior to dominion over oak and ash or any less remote specimens of the world's flora. It was a novel point of view, and its adoption involved a thorough transformation of the whole British attitude towards the oversea possessions of the Crown. Their fathers knew the Colonies rather as regions for the sudden enrichment of unlikely persons than as instruments for the enlargement of national dignity. They had supplied a purely economic Eldorado to which Mr. Micawber might usefully resort or from which Mr. Magwich might unexpectedly return. But the new consciousness of Empire endowed these regions with a fuller meaning, a significance of which Sir John Seeley lecturing at Cambridge on *The Expansion of England* supplied the theory and Mr. Cecil Rhodes the practice.

That was the transformation celebrated in the Diamond Jubilee. It had not been effected without vicissitudes, since new developments on such a scale cannot hope to pass unchallenged. There were still bitter memories of Majuba and Khartoum, although Maiwand had been effaced by the great march to Kandahar. The forward movement in Egypt had been mainly retrograde, until a recent thrust by Sir Herbert Kitchener in the direction of Dongola raised hopes that the Sudan might be redeemed; and the unsuccessful fight of Dr. Jameson and his friends at Krugersdorp was an unpleasant demonstration that empire-builders are not necessarily victorious. But in the public mind a splendid roll of personal heroism afforded ample compensation for military misadventures. Lieutenants Chard and Bromhead at Rorke's Drift had helped their countrymen to overlook the less rewarding aspects of the Zulu War; Colonel Burnaby dying gallantly outside the square at Abu-Klea obscured the unhappy fact that the Desert Column failed to arrive in time; and the heroic end of Major Wilson's party far away among the Matabele was some consolation for the loss of the Shangani patrol. Public interest in these achievements was warmly personal. It was an age that could recite its national heroes as accurately as its Derby winners. It knew precisely where Lord Roberts won the Victoria Cross, which gallant subalterns had rescued the Queen's colour of the 24th, how the Hon. Maurice Gifford lost his arm somewhere north of Buluwayo, and when the admiral had signalled "Well done, *Condor*," to the intrepid gunboat that carried Lord Charles Beresford irrepressibly under the forts at Alexandria. This supplied the favourite reading of its

[175]

young people in handsome illustrated volumes; and as the public mind followed the forward march of Empire with eager pride, it acquired a peculiar intimacy with the armed forces of the Crown which enabled it to know all about the 4.7-inch guns of H.M.S. *Powerful* and to receive with becoming satisfaction the proud announcement that Captain Ames, who was the tallest man in the whole British Army, would lead the Diamond Jubilee procession.

That happy day was coming fast, when it would gaze upon its Service heroes. And they had their counterpart in civil life, where Mr. Chamberlain had unexpectedly emerged as an imperial emblem. This was not altogether illogical, since he had parted from his Liberal associates upon the imperial issue of Home Rule for Ireland, and Unionists rallied eagerly to the lean profile, the single eyeglass, the orchid, and the rasping tongue. When there were sharp things to say about the other side, he said them with unrivalled sharpness; and when angry Irishmen required a face to shake their fists in, his was always ready to their hands. The fires of controversy hardened him. But since the execration of opponents is an unequalled passport to esteem, he mounted steadily in public favour; and as shrill Home Rulers called him 'Judas,' Mr. Chamberlain passed on serenely towards the patriotic pantheon. It was a strange deflection of that Radical career, which had begun in a progressive municipality and ended by seating him beside Lord Salisbury and Mr. Balfour. But his devotion to the Union atoned for those remote republican beginnings. He was a pillar of the Empire now. His social policies must wait until the safety of the Empire had been attended to by the elimination of its Nationalist enemies. That was a congenial pursuit for a politician who loved to use the tomahawk. Not that he altogether ceased to be constructive. For when a coalition sanctified the alliance of Conservatives with

Liberal-Unionists after their second triumph over Home Rule, he chose an office that identified him with the Empire whose unity he had preserved, electing to become Colonial Secretary in the hope, as he explained to the Prime Minister, of doing something for a closer union between Great Britain and the Colonies. There was logic in it, since his political alignment as a star in the Unionist firmament was entirely due to a cold passion for the union between Great Britain and Ireland; and what Unionist could fail to work for its extension to the oversea possessions of the Crown?

Besides, with an expanding and consolidating Empire the Colonial Office was a department in which there might be some activity even under a Unionist Government. In other fields the *status quo* was sacred. The Government, indeed, had been returned by the electors in order to defend it. But in the imperial sphere affairs were not so stationary, and there might be something for Mr. Chamberlain to do. World affairs had always interested him. As he brought to politics the wider outlook of the City, he had been almost the first man in British public life to become aware of the United States as anything more than an immense theatre for hair-breadth escapes from Indians or for slightly laughable experiments in democratic freedom. His early contact with Colonial problems at the Board of Trade had fired his busy fancy, and Mr. Chamberlain was adequately supplied with views about the world and its affairs. The Foreign Office was sacred to Lord Salisbury. But Mr. Chamberlain might have a finger in innumerable pies at the Colonial Office, although it had not hitherto occurred to any politician of the first magnitude that it was a post worth having, and in consequence his predecessors in the office had been an uninspiring list of amiable but unimportant gentlemen. That scarcely mattered now, since it was 1895 and he was Mr. Chamberlain.

The new occupant of the big room in Downing Street, where a large globe stood underneath an ugly chandelier and startled civil servants blinked in the electric light with which he had replaced his predecessors' candles, plunged happily into the racing stream. The globe revolved, and he was soon directing British entrants in the race against the French for West Africa. French pride and energy, recovering from the defeats of 1870, had turned with ardour to colonial activity. That was how France consoled herself for her eclipse in Europe by the bright constellation of United Germany. But since it was no part of current thought to find consolations for unsuccessful rivals, the British *rôle* was a brisk competition; and none was brisker than the new Colonial Secretary. West Africa, where Frenchmen with tricolours and treaties ran races to the homes of native potentates against Englishmen with treaties and Union Jacks, was a comparatively simple field. But South Africa was a more complicated course, the obstacles consisting of two Boer republics, an enterprising British element, some gold-mines, and Mr. Cecil Rhodes.

The Secretary of State was soon kept busy parrying the most embarrassing confidences about impending revolutions in Johannesburg. As he told someone afterwards, "I can hardly say what I knew and what I did not. I did not want to know too much." He knew that something of the kind was contemplated; he informed his High Commissioner at Cape Town that he took "for granted that no movement will take place unless success is certain"; he advised a permanent Under-Secretary that "it should either come *at once* or be postponed for a year or two at least." But when it came a fortnight later and Dr. Jameson trotted across the Transvaal border in the last days of 1895 with a few hundred men and six Maxim guns, he was aghast. He stigmatised the Raid at once as "a flagrant piece of filibustering" and excommunicated its participants. But his thunders were wholly superfluous, as the resourceful Dutchmen rounded up the raiders and returned them scornfully for trial by the British Government. The effect of the event upon South Africa was calamitous, since it confirmed the Boers in their suspicion of the British and left Mr. Rhodes and his associates in the defiant mood of unsuccessful conspirators. Its influence on British politics was to unleash his enemies in hot pursuit of Mr. Chamberlain with loud (and not wholly unconvincing) charges of complicity in the unlawful act. But the result in Europe was still more striking, as the German Emperor, exasperated by his grandmother's ubiquity in world affairs, unburdened himself in an unhappy telegram (he had a *penchant* for sudden and sensational pronouncements), in which the Boer President was congratulated on his victory over the invaders "without calling on the aid of friendly Powers." This was insulting to Great Britain; and British sentiment, relieved from the necessity of arguing an unconvincing case against the Boers, turned happily to the more satisfying task of resenting the Kaiser's telegram, while Chamberlain wrote shrewdly to the Prime Minister that "what is called an 'Act of Vigour' is required to soothe the wounded vanity of the nation. It does not much matter which of our numerous foes we defy, but we ought to defy someone." This was the heroic mood of 1896, in which happy headlines invited England to "Get Ready," warned foreigners to keep "Hands Off," and informed the world that she was "England Yet."

There was a splendid loneliness about Great Britain in the closing years of the Queen's reign, when a minister would write cheerfully that "we have in hand difficulties of the most serious character with France, Russia, and Germany. We are engaged in an important expedition in the Soudan; and it is uncertain as yet whether the war on the

North-west frontier of India has been finally concluded."
The Continent, whose populations were comprehensively
dismissed as *"lesser breeds without the Law,"* was full of
menace. France lay uneasily beneath the shadow of the German armies. Red-trousered sentries in tilted *képis* fingered
their rifles; nerves quivered at the slightest incident; and
eyes were strained towards the 'gap in the Vosges.' Beyond
the frontier a flamboyant Emperor in shining armour with
a silver eagle on his helmet struck splendid attitudes and
made resounding speeches on the subject of his never-to-be-
forgotten grandfather whose main achievement, it must
always be remembered, was the defeat of France. Bismarck
had been discarded, and the Prussian Juggernaut had now a
more impulsive driver. The ramshackle chariot of Austro-
Hungarian policy lumbered in its wake; and the lighter
vehicle in which the fortunes of Italy had been embarked
brought up the rear of the procession. For the *Triplice*
aligned Germany with Italy and Austria; a *bloc* of allied territory ran clear from the North Sea to Sicily and from
Metz to the Russian frontier; and as the Triple Alliance
could mobilise twelve million men, its hand lay heavy on the
Continent. So much power embodied in massed infantry behind the clank and jingle of the guns and line after line of
riding cavalry was intoxicating; and the German Emperor
was responsive to the intoxication. The lesson was not lost
upon the Czar and his advisers in the yellow amphitheatre
of the General Staff building at St. Petersburg. The old connection with Berlin, which Bismarck had once kept sedu-
lously polished by his 'Reinsurance treaty,' was permitted to
grow dull; and the slow processes of Russian policy began
to grope for an ally. Great Britain was excluded by an interminable rivalry in Asia. But there was still the French
Republic, though republicans were strange company for a
Czar to keep; and Russian bands began to learn the *Mar-*

seillaise. A Grand Duke was soon examining the admirable qualities of the Lebel rifle; French investors felt the attractions of a Russian loan; the eccentric silhouettes of French warships slid past the batteries at Cronstadt; and as the low shores of the Gulf of Finland caught the thunder of salutes, the Czar of Russia stepped on to a French quarterdeck beneath the tricolour of the Republic.

It was a striking transformation; and when a Franco-Russian treaty had confirmed the partnership, the European domination of the Triple Alliance was challenged, and France had an ally. That was the new alignment, hallowed by Detaille in patriotic canvases and the delighted pencil of Caran d'Ache. The Cossacks suddenly became the saviours of the Republic, and the imagination of the boulevards heard with effusive gratitude the distant tread of Russian armies. French nerves were still unsteady, and Captain Dreyfus was convicted of espionage on evidence that cooler heads might have found less satisfying. But France had an ally, and the Republic faced the future with new confidence.

These changes in the Continental scene had little influence on British isolation. If anything, indeed, they served to deepen it. For Kipling's Englishman, no less than Gilbert's, remained convinced that

> *He himself has said it,*
> *And it's greatly to his credit,*
> *That he is an Englishman!*
> *For he might have been a Roosian,*
> *A French, or Turk, or Proosian,*
> *Or perhaps Itali-an!*
> *But in spite of all temptations*
> *To belong to other nations,*
> *He remains an Englishman!*

[181]

It was not easy to say which of the available alternatives was most distasteful. But some might be ruled out from the start. For there was a general impression that the Latin races were in decay, since they were largely given over to vainglory, dirty linen suits, and the possession of colonial territories that were deserving of a nobler ownership. The French were altogether too emotional and gravely addicted to the arts; and the Russians were understood to be perpetually up to something quite unmentionable behind the Hindu Kush that threatened the Queen-Empress in her tenure of the most imperial of all her possessions. Of course there were the Germans, for whom the victories of 1870 had created a sound esteem in British minds. It was a notable achievement to defeat the French; and when the conquerors were bearded men addicted to tobacco, beer, and Martin Luther's hymn, they made a strong appeal to British sympathy. Besides, contemporary scholarship in England had a marked tendency to detect Teutonic origins for almost anything; the Line regiments wore a spiked helmet in respectful emulation of von Moltke's conquering heroes; and the Queen's family arrangements had produced a network of affectionate ramifications beyond the Rhine, so that units of the British army were apt to go by such distressing titles as 'Princess Hohenzollern-Sigmaringen-Auspach's Merthyr-Tydfilshire Own Royal Loyal Light Infantry.' Thus it was not surprising that Lord Salisbury had permitted British policy to be drawn into the orbit of the Triple Alliance. There was a good deal to be said for friendship with the big battalions. French restlessness in the colonial sphere was a perpetual source of irritation; and if one must take sides, it seemed natural to Englishmen to side against the French. The Germans, it was felt, were more dependable; and German gratitude was cultivated by mild colonial encouragements and the gift of Heligoland, a slightly supernumerary possession of Great Britain. But this idyll was sharply interrupted by the German Emperor, who had no capacity for playing seconds. Under his rather feverish touch the *tempo* of Teutonic growth accelerated; Anglo-German rivalries developed in distant territories; and his telegram to President Kruger was an offensive declaration of German independence, which shocked the British mind. It had not been unwilling to recognise its Teutonic cousins as deserving recipients of colonial charity. But a dramatic challenge in the face of Europe relegated them once more to the overcrowded category of tiresome and offensive foreigners.

This was the tone of Britain's outlook on the world in 1897, and the world reciprocated with a warm dislike. What could be more irritating to the Continent than the spectacle of Britain's insular prosperity supported on unchallenged sea-power and a strong conviction that its people were the Lord's elect? There was, to foreign minds, something strangely unattractive in British invitations to

> *Walk wide o' the Widow at Windsor,*
> *For 'alf o' Creation she owns.*

Yet that warning and that spectacle were to be publicly repeated in the celebration of her Diamond Jubilee, which was to glorify the Empire in the person of its Empress. For she had become the emblem of imperial unity; and the whole triumph was designed to celebrate

> *One Life, one Flag, one Fleet, one Throne.*

This was to be the whole significance of the great occasion. It was a visible embodiment of Mr. Chamberlain's ambition "to organise an Empire—one may almost say to create an Empire—greater and more potent for peace and the civilisa-

tion of the world than any that history has ever known."
His hand was everywhere that summer—in a Colonial Conference, in the Colonial contingents for the procession, in
his great reception for the Colonial Premiers, in their un-
shakable conviction that "'Joseph' ran the whole thing in
the Jubilee."

The great day came at last. It was a fine Tuesday in the
last week of June, and London was full to bursting-point.
The buildings were quite unrecognisable behind a multiplicity of stands, triumphal arches, allegories in gas-jets,
yards of scarlet drapery, royal cyphers in electric glow-
lamps, and venetian masts. A writer in the *Daily Mail* archly
complained that somebody had boarded up the Law Courts,
covered the pediment of the Royal Exchange with carpen-
try, and substituted a good deal of scaffolding for the
Houses of Parliament. St. James's Street had fallen into a
sort of delirium of beauty. Two Corinthian columns sprouted
inconsequently from the pavement at the corner of Piccadilly, their gilt capitals supporting golden globes and palms
proliferating round their bases. All down the little hill
towards the modest red brick of the palace an alley of venetian masts supported an arcade of evergreen festoons, from
which depended baskets of expensive flowers, stuffed birds
in flight, and coloured globes of red, white, and blue glass
whose patriotic magic transformed the paving-stones beneath into a thoroughfare of Empire. The most urbane of
streets had suddenly turned sylvan, and awestruck visitors
beheld a woodland glade in fairyland—just such a fairyland
as was annually recreated by Sir Augustus Harris in the
pantomime at Drury Lane. The Strand was flagged out of
all recognition; there were more gas-jets on the Mansion
House than anyone could bear to count; the City griffin
ramped at Temple Bar above a bank of hot-house plants
unknown to heraldry; and all along the route inscriptions in

[184]

which lofty sentiment combined with unchallengeable statements of chronology brightened innumerable house-fronts.

The Queen had her first sight of them when she arrived in London on the day before the great procession. She had been at Windsor for the thanksgiving service in St. George's Chapel, when her mind went back to the first morning of her reign at Kensington and she remembered how her dear mamma had fetched her out of bed for the great news of her accession. They sang her husband's *Te Deum* once more and the new hymn for which Sir Arthur Sullivan had written the music, although the words were not by his accustomed collaborator (which was, perhaps, as well). Then she kissed all her children and grandchildren, thought for one melancholy instant of those whom she could no longer kiss, and drove to Frogmore for a sad little session beside her husband's grave. For there is a tragic side to such feats of survival as she had performed; and she was beginning to feel "rather nervous about the coming days, and that all should go off well." True, the Prince of Wales had offered modestly to save her some fatigue by receiving her loyal addresses and giving medals to the troops from India and the Colonies. He would attend the state performance at the Opera on her behalf to hear Melba and the incomparable de Reszkes in *Romeo and Juliet,* and review the Fleet and ride beside her carriage in the great procession. But the heat and burden of the day were hers.

The first blast of the public celebrations fanned her cheek on the next afternoon when she arrived at Paddington. The streets were crowded, and she was much gratified by a triumphal arch which had compressed its loyalty into the elliptical ejaculation, "Our hearts thy Throne." She counted two more arches in the Edgware Road and was impressed by all the beaming faces. The night was rather hot, and there was a good deal of noise outside the palace because

[185]

her subjects showed a remarkable disinclination to go to bed and a good many of them were sleeping in the parks in order to be in time for the procession.

The great day opened with a touch of haze. But at the very instant that she left the palace the sun, no less punctual and always conscious of its duty to the British Empire, shone out resplendently. It saw the head of the procession winding through the roaring streets—Lord Roberts on his little grey, New South Wales Lancers, Queensland Mounted Rifles, Rhodesian Horse led by the Hon. Maurice Gifford with his empty sleeve, black men in forage caps, brown men in turbans, fezzed Zaptiehs from Cyprus, Hausas from the west coast of Africa, broad-faced Dyaks from Borneo, Chinamen from Hongkong in the most unlikely hats, the whole variegated spectrum of the British Empire passing through the streets of London in honour of the small imperial emblem seated behind them in an open landau beneath a parasol. That was her *rôle,* less personal than it had been in former years. For though the crowds acclaimed the little figure in black chiffon and white ostrich feathers, their cheers were less for that miracle of longevity than for their own immense achievement, for the imperial effort which had linked one-fifth of the habitable world in allegiance to the old lady who sat there smiling through her tears and nodding at them with her bonnet.

When she reached St. Paul's, the vast procession halted. The cathedral steps were packed with clergy, choristers, and bandsmen; and as she sat there in her carriage and the sun blazed down on them, there was a short service of thanksgiving and the waiting crowds caught up the solemn air of the Old Hundredth. That was the crowning moment, when she sat beneath her parasol among the standing horses and the halted men and the Archbishop gave thanks to God for her survival. Then he called for cheers; and as St. Paul's

Churchyard rang with her subjects' acclamations, the slow drive resumed. The City roared its gratitude; the Lord Mayor took an emotional farewell outside the Mansion House after his perilous feats of equitation; and the royal carriage with the nodding aigrette and the white parasol crossed London Bridge to taste the welcome of her poorer subjects. If they had any grievances, they were forgotten in the uproar. Six miles of roaring Englishmen acclaimed her before she got back to the palace for a quiet lunch; and in the evening she did her best to speak to all the princes and princesses after a state banquet. But she was very tired. For if it was exhausting to be Queen of England, it was a still heavier burden to have become the emblem of an Empire. That was the strange destiny of Albert's widow and Lord Melbourne's pupil and the granddaughter of George III.

NINETEEN
HUNDRED AND ONE

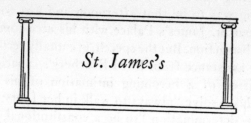

St. James's

THE KING stopped speaking, and the Privy Council looked at one another as they stood there in their uniforms. This time the Accession Council was not 'in a palace in a garden,' as it had been on the last occasion sixty-four years earlier when a slight girl in black addressed them from a paper in Lord Melbourne's handwriting and the sunshine of 1837 played among the leaves outside; but their meeting on that January afternoon in 1901 was behind the red brick and battlements that stood between St. James's Street and the cold alleys of the park. He had been speaking for about eight minutes without notes, and they were all much impressed. But when someone asked him afterwards if they could have the text for publication, he seemed surprised that no one had reported it and replied that he had nothing written down. The speech, it seemed, had been put together on his way up from Osborne that morning; and nobody had been consulted about what he was to say. So the Prime Minister would have no draft of it; and, in any case, it would not be much use asking Lord Salisbury if he remembered what the King had said, as he had almost forgotten where the meeting was to be that afternoon and was found wandering about St. James's Palace with his accustomed air of dignified abstraction. But the speech, eventually reconstructed with some assistance from Lord Rosebery's capacious memory, consisted of a becoming intimation of his mother's death, of his resolve "always to walk in her footsteps," and of his own determination "to be a constitutional sovereign in the strictest sense of the word." But the final announcement was the King's decision, for which nobody had been prepared, "to be known by the name of Edward, which has been borne by six of my ancestors" (a statement subsequently contested with some pedantry by Lord Acton on the strength of an uninteresting anecdote about Macaulay which could be refuted by reference to any dictionary). "In doing so," he had continued, "I do not undervalue the name of Albert, which I inherit from my ever-lamented great and wise father, who by universal consent is I think deservedly known by the name of Albert the Good, and I desire that his name should stand alone."

That grateful intimation, more than any other, marked the dawn of a new era; and it came as a complete surprise. For until the King's accession nobody had known in what name he proposed to reign. As Prince of Wales he had always been known as Albert Edward; and it could not be doubted that his mother would have wished him to succeed as the first of a line of royal Alberts. But the Prince thought otherwise, although he kept it to himself; unless a private reference by Mr. Gladstone four years earlier to "the reign of Edward VII" showed that the old prophet was in the secret. It was still a secret, though, to everyone at Court; and the King's announcement at his Accession Council showed, more than any other fact, that a new reign had opened.

But before it could begin, his country took its leave of the old reign with rich formality. The Queen had wished a little strangely for a military funeral. This was an odd desire on the part of an old lady with markedly domestic tastes. But the imperial mood had grown upon her; her thoughts were filled with her armed forces in South Africa (had not Lord Roberts been the very last of the long line of her official visitors?); and her desires were amply satisfied. A gun-carriage at Osborne; the dull thunder of artillery from a long avenue of warships on the black waters of the Solent; men resting rigidly on their arms reversed; the slow tramp of soldiers in great-coats and the wail of military bands—these were a strange reversal of her Diamond Jubilee. The same waters on which thirty miles of flagged and cheering warships had been aligned on a June day in 1897 in honour of her anniversary lay under a grey sky to watch the Queen go by; and in her capital the same crowds were waiting on the pavements. But they were silent now. This time there were no coloured favours in their coats; and the crowds that waited for the slow march of Chopin's sweetish melancholy to pass along the silent streets wore mourning. But though it was for the old Queen, they wore it just a little for themselves.

The high mood of 1897 had passed, and something had died in them. For they looked with a faint touch of apprehension into the new century. There had been brisk controversy among mathematicians as to whether it would start in 1900 or in 1901. But whenever it began, there could not be the slightest doubt that a new era opened rather formidably with the new reign. The old certainties had vanished; and they looked back a little wistfully across the gulf which separated 1901 from 1897. So much had happened in the interval. The spiritual debauch of the Diamond Jubilee was followed by a mood of penitence. Had not their favourite minstrel warned them at the time against *"frantic boast and foolish word"*? Now he was frankly chastening—

> *Let us admit it fairly, as a business people should.*
> *We have had no end of a lesson: it will do us no end*
> *of good.*

The lesson, which had been of a military character extending *"over eleven degrees of a bare brown continent,"* was inculcated with unkind reflections on

> *the flannelled fools at the wicket or the muddied oafs at*
> *the goals.*

It was handsomely deserved, although before a harsh reminder to his fellow-countrymen that they had

> *fawned on the Younger Nations for the men who could*
> *shoot and ride,*

it might have been fairer to admit that these Colonial paragons were no less addicted to ball-games, though more fitted by their circumstances to the requirements of irregular warfare. But the lesson had been severe. For an expanding Empire encountered two republics in South Africa that were unresponsive to expansion; the cold glare of Mr. Chamberlain's eye-glass confronted Kruger's inexpressive mask; and in the subsequent events the British Empire lost a good many of its more spectacular illusions.

Nothing could have been more light-hearted than the initial strategy, which provoked forty thousand Boers with a British strength of only twenty thousand men to meet them. The more cautious Balfour wished to play for time and reinforcements. But Mr. Chamberlain's imperial diplomacy moved faster than the transports. True, he appreciated that outlying points in British territory would be in some danger for a short time; but nobody had warned him that there would be the slightest need to send more than one army corps. That was the first illusion, which was brutally dispelled in the autumn weeks of 1899. For the Boers moved with indecent promptitude, and the defending forces were unceremoniously shepherded into Ladysmith and Kimberley, where British soldiers were positively besieged in British towns by an enemy with guns that outranged them and unpleasant habits of mobility and marksmanship which seemed to indicate that Aldershot was an imperfect training for the more complicated happenings of Elandslaagte and Nicholson's Nek. The next phase, which opened with a hopeful feeling that things would be much better when the troops arrived, was even more instructive. For the troops arrived; Lord Methuen's command tramped through a rainy night across the veldt to Magersfontein in quarter-column, guides holding ropes along the flank in case they lost formation, and stumbled straight into an enemy who shot them down at ease from trenches; two hundred miles away that week the same romantic taste for night attacks cut Gatacre's command to ribbons at Stormberg; and on the right of the extended front, where Buller fumbled at the gates of Ladysmith, his first attempt to find a way across a river which nobody had reconnoitred very much, preferring to advance in solid columns with impeccable alignment and field-guns spinning merrily ahead, like Mercer's battery at Waterloo, with the incomparable dash and jingle annually admired by happy patrons of the Military Tournament in the Agricultural Hall at Islington, had ended on the melancholy banks of the Tugela in the harsh awakening at Colenso, which left the country counting casualties and lost guns and wondering a little ruefully if methods admirably suited for disposing of Dervishes in the Sudan were equally adapted to a contest against Mauser rifles, smokeless powder, and Krupp guns.

That triple bill of defeat was the unpleasant harvest of a single black December week in 1899. The country reeled, and its European neighbours could be heard tittering at the discomfiture of a large Empire by a few determined amateurs. There was something disconcerting in the spectacle of their defeat by the invisible activities of an agricultural community which brought its coffee-pots and Bibles into the field and went to war by the simple expedient of wearing bandoliers over its everyday clothes. But they recovered swiftly. Within a week of the disasters Roberts and Kitchener were in command; there was a call for volunteers; the Colonies were asked to take a hand; and the immense, if slightly inaccessible, resources of the British Empire came gradually into play. There was a breathless interlude, as the slow transports steamed past Madeira and down into the South Atlantic, while patriotic statisticians estimated with increasing gloom the diminishing supplies of their beleaguered countrymen in Ladysmith and Kimberley and further to the north at Mafeking, where Colonel Baden-Powell sustained a gallant siege upon a heartening diet of gaiety and wild improvisation. The persevering Buller gave one more depressing demonstration of his quality at Spion Kop. But now his countrymen, attuned to military ineptitude, were less painfully surprised at finding his command still on the wrong side of the Tugela. For England waited cheerfully for "Bobs" and "Fighting Mac" to change the situation; and it did not wait in vain, since a swift fortnight of manœuvre sufficed for the wrinkled little man to relieve Kimberley and round up the Boers in the insanitary trap at Paardeberg; and the contagion of success swept Buller's weary columns into the incredulous and battered streets of Ladysmith.

The tide had turned at last; the slow machine of war creaked painfully towards the inevitable British victory over an agile but insubstantial enemy; and the end came in sight. There were still awkward moments, when Sanna's Post obtained unpleasant notoriety and De Wet became synonymous with the intangible, while less satisfactory exhibitions were still given on the higher levels of the British side by

> the old men
> ('Eavy-sterned amateur old men!)
> That 'amper an' 'inder an' scold men.

It was a trying time for elderly professionals, to whom it was revealed with uncomfortable iteration that their professional equipment was only distantly related to the requirements of real warfare against well-armed and civilised opponents. For the familiar lessons of Aldershot and savage warfare were both equally inapplicable in South Africa; and well-meant efforts to apply them ended in the depressing and recurrent lilt of

> Only a Kensington draper
> Only pretending to scout . . .
> Only bad news for the paper,
> Only another knock-out.

That phase was over now, and the war closed with the less orthodox methods of "A section, a pompom, an' six 'undred men," unnumbered blockhouses, and unlimited barbed wire, to the impressive ground-bass of two hundred thousand men

> foot-slog-slog-slog-sloggin' over Africa!
> Foot-foot-foot-foot-sloggin' over Africa—
> (Boots-boots-boots-boots movin' up and down again!) . . .

[197]

Now the war was over, and the British Empire settled comfortably down to the congenial exercise of absorbing the indigestible morsel of South Africa. But the scar remained. The nation's pride was deeply scarred by the discovery that it had taken years, rather than months, to eliminate two insignificant republics in a distant continent. This pointed to deficiencies in those splendid images of war that had figured so prominently in the Diamond Jubilee procession. For if it really took as long as that to deal with Kruger, the British taxpayer began to wonder if the War Office was equal to disposing of the Russians or the French or the increasingly disturbing figure of the Kaiser. The nation had gone wild with joy at the relief of Mafeking; but it was a sobering reflection that the defence of a small town by seven hundred men with two field-guns, some Maxims, and a home-made howitzer of uncertain habits was a slightly disproportionate occasion for a whole Empire's exultation, which seemed to indicate that its opportunities for public rejoicing were likely to be restricted in the event of warfare on a more considerable scale. This mood precipitated a good deal of angry heart-searching on the part of self-appointed experts, who publicly deplored the fact that in five months' observation of British officers they were unable to recall more than one occasion on which a single one of them had been detected in the act of reading a military book; and Royal Commissions wrestled with the divinely appointed obstinacy of a military caste which was reluctant to believe that anything could ever modify the operations of war, as they had been in the habit of conducting them in the Long Valley at Aldershot and proposed, by God's help, to reproduce them in whatever quarter of the world their country's enemies might dare to challenge it. The warning had been costly. But mercifully it was audible; and a relatively minor fiasco in South Africa encouraged the application of intelligence to military matters which spared the nation far graver trials nearer home upon a subsequent occasion.

Nor was the temper of self-criticism inspired by the events of 1900 confined to the imperfect apparatus of national defence. For the whole edifice of Jubilee complacency was plainly challenged. It was unpleasantly evident that there were imperfections in the order bequeathed by Queen Victoria to her son; and his subjects began to feel the breath of change. A well-timed election before the war was over had enabled the Conservatives to capitalise the prevailing patriotism in a party victory. But the ensuing mood was inadequately represented in the Parliament of 1900, though it found utterance a few months after the new reign began in a pronouncement by Lord Rosebery. That statesman had succeeded Mr. Gladstone in the exacting leadership of a fractious party and weakly repudiated his succession, subsequently reappearing at intervals in public life in the disturbing, though congenial, *rôle* of Hamlet's father's ghost. He now consented to address an audience at Chesterfield in terms to which that township owes its chief distinction, apart from the unpleasing circumstance that its church steeple is distinctly crooked. For he informed his hearers that the country's need was for "a condition of national fitness equal to the demands of our Empire," adding that it owed to Lord Salisbury and his colleagues "seven years lost for all social and human causes; seven years lost for all measures which make for national health and national efficiency; seven years lost in our training and preparation for the keen race of nations, both in commerce and in dominion." This was a tone, with its confession that Great Britain had competitors abroad and that there was room for improvement in her affairs at home, which Queen Victoria would scarcely recognise. But a new reign had opened; and King Edward's subjects stared about them in a new world.

NINETEEN
HUNDRED AND FIVE

1. Winter Palace Square

THE SHOUTING in the square came nearer. Now they could hear it quite distinctly from the palace; and the Admiralty spire that hung like a gold spectre in the sky above St. Petersburg looked down at the procession as it shuffled slowly through the streets towards the Winter Palace on its way to see the Czar. They had been gathering all through the January morning from the dilapidated wooden cabins that huddled in the shadow of the tall, thin chimneys of the Putiloff works. Some of them were carrying ikons and portraits of the Czar, and a few had brought their wives and children with them for an outing. For how could it be more than a respectful outing to present the Czar with their petition against the capitalists and bureaucrats who denied them everything? Its tone was humble and its bearers were pathetically law-abiding, as they shuffled through the winter streets to see the Czar, whom Father Gapon had invited to meet his subjects in the Winter Palace Square that afternoon at two o'clock.

But the Czar was not in St. Petersburg. His ministers,

alarmed by the unusual nature of the communication, had withdrawn their master to the safe seclusion of Czarskoye Selo, where he could be happy in his own surroundings. His other palaces were heavy with the accumulated air of Russian history, and there was not much in Russian history to cheer a Czar. Their rooms were full of memories. Elizabeth and Catherine still lived in their swaggering rococo; there were dark corners at Gatchina where Paul grimaced among his grenadiers; and the shadows were full of hunted figures—of his own grandfather's drawn features and his father's sullen scowl. But at Czarskoye Selo he could escape from history into a safe domesticity. The lace frills on the cushions, the innumerable photographs, the English novels in the revolving bookcase all spoke to him of life in comfortable country-houses, where life was less exacting for royal personages. His mother's hand appeared in the pale colouring of endless Copenhagen china ornaments which she invariably brought them from her Danish holidays; and his own preferences covered the walls with marine paintings to remind them of happy days on board the *Standart*. For they could be so happy when they were not on Russian soil. But life was always difficult at home; and the slightly liner-like conformation of more than one room at Czarskoye Selo recalled happy days at sea. It was an innocent escape from their surroundings, in which the Czar of All the Russias sought comfort in the inimitable dowdiness of framed photographs and frilled lampshades in the taste of the best boarding-houses of the time of Queen Victoria's first Jubilee.

This unimpressive little man with a small pointed beard, a kindly eye, and nearly all the private virtues was strangely inadequate to his enormous *rôle*. An ardent bicyclist, a devotee of amateur photography, he had kept a diary with blameless regularity since he was thirteen; and its unexcit-

ing pages with their invariable record of the weather and
the names of gentlemen in waiting reflected him with the unmeaning accuracy of a mirror. He was not far off forty now.
But the rather backward schoolboy who had begun to keep
a diary in 1881 still made his daily entry as Czar of All the
Russias, recording with mechanical precision the hour of his
appointments, the temperature, and the titles of the books
he read. His observation was a schoolboy's; and his reading,
in which Conan Doyle competed with occasional excursions
into Robert Hichens and Baroness Orczy, would have filled
a house-master with some misgivings. His foreign languages
were good, and his military education had included a brief
course in manly gaiety at the experienced hands of an Imperial *ballerina* who lived in a monstrosity of *art nouveau*
across the river from the Winter Palace. But there was
something listless in him which omitted to grow up. Where
other men are formed by action, this ageing process was
denied him. For the Czar, disbelieving in his own ability to
influence events, was possessed by an immense fatalism;
and this passive creed retarded his development. If it was
no use to interfere with destiny, there was little to be said
for thinking very hard or doing very much. So Nicholas
resigned himself to an uncontemplative life, in which most
of his actions were mechanically impelled by circumstances
or advisers. His fatalism, as it grew upon him, was noted
by observers. An Englishman commented later that "the
Emperor of Russia has positively not a nerve in his body.
He is a profound fatalist." Even a Grand Duchess noticed
his fatalism. Such passivity was unlikely to accelerate his
growth; and as his life went by, there was only one respect
in which he seemed to grow to man's estate. For an unclouded marriage had made him an adoring husband and
a devoted father. A granddaughter of Queen Victoria gave
him the felicity of an English home, four daughters, and

—at last—a son. Their harmony was quite unbroken; but her deep religious sense, in which mysticism bordered dangerously upon magic, served only to increase her husband's feeling that he was a passive instrument of Providence; and in this belief he became less capable than ever of independent volition. But resignation and a blameless life formed an inadequate equipment for the part he had to play. For insignificance may be a royal virtue where political development has relieved the monarch of more complicated duties; but the Russian monarchy had not yet evolved so far. Its occupant was asked to be an autocrat; and autocracy demands more than a passive faith that the will of God will somehow prevail.

The will of God was manifested at the moment in his residence at Czarskoye Selo whilst a considerable number of his subjects, who believed him to be in St. Petersburg, shuffled respectfully towards the Winter Palace through the Sunday streets. They were on strike because the management of the Putiloff works had recently dismissed some of its employees for the grave offence of joining Father Gapon's organisation. This well-meaning group, which went so far as to explore the dizzy possibilities of an eight-hour day and Parliamentary government, was (like its leader) quite familiar to the police, who thoughtfully supported its finances and followed it with close attention. But when its leader intimated a few days before the demonstration that his followers desired to take their troubles to the Czar himself in the great square before his palace, it was felt that Father Gapon went too far. True, the petition that they were to bring with them asked for nothing more than recognition of trade unions, the right to discuss wages and working conditions, and a Constituent Assembly elected on a democratic franchise. But it had found unpleasant things to say about official honesty. Its innocent appeal to the Czar's sympathy against his stern administrators was tactlessly expressed; and there was something dangerously like a threat in its last despairing statement that if he left their prayer unanswered, there would be nothing left for them but to die there on the square outside his palace. (That passage, it subsequently appeared, was the sole portion of the document found worthy of official notice.) It was the mildest manifesto drafted since the Middle Ages. The programme of industrial and Parliamentary reform was drawn within the frame of loyalty to the Russian monarchy. There were no proposals subversive of the capitalist basis of society in its modest statement of their bare request for a few elementary human rights. For who could quarrel with their accuracy when the petitioners announced that they "have the appearance of human beings, but in fact we have no human rights at all, not even the right to speak, to think, or to meet for discussion of our requirements or the steps to be taken for the improvement of our conditions"?

This was all the simple consequence of the industrial development of Russia, which had superimposed the discipline of the machines on a society emerging slowly from a state of rural slavery; and the *malaise* of Russian industry was accelerated by the unhappy circumstance which had concentrated so much of it in the unpropitious region of St. Petersburg. That neighbourhood, designed by Providence for the support of a few Finnish fishermen and fur-trappers, had been selected by Czar Peter for his capital. His energy, defying economics and geography, had raised a city from its swamps. But though the stately buildings on their driven piles lined the rushing Neva and the broad avenues of St. Petersburg proclaimed a capital, nothing could render it congenial to a large population. For the autumn mists still crept up from the hidden marshes, and a cutting wind off Lake Ladoga swept down towards the sea. It was a climate in which wealth might find a way to make life tolerable. But it was unbearable for poverty; and since industrialism in its early stage bred abject poverty, St. Petersburg was always restless. Avid of any shift in their discomfort, an uneasy population huddled precariously in wooden cabins round the Putiloff works and in their rookeries on the Viborg side. Change—any change—could hardly fail to be for the better; and Father Gapon's mild incitements brought St. Petersburg into the streets that Sunday afternoon.

As they tramped hopefully along towards the Winter Palace with their petition, they saw that there were a good many troops about. But what was that to them, since their business was with the Czar himself and they were carrying his portrait as an emblem of their loyalty? Some of them had brought their ikons with them to give a pious tone to the procession. It was a Sunday afternoon; and as they were Russians, they were singing as they marched. There was a gleam of holy pictures, and the deep Russian voices sounded above the tramp of heavy boots. But they were not singing those revolutionary songs whose sentiments were so distasteful to the Czar's police. For as the sound came nearer, they were singing hymns. A few had brought their wives and children; and the long column tramped through the Sunday streets to meet the Czar, where his rust-red palace waited and all the statues of the great façade looked out across the square. But the Czar was not there to meet them, since he was a dozen miles away at Czarskoye Selo. It had been thought better that the appointment should be kept for him by others. So the soldiers were waiting in their ranks outside the Winter Palace; and when his subjects tramped into the square, someone ordered them to go away. This was not in the least what they had expected, since Father Gapon was to go inside with their petition and then come out to tell them all about the Czar's reply. But he had vanished, and somebody was ordering them to disperse. Then a bugle rang out; they were looking into rows of rifle barrels; the volleys crashed; the air was full of singing bullets; and whips cracked and whistled, as the Cossacks rode them down. There was a dreadful panic, as the procession broke and ran for safety. They were all running now, except some of them who lay quite still on the cobbles, where the palace statues looked out across the square. That afternoon St. Petersburg had learnt among its dead that it was unrewarding to approach the Czar: the lesson was remembered.

Its immediate consequence was an explosion in the provinces. For the unpleasant rhythm of Russian history, which compelled an alternation of defeat abroad with revolution nearer home, was felt once more. It was January, 1905; and Kuropatkin, beaten on the Yalu, had failed to hold the Japanese at Liaoyang and the Shaho, while Nogi battered Port Arthur into surrender. That was the unhappy state of Russian enterprise in the Far East, which had appeared to promise a new empire at the gates of China with ports on summer seas, a regency for Admiral Alexeieff, the glories of the Trans-Siberian Railway, and wealth for highly-placed concessionaires. But the decisive word was spoken by the Japs; and the Czar's dream had crumbled into the ashes of Port Arthur and the freezing trenches before Mukden, whilst his Pacific Fleet lay rusting on the sea-floor and Rojdestvensky dragged his crews half-way round the world from Cronstadt through the fogs of the North Sea (where they nearly started a war with England by some hysterical night-firing among startled fishing-boats on the Dogger Bank), by way of Madagascar and the China Seas, to their inevitable doom at Tsushima. It was a depressing demonstration of the truth of a French general's opinion that the Russian way in war is to make a good start, but a poor finish—with the exception that in the present instance they had not even started well.

A military empire cannot be sustained indefinitely upon a diet of defeat. The imperial eagles, whose air was so magnificent in time of peace, began to look distinctly draggled; and Russia swerved, as usual, from defeat towards revolution. The heartless massacre of 'Bloody Sunday' fired the long train, and all Europe waited for the explosion. But the explosion never came. For though that solitary act assembled all the elements of a successful revolution, stripping the silent masses of their last illusion as to the possibilities of any betterment within the framework of the Czar's authority and aligning on their side the decent impulses of an articulate and educated middle class, the chemistry of 1905 failed to produce the necessary spark; and the ensuing episodes were little more than an unsatisfactory dress-rehearsal of a revolution, in which the scenery stuck, properties failed to appear at the right moment, and the actors were not word-perfect. The cast was adequate, since Trotsky took the chair at meetings of a Soviet of workers in St. Petersburg, and Lenin, who had heard the news in Switzerland when all the *émigrés* sang the Revolutionary Funeral March in a Geneva restaurant and he went home to write excited articles and plunge happily into the details of gun-running, was flitting up and down the capital in a false name, hoping that the police would fail to recognise him without his beard and hoping against hope that the prevailing atmosphere of revolutionary eloquence might be succeeded by a more practical epoch of competent street-fighting with barbed wire, trenching-tools, and long nails for use against the Cossacks' horses.

This formidable man of thirty-five, whose whole life changed when the Czar's executioners hanged an adored elder brother behind the bastions of the Fortress of St.

Peter and St. Paul, had mastered the full dialect of Marxist Socialism at an early age, and his utterance abounded in its strange incantations. A free use of the words 'inevitable,' 'objective,' and 'materialist' marked his proficiency; and he acquired an easy familiarity with such things as "the objective meaning of the historic process" and the "objective contents of historical phenomena." But though his mastery of revolutionary theory was unsurpassable, he never lost a grip of revolutionary practice. His mind was eminently practical. The sacred calendar of European revolutions indicated that the English Chartists, the June barricades of 1848, and the Paris Commune were to be followed by something more decisive; and his whole life was a conscious preparation for that event, for the development in which (as Marx wrote to Engels) "twenty years are but as one day—and there may come days which are the concentrated essence of twenty years."

The thoughtful measures of the Czar's police ensured his preparation for the part by relegating him to the endless leisure of exile. That was the university in which a revolutionary graduated. Long hours of reading formed him in the lamplight of innumerable little rooms, first on the outer edge of Siberia beyond the Yenisei, where his honeymoon took the unappetising form of a joint translation of the Webbs' *Industrial Democracy,* and the cold hillsides looked out across Mongolia; then in German lodgings, which they shared with a revolutionary lady who dropped cigarette ash over everything and had a tendency to use her scissors for clipping pieces off the joint; in London, where he spent half his time in the reading-room of the British Museum and went for endless rides on top of omnibuses or made pilgrimages to Primrose Hill, because they liked the view and found comfort in the proximity to Marx at Highgate Cemetery and he took Trotsky for a walk to see "their famous Westminster"; and finally in Switzerland, where there was a perpetual smell of burnt papers in Krupskaya's room and he wrote steadily—the "cold fanatic who wrote little articles in a little newspaper"—and nearly lost an eye by cycling absent-mindedly into the back of a Geneva tram and read endless books about street-fighting, as he smoothed his thinning hair and made notes in his small handwriting on tiny squares of paper, or went off for long tramps in the mountains and came back again for interminable arguments with fellow-exiles, whose obtuseness on the finer shades of Marxism was an undying source of irritation.

His orthodoxy revelled in excommunications, for which the strictness of his creed afforded ample opportunity. The votaries of Marx appeared to view their prophet's writings in a positively religious light; and a wealth of exegesis and apologetics was expended on those copious outpourings, in which economics were drastically revised, whilst history was subjected to a process of simplification by the bold expedient of misreading nearly everybody's motives and ignoring a good deal of history. But the Marxian revelation impressed its devotees with the completeness of a faith; and though Marx himself had been as adaptable as Mahomet, Marxism was as rigid as Islam. Indeed, its votaries working and waiting for the inevitable event of a world-revolution prescribed by the unchanging laws of history caught something of Moslem fatalism; and disputing sects quoted the sacred writings against one another with the ingenuity of learned mullahs bandying stray fragments of the Koran. It was a religious atmosphere, in which orthodoxy was computed with rabbinical exactitude and heresies were gleefully denounced. The faithful, certain of a martyr's crown from the police, enlarged their opportunities for martyrdom by persecuting one another with enormous gusto. Excommunications thundered on all sides; rival Popes abounded; and the Socialist devotions of competing sects proceeded in a refreshing air of intellectual contempt and personal abuse.

Formed by these spiritual exercises, Lenin never hesitated to prefer strict orthodoxy to mere strength of numbers, and gaily split the Social Democratic Party on a point of doctrine. The sequel left him with a tiny group of Bolsheviks. But that did not disturb him, since his faith was pinned for practical purposes on a small body of whole-timed professional revolutionaries, of "people whose profession consists of revolutionary activity. This organisation must not be very broad and as conspirative as possible. . . . Give us an organisation of revolutionaries—and we shall turn Russia upside down."

But Russia in 1905 was disinclined to face the bold experiment, though Lenin pelted it with arguments and Trotsky regaled a Soviet of workers with his nightly thunders. Perhaps the situation was not quite sufficiently confused to produce one of those apocalyptic "days which are the concentrated essence of twenty years." The horror in the palace square was promptly followed by an impressive outbreak of strikes. A cruiser mutinied and steamed into Odessa under the red flag; and the news set Lenin dreaming happily of extensive trouble in the Black Sea Fleet. He was still in Switzerland, and a Bolshevik was startled by his orders to "act decisively and boldly. Then send a torpedo-boat for me at once." (There was no indication whether it was to proceed straight to Geneva or to force the Dardanelles.) But when he finally reached Russia by the less romantic route of Sweden and Helsingfors, he found the disappointing spectacle of a distracted country which was to be permitted to elect some sort of Duma upon some sort of franchise, while the Czar's police proceeded with wholesale arrests and amused his subjects with the organised and highly patriotic pastime of massacring the Jews. It was a depressing outcome of so much tragedy and so much hope; and as Lenin stumbled through a winter night across the frozen sea off the Finnish coast to catch a steamer on his way back to exile, the ice began to move beneath him and he reflected that it was a silly way to have to die.

But the lesson had been lost upon the Czar. Not that he was afforded great facilities for learning it. For shortly after 'Bloody Sunday' he was waited on in the suburban safety of Czarskoye Selo by a respectful deputation of carefully selected workmen. Their demeanour, to which a prescient police had given some attention, was impeccable, conforming closely to their orders "to remain silent when he talks to you and go on bowing." After a preliminary search of all their clothes at a police station, a two-hours wait, a short journey in a special train, and an uneasy interval the Czar appeared and read a little speech. They bowed extremely low, as he informed them that they were forgiven and that something would be done; meanwhile they must be patient and go back to work. This exhilarating audience was followed by a large dinner in the palace kitchen. But their reception in the factories was not encouraging. For the factories, unlike the Czar, had learnt their lesson. The sad-eyed automaton at Czarskoye Selo still made its little entries in the royal diary. The war dragged on six thousand miles away. Mukden was lost. But he revived sufficiently to record that he had "shot a cat"; and as the Russian Navy went to destruction at Tsushima, their home-loving Emperor had a "very nice picnic."

2. Tangier

O<small>N THE LAST DAY</small> of March the white houses of the little town crowded along the waterfront to watch the big German steamer anchor in the bay. It was blowing hard; and a respectful diplomat who went alongside had some difficulty on a heaving rope-ladder, as he was wearing the full uniform of a Bavarian Uhlan. Tight breeches, riding-boots, and rakish headgear were equally unsuitable for feats of maritime agility. But the occasion fully warranted his inconvenient costume, since the ship's company comprised no less than forty persons of extreme distinction, including nine retired admirals and his sovereign; and as he climbed on board all over spray, von Kühlmann's acrobatic feat was highly gratifying to the Kaiser. They had arrived from Lisbon, because a letter from his Chancellor advised the Emperor to make a landing at Tangier. It would have diplomatic implications of the gravest order; and though he had an overwhelming taste for theatrical diplomacy, on this occasion the Emperor was not quite sure of his effect. His sudden emergence from a trap-door at Tangier would be extremely striking; but there was some room for uncertainty as to who would be struck. He viewed the prospect with misgiving on other grounds as well, since they had just discovered that one could not drive a carriage through Tangier. Besides, the wind was fresh and they were separated from the land by an extremely lively interval of water. A French naval officer, whom he interrogated anxiously, assured him that there was no danger, but was not prepared to guarantee the weather until five o'clock that afternoon. This was unfortunate, as he was due on shore that morning for a reception at the German Legation on the hill, followed by a round of celebrations with the Moors which would not permit him to return on board before five o'clock. The sky was scrutinised; and after some delay he left his rolling liner for the shore in a small boat that bounced uncomfortably across the bay. This heartening experience was an indifferent preparation for a crowded day; and the imperial composure barely survived the courtesies of landing, which were abbreviated by his prompt departure for the town. He went on horseback, since it was felt that a pedestrian progress would be too undistinguished. Other visitors passed through the steep and narrow streets of Tangier on foot; but it was only fitting that, where ordinary mortals walked, the German Emperor should ride. Unhappily its streets are singularly ill-adapted for equitation; and the white charger which had been provided for the great occasion was unduly aware of its responsibilities or else disconcerted by the unusual spectacle of its imperial master in a white helmet which, though picturesque, was hardly called for by the climate of Tangier in March. The consequence was a precarious interlude, in which the visiting grandee looked far from well and snapped at somebody beside him because there was some cheering in the narrow street that upset him greatly and might, still worse, upset his mount. Arrived at the Legation, he made a fretful speech with pointed references to the independence of Morocco, with which the French were tampering, cancelled his lunch and the subsequent festivities arranged by the hospitable Moors, and hurried back on board his liner, which lay rolling comfortably in the bay. The imperial visit to Tangier was over; and within half an hour the *Hamburg's* smoke was heading for the Straits.

This ill-tempered episode, contrived in the best tradition of German diplomacy, managed to annoy the largest possible number of persons. The local Germans were embarrassed, the French alarmed, the British irritated. Even the Moors, who were to be the beneficiaries of his sudden gesture, were left with a large lunch on their hands and a disappointed crowd of horsemen, who had lost the chance of showing off their paces at full gallop with a satisfying expenditure of blank cartridges in a *fantasia* before the royal guest. But tact was a vulgarism into which the Kaiser rarely lapsed. Acutely conscious of his international importance and seeming sometimes to confuse international relations with an exciting form of amateur theatricals, he was the evident despair of statesmen and the constant joy of political cartoonists. The variety and vividness of his public appearances startled observers, whose uncertainty as to what he was going to say next was only equalled by his own; and in 1905 the German Emperor was the cynosure of Europe.

This problem-child was now approaching middle-age. But he retained a taste for dressing up, for which supreme command of the armed forces of a military empire (to say nothing of his foreign regiments) afforded ample opportunity. Owning a splendid repertory of martial costume and spared the necessity (so wearing to self-made autocrats) of inventing his own uniforms, his striking figure was seen to advantage in every known form of tunic, plastron, and cuirass, whilst an imposing galaxy of nautical and military headgear crowned the stern majesty of the imperial features. Their

[217]

gravity was emphasised on suitable occasions by a cultivated glare; and a bold tonsorial experiment provided a moustache which seemed to challenge gravitation by its almost vertical ascent. (Strange that pre-eminence in Germany has more than once been indicated by an eccentric pattern in the hair upon the upper lip.) This splendid effigy was all his own creation; but his interest was not confined to its spectacular aspects, since he was no less actively concerned with what it said than with what it looked like. A religious sense of monarchy inspired him and combined with considerable powers of speech to lend excitement to his public utterances, which were both frequent and emphatic. The imperial vehemence would have been less significant on the part of a less influential person. But when it came from the supreme warlord of an army of three million men and a rapidly growing navy in a country whose monarchy was anything but constitutional, his slightly enigmatic personality became a fact of international importance.

His moods were always trying and his manners never good. The Emperor had been a grief to his mother, an anxiety to his grandmother, and an unfailing source of irritation to his uncle. For it was a sad disappointment to his royal relatives in England that a grandson of Queen Victoria could turn out quite so badly, and they were always ready to misread his noblest impulses. Anxious diplomats appraised his lightest utterances; and their task was not rendered easier by his vivid taste for over-emphasis and an occasional indulgence in royal jokes of which the point was not always readily discernible. Humour in high places is apt to be a perilous accomplishment; and when the Emperor sought to convey to an ambassador his satisfaction with a recent decision of the British Government in the picturesque ejaculation that "the noodles seem to have had a lucid interval," the strain upon diplomacy was almost more than it could bear. His tactlessness on that occasion was not ill-meant. But the imperial dictum stood in considerable need of judicious interpretation before it could be suitably transmitted to its recipients in London; and as their interpreters are not invariably sympathetic, exalted personages would be well-advised to abstain from sayings that are not literally true. His cheerful habit of exaggeration was an obstacle to just comprehension; and his mysticism, which was perfectly sincere, baffled observers almost equally. It was bewildering to meet a monarch with a genuine belief in the divine right of kings; and when he publicly announced a recent visit by his grandfather (who had died nine years before) to some regimental colours in a room at Potsdam which had been unoccupied since 1888, the temptation to irreverence was almost irresistible. Indeed, light-minded persons whispered that the Emperor had gone so far as to appoint himself aide-de-camp to his august predecessor for the occasion.

These strange beliefs formed an essential part of the impressive apparatus with which the Kaiser fortified himself to do his duty. His sense of that was high—as high as might have been expected in a descendant of Frederick the Great and Queen Victoria. But a sense of duty merely indicates what has to be done and leaves its owner to discover in himself the strength to do it. Never a strong man, he fought a creditable battle with pain and a severe physical disability, from which he emerged with an impersonation of rude health supported on a disproportionate expenditure of nervous energy. For there was always a large element of unreality about his health. The Kaiser's vigour was a histrionic triumph; and the underlying strain betrayed itself in the impaired condition of his nerves. Sudden impulses and a continual restlessness disclosed his true condition, and the Kaiser often bordered on hysteria. His brittle nerves inclined him to association with other neurasthenics, and the tone of the imperial circle was a trifle shrill. For he was anything but strong. Yet if he could convince himself (and others) that he was under God's protection, that would be a welcome substitute for strength; and if the divine custody were only supplemented by the benevolent activity of his ancestral spirits, this additional collaboration might enable him to discharge his task. That was, perhaps, the source of his reiterated and eccentric faith in God's collaboration in the unfamiliar detail of administering the German Empire and the steadily recurring references to his never-to-be-forgotten grandfather. (Allusions to his father's spirit were less frequent, since it was doubtful how far his current actions were likely to commend themselves in that spectral quarter; and his mother, to whom they were evidently distasteful, was not yet a spirit.)

Fortified by these beliefs, he faced the burden of his public duty and proceeded with his bold impersonation of a burly emperor in uninterrupted enjoyment of the rudest health. His make-up for the part was formidable; and much of his apparent violence is traceable to histrionic motives. The martial air, the frozen eye, the uniforms were all in character; and his strident utterance was an attempt to satisfy himself first, and the world afterwards, that he was equal to the *rôle*. The danger was that innocent spectators of the imperial performance might take the terrifying mask which he assumed at its face value. Europe, indeed, was apt to diagnose him as the cause of more than half its troubles and to mistake his stage-effects for the approaching mutter of a storm. He did his best to dissipate the impression with his pathetic avowal to a French diplomat, *"Ich bin doch kein böser Mensch."* But the harm was done, since fear is the most perilous of international moods; and he exhaled an atmosphere of fear, in which other nations drew nervously together and began to scrutinise their armaments (and his) with anxious eyes. For Europe was frankly afraid of him; and it is no extenuation that, if the truth were known, they had not much to be afraid of. The truth could not be known till afterwards; and since it had been his ambition to keep Europe guessing, Europe could not be blamed for guessing wrong.

Besides, the German Emperor was highly typical of the nation over which he ruled. Emerging from long centuries of fragmentary local history, the Germans had become a nation within the memory of men still living, since Bismarck's work was less than forty years away. Their international significance was a new and gratifying fact, to which they called their own attention with an emphasis and stridency that other nations, who were less acutely conscious of their own importance, found a little tiresome. (But then their own importance was not quite such a novelty to other nations.) Few neighbours have sufficient charity to recognise the blatancy of *parvenus* as a form of diffidence; and when German tongues informed the listening spheres with painful regularity of German excellence, the Continent omitted to observe that a shy nation was only trying hard to reassure itself. Perhaps the error was excusable, since German contacts were not rendered easier by an extreme sensitiveness combined with a complete unawareness of other people's feelings. A wise diplomat commented that "they were the most sensitive people in the world, and at the same time it would never enter into their heads that they could by any possibility be offensive themselves, although in reality they very often were." That was the impenetrable screen of misconception behind which the Germans moved. The suddenness of their promotion to a place of international importance made them unnaturally anxious to impress the world. It was all so very recent; and there must be no excuse for European neighbours with inconveniently long memories to confuse the drilled magnificence of the new *Reich* with the kindly but unimpressive Germany of 1850. Unduly anxious to impress, the newcomers were more preoccupied than older residents with what the world might think of them. But by some mischance their simple make-up omitted to include those organs of perception by which more normal persons are informed of the effect which they produce on other people. It followed that their international career was marked by an unfortunate duality, in which the German ear supposed the German voice to be insisting mildly that Germany was not wholly negligible, while the neighbourhood was almost deafened by the noise.

The Kaiser's utterances were a vivid instance of this unhappy failing. When he desired to impress his fleet with its duty to protect German interests in Chinese waters, his peroration invited them to "strike out with mailed fist"; when there was something to be said that might encourage naval construction without causing undue apprehension in British minds, his German hearers were informed that the trident was within their grasp; and when he wished to hearten his marines on their departure for a punitive expedition directed against Chinese barbarism, an unhappy taste in historical analogy impelled him to express the hope that "even as, a thousand years ago, the Huns under their King Attila made such a name for themselves as still resounds in terror through legend and fable, so may the name of Germany resound through Chinese history a thousand years from now." The echo, alas! was not confined to China; and the Kaiser's eloquence supplied the enemies of Germany with an invaluable weapon of which no explanations could deprive them. The Kaiser, it must be confessed, was often in need of explanation; and the task provided German diplomats with ample occupation, since it was his melancholy

fate to be almost perpetually misunderstood. Thus, his disinterested action at the darkest moment of the Boer War in
supplying the Prince of Wales with helpful memoranda to
show him the best way of winning it failed unaccountably to
earn his uncle's gratitude. Few uncles relish good advice
from nephews, especially when their own affairs are rather
critical. But the Kaiser was the last man to grow weary in
well-doing from any diffidence as to the feelings of his beneficiary. Acutely conscious of his own, he was completely unaware of other people's feelings; and, like his subjects, the
German Emperor was painfully surprised that nobody in
Europe seemed to like him.

The fact, one must confess, was hardly to be wondered
at, since the Continent was asked to live in a state of perpetual uncertainty because the Kaiser and his people were
uncertain of themselves. Europe was expected to permit
the prospect of continued peace to depend on German
moods, which varied with a girlish frequency. But adult
nations are unresponsive to a cave-man's wooing; and his
antics had already led to one grave and significant result.
For the growing sense of insecurity had drawn France and
Russia together in the bold paradox of an alliance between
the Third Republic and the Czar; and Nicholas II was now
happily united with the political descendants of Marat. Yet
such distinctions were easily effaced by German heavy-
handedness, and as a result Bismarck's life-work was threatened by the combination that he dreaded most. For war on
two fronts had been the nightmare of Prussian statesmanship throughout Prussian history. But the Kaiser's unaccountable behaviour and the neurotic diplomacy of Holstein
precipitated Russia into the waiting arms of France, since
Teutonic methods, which rarely made a friend for Germany, had an almost magic power of persuading other nations to forget their differences.

[223]

The same lubricant was soon at work on Anglo-French relations, although these had been exacerbated by centuries of war and rivalry, by colonial competition and vast differences of temperament, to say nothing of the inability of French caricaturists to refrain from availing themselves without undue chivalry of the pictorial possibilities presented by the aged silhouette of Queen Victoria. Nothing was more improbable in 1900 than a *rapprochement* between England—Queen Victoria's, Lord Salisbury's, General Buller's, Colonel Baden-Powell's, Mr. Kipling's England—and the France of President Loubet, where the air was still heavy with the acrid fumes of the Dreyfus affair and angry disputants assessed the credibility of Major Esterhazy, the rectitude of Colonel Picquart, the eloquence of MM. Clemenceau and Zola, the adroitness of Maître Labori, and the equivocal behaviour of Colonel du Paty de Clam. To Englishmen the French were still an object of mild ridicule and real apprehension, who made indifferent sportsmen, constructed warships that looked absurdly like Chinese pagodas, sympathised offensively with the Boers, and deliberately planted tricolours in places where the Union Jack was manifestly called for; while the luminous intelligence of France saw little more in England than the white cliffs of a perpetual and ruthless enemy, whose cold brutality deprived the gallant Marchand of his hard-earned triumph on the White Nile and effaced the Boer republics with an unpleasing combination of low cunning, high finance, and larger numbers. Fashoda was still a bitter memory in Paris; and Englishmen could not forgive the French capacity for repartee.

In this heart-felt and mutual distaste nothing was more unlikely than a dawn of Franco-British harmony. There were too many awkward questions to be settled between the Cape and Cairo, and indignant patriots of either nation glared suspiciously at one another across the Channel. Besides, there was a strong prevailing tendency towards Anglo-German friendship. Large-minded Englishmen, who confessed in private that it would really be too much to hope that the whole future of the world could remain indefinitely in British hands, were generously prepared to admit persons claiming a common origin to the high duty of conducting its affairs. This palpably included Germany and (overlooking their one unhappy lapse into disloyalty) the United States; and visionaries of the calibre of Mr. Chamberlain and Mr. Rhodes played with the notion of an Anglo-Saxon *bloc* combining all the virtues with the world's greatest armaments and a large proportion of its habitable land. An Anglo-German understanding was to provide the diplomatic base of this happy combination. But somehow the foundation-stone was never laid, in spite of strenuous attempts by well-meaning statesmen. The Kaiser had performed with fair success the part of a devoted grandson to Queen Victoria; but he was never equal to the *rôle* of a respectful nephew to King Edward. Unable to persuade himself that the frivolity of his beginnings had produced anything more formidable than an elderly *viveur,* he failed to notice that his uncle's smile was quite as kingly as his own frown. This under-estimate was fatal to their understanding; and as the Kaiser's manners never failed to jar upon the King, their lack of sympathy was mutual. Indeed, the Kaiser's efforts to repair it were still more infelicitous than usual, since he devoted at least one important interview with his royal uncle to an irritable outburst upon the practice of "treachery" by "perfidious Albion." This happy touch was hardly obliterated by eager letters on the subject of "the great Teutonic race which Heaven has entrusted with the culture of the world" and the conferment on King Edward of the rank of honorary Admiral *à la suite* of the

Germany Navy, since King Edward was unlikely to be much impressed by cultural considerations which totally omitted Paris from the Continent of Europe and, though young, the German Navy had other possibilities for England than honorary rank. The sad truth was that the Kaiser's Anglomania, which was quite genuine, had taken the unhappy form of a determination to amplify the German Empire on the British model. He had inherited a continental state with an unequalled army. But if he was to follow British precedent, he must have colonies and coaling stations, foreign trade, and a considerable fleet. These were his objectives now; and Germany had changed direction at an angle which might bring it into collision with Great Britain. For respectful imitation soon degenerated into competition; and the directors of British policy, who had once viewed Germany as a potential ally, began to see a rival.

The consequences were immediate, since if Great Britain had a rival, it would be just as well to have some friends. The Anglo-Japanese alliance might serve to stabilise affairs in the Far East. But there was something to be done a little nearer home; and British ministers, who had found their courtship of Germany extremely trying and unfruitful, assuaged their feelings in conversations with the French. As France was tolerably satisfied with the extent of her possessions, these were less arduous; and it was presently discovered that outstanding questions could be adjusted without undue sacrifice. M. Delcassé was eminently reasonable, and Lord Lansdowne moved through diplomacy with the grace becoming a great-grandson of Talleyrand. But their tentative approaches were powerfully aided by the King. He had always had a taste for foreign travel, and he combined it with an unusual grasp of foreign policy and a rare power to please. His first programme in 1903 was a Mediterranean cruise, which included an innocuous visit to Lisbon and the graver spiritual perils of a call upon the Pope. But though the King had faced the Bay of Biscay on his outward voyage in the month of April, he preferred to return overland in May, going by way of Paris. There was some apprehension as to how he would be received. As they drove down the Champs Elysées, a silent crowd stared at the carriages with a few disrespectful shouts of *"Vive Marchand,"* *"Vivent les Boers,"* and *"Vive Fashoda,"* recalling old unhappy things. But the smiling figure in its scarlet uniform saluted punctually; and when someone said, "The French don't like us," he replied, "Why should they?" Indeed, they had not yet much occasion to. But after an official speech in which he touched with positively unofficial friendliness upon his pleasure in finding himself once again in Paris as well as on the dual *rôle* of France and England "as the champions and pioneers of peaceful progress and civilisation and as the homes of all that is best and noblest in literature, art, and science" (an assertion in grave conflict with the Teutonic monopoly of culture), the atmosphere grew warmer; and it grew warmer still, when he was seen genially recognising friends in the *foyer* at the Français. There was a pleasant round of banquets, races, and reviews; and it began to dawn upon the French that King Edward was a good Parisian. His official utterances continued to be emphatic on the theme of Anglo-French collaboration; and when he drove away, they cheered him wildly in the streets.

That urbane personage had sounded the *trois coups* with an accomplished hand, and the curtain rose upon a Franco-British transformation-scene. For the two countries had discovered that they did not dislike each other quite so much as they supposed—or possibly that there was a third party whom both of them disliked far more. Diplomacy filled in the details; and the world was presently apprised in the

Anglo-French Conventions of 1904 that they had settled all outstanding controversies. In broad outline, it was understood that France abandoned her resentment of Great Britain's interest in Egypt in exchange for recognition of her own privileged position in Morocco. This settlement caused no immediate alarm. The German Chancellor raised no objection; the King went to Kiel, dined on board the *Hohenzollern,* and listened to a disquisition on the Yellow Peril with his customary courtesy. But an uneasy feeling had begun to grow on German minds that British policy was no longer quite so passive as it used to be. Its attention seemed no longer to be monopolised by distant problems in remote corners of the earth. The King was now a star performer on the European stage; his influence was felt in Continental capitals; and this development was hardly welcome to the Kaiser, since no *prima donna* welcomes a star of comparable magnitude. France and Great Britain had presumed to settle their affairs without consulting Germany; and it was just the moment for an impressive demonstration that Berlin could not be ignored. It might unseat Delcassé, who was the chief weaver of the Franco-British web; it might even scare Great Britain back to the path of duty. A sudden intervention would serve to remind anyone who had forgotten that Germany still existed, though the precise consequences of the reminder might be a matter of some uncertainty. But to the German mind, congenitally incapable of estimating the effects of their proceedings upon other people, there was no doubt of its desirability. The world must be reminded that the German Empire was still there; and the world, no doubt, would receive the glad tidings in a becoming attitude. The only question was the choice of an effective entrance for the bearer of the news. As the stage was slightly overcrowded, there seemed nothing left but the trap-door; and the trap-door was at Tangier.

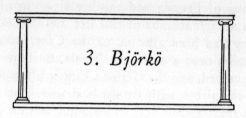

3. Björkö

THE BALTIC TIDE ran steadily behind the Finnish Skerries under a midsummer sky of blinding blue. It was a still morning. All the islands and the avenues of gleaming water and the silent trees along the shore swam in the clear northern light; and a boat came alongside the *Polar Star*. An eager figure bounded up the ladder, and the Kaiser fell into the Czar's embrace. A happy thought had sent him into northern waters; and whilst he was off the Swedish coast, an invitation from the Czar brought the *Hohenzollern* to Björkö. These were happier surroundings than Tangier, where he had been expected to ride a strange horse up a narrow street between Spanish anarchists in order to impress a crowd of Moors. His duty now was more congenial, since he had only to impress the Czar; and that, if he knew anything of Nicholas, was easier. He was at his best with Nicholas, especially when he could patronise the Russian Empire, which seemed to hang uncomfortably between revolution and defeat. Besides, the royal missionary breathed once more the air of history that he enjoyed so much, because his mission

[229]

bore a distinct resemblance to the noble interview between another King of Prussia and another Czar, in which there had been a notable display of chivalry. On that occasion all the chivalry had been allotted to the Czar, who stood in noble attitudes over a defeated Prussia. But now the situation was reversed, and the German Emperor proposed to be extremely chivalrous with Russia in defeat. That would be most enjoyable; and he left Swinemünde with a gay determination to recall Russia to the side of Germany by a vigorous display of his compelling personality. Indeed, he went so far as to copy out the draft of a Russo-German treaty in his own handwriting in case there was a chance of using it; and when he went on board the *Polar Star,* he had it in his pocket.

Their conversation was a little slow at lunch, although the Czar was in the best of spirits. But the Kaiser seemed a trifle moody, though Nicholas had told him on the day before that King Edward was a mischief-maker and that he would never lend himself to an anti-German combination. This looked promising; and when the Kaiser hinted after lunch that his incorrigible uncle might have made some deal with France without a word to their allies in Russia, the Czar looked dejected and asked what he should do in this unpleasant situation. The Kaiser saw his chance, proposing eagerly that they should follow suit. For if the French chose to come to terms with England, there was no reason why the Czar should not do the same with Germany. By a happy chance, he said, he had a treaty in his pocket which met the case exactly. The two men were talking in the yacht's saloon. But the Czar took him by the hand and drew him hurriedly into his stateroom. Then he shut all the doors and asked to see the treaty. The Kaiser laid it on the table, and his host studied the document with care. It was a defensive alliance between Ger-

many and Russia, which provided that each ally would aid
the other, if attacked, with all his European forces. While
the Czar re-read the treaty, the German Emperor was praying hard that God would guide him to a right decision; and
he was gratified to notice, as his eye strayed to the port-hole,
that he could read the letters on the ensign of the *Hohenzollern,* anchored a few cable-lengths away, with its encouraging inscription *'Gott mit Uns,'* which seemed to
indicate that His responsibility for German policy was duly
realised. Then the Czar signed the treaty, and the Kaiser
signed after him. The two men embraced; and when the
strain was over, the Kaiser's eyes were full of tears and he
was quite damp with perspiration. But his thoughts were
still on higher things, since he reflected happily that their
proceedings in the little cabin had been watched from above
by a spectral audience consisting of no less than two Kings
and one Queen of Prussia, as well as the last Czar but two.
The presence of these ghostly witnesses (including his inevitable grandfather) was most gratifying to the Kaiser;
his sense of history was richly satisfied; and as the sunshine
filled the cabin and the tide went whispering among the reeds
along the Finnish shore, he was convinced that "the morning of July 24, 1905, at Björkö is a turning-point in the
history of Europe, and a great relief for my beloved Fatherland, which will at last be emancipated from the Russo-
Gallic strangle-grip."

The sequel was not nearly so dramatic. For when the
heroes of that eventful day returned to their respective
countries, they found their ministers inclined to be distinctly
sceptical as to the precise value of the sheaves they had
brought home with them. The German Chancellor observed without enthusiasm that as the military intervention
of their new ally was to be confined to Europe, it was not
the slightest use. The German army could, he hoped,

account for France without Russian aid; and the one operation in which Russian forces could be of the least assistance
was an attack on India, which had been carefully excluded
from the treaty. In these distressing circumstances von
Bülow threatened to resign. But such ingratitude reduced
his master to an almost whimpering avowal of his de-
pendence on the Chancellor. The iron mood had passed;
and the Kaiser, always a little apt to overdo it, was rarely
happy in an emotional appeal. Alluding tearfully to his
reluctant feats with his crippled arm on a strange horse at
Tangier in deference to Bülow's wishes, he begged him to
remain in office, adding in a fevered postscript that he
should not survive a resignation and that the Chancellor
must think of the imperial widow and orphans. Von Bülow
melted, and his master breathed again. But that was almost
the last that diplomatic circles in Berlin heard about the
Treaty of Björkö.

Its obsequies were no less summary in Russia, since the
Czar's ministers felt no enthusiasm for a change of partners
at a particularly awkward moment. The country was disturbed; the war in the Far East had dragged through its
humiliating course to an uncomfortable standstill; and
peace negotiations were proceeding under the presiding
smile of President Roosevelt, who had surprised the world
by his emergence as an international *deus ex machina*. Unwearied by his onslaughts on the dark powers of American
finance and industry and the more yielding obstacles that
stood between his country and the Panama Canal, he filled
his leisure by the prompt and capable transaction of other
people's business. His mediation had brought the Russo-
Japanese belligerents to a round table; and his hand was
heavy on the uncomfortable exchanges which preceded a
settlement of the Morocco question by the same method.
Delcassé had been discarded in deference to German threats

and a conference at Algeciras would, it was hoped, adjust matters peaceably. The Russians were disinclined to sacrifice their French allies in order to grasp Germany's outstretched, if slightly condescending, hand. When Count Witte saw the treaty, he asked bleakly if the Czar knew that Russia had a treaty with the French; and Berlin was presently informed that the historic act of Björkö was of no effect. Indeed, if it had any consequence, its sole result was to unite more closely those governments whose concert had been threatened by the Kaiser's crude manœuvre. King Edward was confirmed in his opinion that his nephew was "the most brilliant failure in history" and an exceedingly uncomfortable neighbour, while the Czar was soon having less exciting conversations on the possibility of eliminating outstanding difficulties with Great Britain. For the German method, which had failed once more to make a friend for Germany, was singularly successful in persuading other nations to forget their differences.

4. Westminster

M<small>R.</small> BALFOUR had not been a great success. There could be no two opinions as to his ability which, with a comfortable touch of nepotism, had brought him into the apostolic line of Conservative succession twenty years before. Lord Salisbury had needed someone to lead the House of Commons without being quite so old as Sir Stafford Northcote and Mr. W. H. Smith or quite so incalculable as Lord Randolph Churchill; and his nephew Arthur seemed to meet the situation. He was extremely intelligent, debated admirably, and adorned a little circle whose main conviction was their certainty of one another's brilliance. Besides, his conduct at the Irish Office, where a Chief Secretary's duty consisted largely of doing unpleasant things to Irishmen and then justifying them still more unpleasantly to Irish members, betrayed a steely quality that Conservatives found reassuring. A languid manner sat gracefully on a reactionary policy; and there was no doubt of his intelligence or, in the larger country-houses from which England was still governed at week-ends, of his charm. It captivated the

[234]

adolescent fancy of Mr. H. G. Wells, who dwelt lovingly upon "his tall, bent body, his little-featured almost elvish face, his unequal mild brown eyes, his gentle manner, his sweet, amazing oratory" and loved to watch him "swaying forward with a grip upon his coat lapel," to "listen to his urbane voice," to wonder if he really cared—"Did anything matter to him? And if it really mattered nothing, why did he trouble to serve the narrowness and passion of his side?"

This elegant enigma, whose *insouciance* was admirably suited to the calm years of Conservative supremacy, still governed England. His intelligence was still conspicuous; but by 1905 the charm had somehow ceased to work. The world, to all appearances, was still the same. The Liberals were out of office; Ireland was still left in full possession of its grievances; enquiries still explored the army's imperfections at enormous length; and Lord Rosebery was just about to make a speech that would make all the difference. But there was an uneasy feeling that time was not on Mr. Balfour's side. For time was getting on, and a harsh sense of new realities invaded politics. This was unfortunate for Mr. Balfour, whose *forte* was dialectics; and now there were so many problems that dialectics could not solve. His party was no more at home than he was in the new urgencies of social questions, since the Conservatives were singularly ill-equipped with any social creed apart from an imperfect recollection of something that Lord Beaconsfield had said exemplifying something he had thought in his Young England days. But Lord Beaconsfield had been in his grave a quarter of a century, and his successors were almost unprovided with ideas about the world in which they lived. Their unparalleled good fortune had condemned their Liberal antagonists to the divisions and unpopularity which were the consequence of Mr. Gladstone's single-minded ardour in the Irish cause; and an unhappy failure to take the patriotic side in the Boer War prolonged the Opposition's weakness. Besides, the schism on Home Rule deprived the Liberals of Mr. Chamberlain's incomparable drive towards reform. This was diverted by his political apostasy towards imperial adventures apart from his recurring reference to Old Age Pensions, which faded into a steadily receding distance. The issues upon which Liberals had failed to win with Mr. Gladstone were a foregone conclusion when they fought without him; and so long as Unionists were confronted with nothing more than the inadequate executors of his political inheritance, their victory was certain. It had been confirmed once more in the patriotic ardours of a war-time election, and Mr. Balfour was the comfortable heir of that majority.

But their good fortune could not last for ever; and the public mind of 1905 was ill-represented by the House of Commons which it had elected in 1900. It had ceased to be impressed by military glories, and it had seen too much of the seamy side of empire-building. Far-flung battle-lines were at a discount; and it was apt to trace ignoble motives, where once it had been quite content to cheer and to apply for still more Chartered shares. For it viewed the Rand with slight misgivings and was prepared to use harsh language when indentured labourers were introduced from China under conditions bearing an unpleasant resemblance to slavery. Its interests, indeed, were concentrating once again upon the country that it lived in; and the term 'Little Englander' began to lose its sting.

The new seriousness of this growing mood was unfriendly to Mr. Balfour's bland direction of affairs. It began to be felt that airiness, perhaps, was not enough; and in the public mind his graceful image was replaced by a less estimable figure which, though a Cecil, seemed to lack the more solid qualities associated with that respected name. The times, it must be confessed, were scarcely favourable to a straightforward rendering of the old negations that composed traditional Conservatism; and even if they had been, Mr. Balfour was not the man to give one. It had once been quite enough for Tories to deny with emphasis that the Corn Laws should be repealed, that the franchise needed enlargement, that Ireland needed anything for which it asked, and that Mr. Gladstone could by any chance be right in anything he said. These simple negatives had formed a practicable creed for many years. But the 'Everlasting Nay' was ceasing to be applicable in 1905, since it involved unpopular asseverations that there was nothing to be done about anything in particular and that the condition of the people left nothing much to be desired. Besides, the mind of Mr. Balfour was incurably philosophical, and he displayed an irritating incapacity to distinguish his own policy from that to which he was supposed to be unalterably opposed. There was so much that could be said for and against either course (and he was so brilliantly equipped for saying both) that his intelligence was often baffled by the vulgar problem of what he should do. A popular demand for action was the last thing that he could meet; and as he faced the harsh realities of politics with an increasing subtlety, impatience grew upon the public mind. His mental processes were exquisite; but all that his less enlightened countrymen could see was a Prime Minister who was unwilling or unable to make up his mind and yet insisted on retaining office.

Even the Liberals began to overlook their differences in the bright prospect of a victory, since there is nothing like a share-out for inducing prospective colleagues to become less critical of one another. The endless leisure of their long sojourn in the wilderness had been amused by disputations of the most complicated order. They had challenged one another's orthodoxy with enormous gusto and frequent excommunications. The relative importance of Home Rule was a rich theme of controversy; the Boer War deepened their dissensions; and an intellectual *élite* withdrew itself behind Lord Rosebery's elusive oriflamme of Liberal Imperialism, while the more orthodox preferred the narrow path of Sir Henry Campbell-Bannerman's amiable leadership. But an external cause impelled their reconciliation. Mr. Chamberlain, who had once destroyed the Liberal Party, inadvertently reunited it by discovering a policy which was even more distasteful to the Liberals than one another's heresies; and his sudden advocacy of Protection made Free Traders of them all.

This strange departure was the consequence of his imperial reflections, since his active mind favoured a British *Zollverein*, a tariff union of the Empire; and as its first requirement was a tariff, he emerged as a Protectionist. The Government of which he was the leading member was uncommitted to his policy; and Mr. Balfour was confronted by the unpleasant necessity of making up his mind. This unaccustomed exercise afforded him an opportunity for the least satisfactory of all his public exhibitions. While the philosophic mind was baffled by the crude antithesis of Free Trade and Protection, he retired into a cobweb of dialectics from the heart of which he professed his inability to see the difference between them; and a graceful ambiguity relieved him of those colleagues who were afflicted with more decided views by methods which increased a general suspicion of undue cleverness. The Free Traders left him, as they were assailed by doubts of his devotion to Free Trade; and Mr. Chamberlain resigned, because he was not yet a convert to Protection. Irreverent spectators guessed that the Prime Minister would shortly dance a few reluctant steps to Mr. Chamberlain's insistent piping and enjoyed the disrespectful image of

> *Old Joe a-kicking up behind and before,*
> *And a yellow gal a-kicking up behind*
> *Old Joe.*

Such speculations were profoundly damaging to the Prime Minister's prestige. His attitude was unheroic, and his hesitations might be attributed to a want of settled convictions. Democracies prefer distinct alternatives, and Mr. Balfour's utterances on the fiscal question were lamentably indistinct. Not that the greater clarity of Mr. Chamberlain's Protectionist appeal fared better in the public mind. The economic triumphs of Free Trade were still too recent for his audience to be disturbed by jeremiads on the state of British industry. The country was extremely prosperous and disinclined to sacrifice cheap raw material and a low cost of living for a vague imperial dawn. Besides, it had its doubts about the Empire; and the controversy degenerated into a statistical debate, in which Mr. Chamberlain was soon reduced to a lame avowal that his figures were no more than illustrations of his argument. The proof, he said, was in the argument and not in the figures, which were only used as illustrations to show what the argument might be. A hard-headed business community was unimpressed, and working men were mainly interested in the unpleasant prospect of a diminution in the size of their domestic loaf. Delighted Liberals, abandoning the arid pastures of their old disputes, hurled themselves gleefully into a Promised Land of controversy, in which success was a foregone conclusion. For this was infinitely more rewarding than expatiating on the woes of Ireland or licensing reform; and a strange irony devoted Mr. Chamberlain's declining years to a crusade that was no less foredoomed to failure than Mr. Gladstone's never-ending campaign for Home Rule.

The end came swiftly. When the Prime Minister resigned, the King sent for Campbell-Bannerman (who quite forgot the ritual of kissing hands at his first audience); and before the year was out, the Opposition braves, forgetting their doctrinal differences in the new dignity of office, were all installed as ministers. The stage was cleared for a General Election in which hopeful Liberals promised themselves a triumphal progress round the constituencies in the first weeks of 1906 and smiled indulgently at the harmless aspirations of an infant Labour Party. Just before New Year a demonstration in the Albert Hall heard the first interjections of those eager ladies, who had resolved to earn the suffrage by a policy of interruption, and listened while the new Prime Minister informed his adversaries that "they have lived for some years on nothing but tactics, and now they have died of tactics." It was a cruel epitaph on Mr. Balfour.

NINETEEN
HUNDRED AND TEN

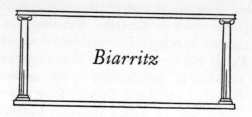

Biarritz

THE KING was not so well that year. His cough was troublesome; and when he got away from England in the second week of March, he was more pulled down than usual. Not that the world knew anything to indicate that King Edward might be out of sorts. He had been all smiles at a big dinner-party on the night before he left; and Paris saw the faithful playgoer in his seat once more at the Porte St. Martin, where they were playing Rostand's interminable apologue about *Chantecler*. But a draughty theatre and a long railway journey were a bad beginning for his holiday; and a cold caught in Paris had become severe bronchitis before he got to Biarritz. Outside his windows the waves thundered on the coast; Spain was a dim line of mountains twenty miles away; and nearer home the shoppers strolled in the Rue Mazagran, or went down to watch the endless duel of the brown rocks beyond the harbour with the big Biscayan rollers that came creaming in from mid-Atlantic. The King was always fond of Biarritz in spite of the rude things he wrote to M. Clemenceau about the drains. He liked the views; he liked the big hotel; and, as he wrote with royal approbation, "the continual roll of the Atlantic is not unpleasant." But that was about all he was permitted to enjoy this time, since the doctors at the Hôtel du Palais were more anxious than they cared to say, and there could be no question yet of his customary drives across the Bidassoa into Spain. For the King was really very ill indeed. This time he pulled through; but his recovery had been precarious, and the sharp bout of illness left him thoroughly depressed about affairs.

There was enough to worry him that spring, since English politics were growing more bad-tempered every year and more complicated every month. Indeed, their latest complications positively threatened the time-honoured outline of the constitution, and in certain eventualities action by the Crown itself was called for. Four years of office had done little to appease the more disturbing elements among the Liberals, since the great victory of 1906 some- how failed to usher in the dawn of progress. It had been a pleasant change for Liberals to crowd into the House of Commons and to pass their good intentions into law with- out regard to the thin protest of the Tory remnant on the empty benches opposite. Ten years of ineffective Opposi- tion seemed to be avenged by this enjoyable experience; and as the Bills went through the House of Commons, eager Radicals approached a Promised Land of licensing reform and education and even, at long last, of something in the nature of self-government for Ireland. But that was not the end, since the wisdom of their forefathers had pro- vided no less than two Houses of Parliament, of which the second was perpetually immune from those progressive in- fluences by which the first was intermittently beguiled; and nothing was more galling, when they reached the next stage in the legislative process, than to watch the mutilation of

their blameless offspring in the House of Lords at the unsympathetic hands of an immutable Conservative majority
entrenched behind the obsolescent battlements of the hereditary system. As the House of Lords obeyed its instincts,
an awkward feeling grew upon the Liberals that the dice
were loaded against them. What was the use of beating the
Conservatives so soundly, if an undefeated remnant in the
Upper House was permanently in a position to deprive the
victors of the legislative fruits of victory? This result was
hardly shocking to those virile intelligences which conceived
it to be the purpose of Providence that England should be
governed for so long as possible on Conservative principles
and, when this was no longer practicable, that it should not
be governed at all. But the effect on Liberals was more disturbing, since they believed with equal fervour that the will
of God was manifested in their programme and that, if the
House of Lords obstructed it, their action was a scandalous
misuse of privilege. The Upper House, it was remembered,
had thwarted Mr. Gladstone in his last crusade; and now,
to all appearances, it could deprive the sweeping verdict of
1906 of any practical significance.

The deadlock was complete, and tempers mounted angrily
on both sides. Of the two the Liberals were angrier, because
their situation was more irritating. It was intolerable to be
denied a victory, which they had actually won, by a referee
who did not even pretend to be impartial; and as each successive item of their programme foundered in the House of
Lords, their indignation was expressed in sombre hints that
they were 'filling up the cup.' But as the game proceeded,
their tone grew more menacing; and when the House of
Lords, improving on its past performances, proposed to
tamper with the Budget of 1909, the cup overflowed. That
measure, which included an Income Tax at the unassuming
rate of 1s. 2d. in the pound, death duties of 10 per cent., a

daring supertax on incomes above £5,000 a year, and a
small duty on the increment value of land, became a battle-
cry; and as Mr. Lloyd George was Chancellor of the Exchequer, the cry lost nothing in its utterance. The bland
presence of Sir Henry Campbell-Bannerman had been removed, and his successor as Prime Minister was Mr.
Asquith. This level-headed advocate had achieved his eminence by a fine intellectual equipment, improved by Dr.
Jowett's Balliol and demonstrated in his lucid demolition of
Mr. Chamberlain's economic eccentricities. Inclining slightly
to the more Whiggish element among his followers, his
leadership was ably supplemented by the more spectacular
appeal of Mr. Lloyd George. That gesticulating little figure
derived directly from the throbbing power-house of political
Nonconformity and professed a highly attractive form of
emotional Radicalism. His occupation of the Treasury was
prefaced by a gay intimation that he was "looking for
someone's hen-roost to rob next year"; and when the
House of Lords proposed to interfere, his voice became the
dominating note in the ensuing uproar. His indignation
and his raillery, his honest sympathy with lowly suffering,
the rasping note of his invective, and his inimitable comedy
assailed the nation's ear by turns; and that unwearied voice
set the whole tone of politics to its incomparable tune. A
delighted audience in the East End of London was told that
"the landlord is a gentleman who does not earn his wealth,"
while their tears were asked for Old Age pensioners on
their way "to the gates of the tomb, bleeding and footsore,
through the brambles and thorns of poverty." A change
of metaphor informed another audience that, with their
support, there was a prospect of "rare and refreshing fruit
for the parched lips of the multitude who have been tread-
ing the dusty road along which the people have marched
through the dark ages which are now merging into the

light"; and a happy use of mountain scenery, to which he was unusually addicted, inspired a peroration in which "the clouds are lifting from the valleys, from the lowly and humble homes of the people, and they are gathering round the tops. There is a fine day coming." These rousing invocations, in which Mr. Lloyd George found his voice (and slightly scandalised his sovereign), quickened the nation's pulse; and the contributions of his adversaries were scarcely more friendly to reflection, since Lord Rosebery, aroused to disapproval, informed a Scottish audience that taxation on such a scale was tantamount to Socialism and that Socialism was "the end of all, the negation of faith, of family, of property, of monarchy, of Empire;" while Lord Milner, with a touch of that hysteria which had impaired his dealings with the Boers, called on the House of Lords to kill the Budget and to "damn the consequences." The temperature rose uncomfortably. The Budget was rejected; Parliament dissolved; and the Liberals were left in office by a majority that would be safe only so long as they could prevent the Irish from voting with their natural enemies.

The year opened upon these uncertainties, with politics at an unprecedented pitch of bitterness and Tory dowagers exiling Liberals from their drawing-rooms and Liberals retorting with the most unpleasant comments on the sources from which Tory incomes were derived and an increasing tendency among Conservatives to grow restless in the silken leading-strings of Mr. Balfour's leadership with a view to substituting something a little ruder (which they eventually found in the unimpressive person of Mr. Bonar Law). In this uncomfortable situation the Government was pressed by anxious Tories to state what it proposed to do about the House of Lords. The Prime Minister replied with a faint touch of mockery that his eager questioners must "wait and see." That judicious counsel followed Mr. Asquith through the remaining years of a prolonged career as evidence of some undue reluctance on his part to take swift decisions. But to its first hearers in 1910 the phrase had an unpleasant ring of menace, since the Prime Minister was plainly going to do something, though he was unwilling to say what it was. There was an uneasy interval, in which the Cabinet balanced the constitutional expedients and leader-writers looked up old precedents about Lord Grey and the Reform Bill and 'King Billy's' stormy reign. Could the new House of Commons pass the Budget, if the Irish asked for terms which the Government would not concede? And if it did, would the House of Lords throw it out again? If so, should they advise the Crown to create sufficient peers to pass it? And if they did, would the King act upon the Cabinet's advice? Their immediate problem bristled with disagreeable alternatives; and as they faced them in the late winter days of 1910, the King went off to Biarritz.

Not that the situation on the Continent was more reassuring than affairs at home. For its leading feature was the state of Anglo-German relations, and these failed to show the slightest sign of improvement. Indeed, if anything, they had deteriorated. This unhappy tendency was the direct consequence of German policy in the excitable control of Kaiser Wilhelm and his advisers. Not that their restless diplomacy was unsuccessful in its way, since the world was forced with gratifying frequency to admit the ubiquity and weight of German influence. This was a source of consolation to German diffidence, which concealed itself with some success behind an overbearing manner. But other nations found it extremely irritating; and German exploits in the diplomatic field left an unpleasant legacy of bitterness on every side with the recurrent consequence that Germany alarmed her neighbours into hostility and was alarmed in turn by the discovery of her own unpopularity. Few nations were less bellicose than France in the first decade of the Twentieth Century. The bitterness of 1870 had almost passed away with the war generation; the Dreyfus controversy had dealt hardly with the more extreme forms of patriotism; and cherished grievances in Egypt had been sacrificed without a pang in order to secure a settlement with England and a fair measure of compensation in Morocco. But when this eminently reasonable settlement was dramatically challenged by the Kaiser and his brusque intervention imposed the tiresome formality of a European conference as well as the brutal sacrifice of M. Delcassé, the German triumph was far less real than apparent. For there was no tangible result beyond a deepening of French apprehensions and a further underlining of the Anglo-French *Entente,* since Germany's explosive quality was the most powerful inducement to all her neighbours to reach a better understanding.

Its solvent powers were even demonstrated in a determined effort at Anglo-Russian reconciliation. Nothing like that had been seen since the Congress of Vienna, since both Powers had persistently misunderstood each other's motives through a long century of Asiatic competition. But German methods had an almost magic power to remove other people's misunderstandings; and the world was presently confronted with the paradox of an Anglo-Russian Convention amiably negotiated between the Czar's ministers and a Cabinet of English Liberals. This happy consummation was completed by the besetting imbecility of Austria, which chose that moment for a sudden violation of the Treaty of Berlin by the annexation of Bosnia and Herzegovina. The impact of this proceeding upon Russia, as the protector of all Slavs, at a moment when she was in no position to resent it actively was deeply humiliating; and the humiliation was still further deepened, when Germany abetted the misdeed by something very like an ultimatum to St. Petersburg and the German Emperor made a sensational appearance "in shining armour" beside his treaty-breaking allies. The Czar had no alternative, since war in the Far East had left his forces too disorganised to accept European challenges. But once again a triumph of Teutonic policy had scored a point and made an enemy.

Yet the prime factor in the European sum was the unfortunate condition of Anglo-German relations. Alarms of war were customary on the Continent. It had grown to be quite natural for Germany to threaten France at intervals and for wiseacres to predict trouble when the snow melted in the Balkans. But it had melted thirty times without a European war; and if Great Britain helped to keep the ring, the trouble might be localised in the more inflammable *vilayets* of the Turkish Empire without a general conflagration. This equilibrium depended largely on the maintenance of British indifference to Continental issues. But if that was once disturbed, if England was alarmed into participation in the European game, the consequences might be grave. That was the problem by which the Kaiser was confronted, and he conspicuously failed to solve it. For his erratic efforts to reassure his shrinking countrymen as to their international importance by a policy of sudden jerks and diplomatic melodrama alarmed his uncle, startled British ministers, inoculated Liberals with suspicions which had been hitherto confined to Conservatives, and left the public mind of England with a vague feeling that they lived uncomfortably close to a serio-comic jack-in-the-box upon which, though the element of comedy might be prolonged for a few years, they would eventually have to shut the lid. This was a sad declension from the happy days of holidays in England in his chosen *rôle* of Queen Victoria's favourite

[250]

grandson; and it was the direct consequence of his unhappy admiration of the British Empire. For if there had been one thing about it of which his admiration was whole-hearted, it was the Royal Navy; and when he got an empire of his own, the eager hero-worshipper resolved that it must have a navy too.

That was the fundamental error into which the Emperor betrayed his country. So long as their expansion proceeded on the lines laid down by Bismarck—a land empire, an unconquerable army, and a few colonies for purposes of exhibition rather than of utility—Europe was fairly reconciled to Germany's accession to a place of Continental eminence, and England watched developments with that benevolence which she reserved for operations in which she was not a competitor, slightly accentuated by a vague sense of kinship and her age-long tendency to side against the French. But when the German appetite extended to include an overseas empire, expanding foreign trade, and a sufficient navy to defend them both, it dawned upon the British mind that Germany was making efforts to emerge from that station to which it had pleased God to call her. Hegemony upon the Continent maintained by an indisputable preponderance of land forces was one thing. But to supplement her overwhelming army with a considerable navy was quite another matter; and when Germany attempted something of the kind, British caution could not help inclining to the other side. For the whale had always tolerated elephants; but if such monsters of the land began to be amphibious, the whale grew anxious.

That anxiety was stimulated by the formidable growth of the German navy. It was quite comprehensible that German patriots, accustomed to strike terror into Continental governments, should feel an irritating helplessness when British cruisers cheerfully stopped German merchant vessels on their way to South Africa during the Boer War and searched them for contraband. Their irritation found practical expression in a programme of naval construction and a slightly premature announcement by their sovereign that "the ocean proves that on it and beyond it no great decision can be taken without the German Kaiser." The first consequence was the alignment of Great Britain with his Continental adversaries. For the Kaiser was the true architect of the *Entente Cordiale,* which owed far more to the growth of English misgivings about Germany than to any British taste for French society. In the next phase, as Germany continued to build warships at a steadily accelerated pace, the naval forces of Great Britain were frankly rearranged to face a menace in the North Sea. A new naval base appeared on the east coast of Scotland; ships were concentrated in home waters; and Sir John Fisher's ingenuity evolved the "all-big-gun ship," with the pleasing consequence that British supremacy at sea was quite unchallengeable so long as the *Dreadnought,* a 'floating guncarriage' in which Sir John Fisher had embodied the ballistic dreams of Sir Percy Scott, was the sole example of its type afloat, and followed by the less pleasing corollary that it could be gravely challenged if any other nation chose to follow suit by building ships of the new pattern, which effectively destroyed the military value of Great Britain's vast preponderance in ships of older types. An uncomfortable era dawned, in which the public mind was exercised by an exciting race in naval armaments and politicians fought by-elections about battleships and rival admirals indicated one another's imperfections with the refreshing freedom of the quarter-deck, while British ministers consulted experts on the problem of invasion, emerging with the comforting conclusion that the home forces could dispose of an invading army, provided that its strength did not exceed 70,000 men, and that if it did, its transports would be too numerous to elude the Fleet (a calculation challenged at the time by the advocates of conscription, but subsequently justified by war experience); and Mr. Haldane, whose pursuits had hitherto been purely intellectual, displayed a practical intelligence in the creation of a Territorial Force for home defence and an Expeditionary Force, rearmed with quick-firing artillery, for Continental use.

But the main focus of anxiety was maritime; and the public mind was shadowed by the tripod masts and mis-shapen silhouettes of the new battleships, whose twelve-inch guns ranged for six miles or more into the mists of the North Sea. A large proportion of its interests was represented by the eager computation of muzzle velocity and weight of broadside, dimensions, turning-circle, horse-power, and estimated speed of naval units; and in these calculations, official and unofficial, there was not the least effort at concealment of the fact that, for purposes of hostile comparison, the German High Seas Fleet was the chosen adversary of the Royal Navy. The Kiel Canal, the defences of Heligoland, and the capacity of the Brunsbüttel Locks became objects of interest to British minds, while readers were delighted by the best spy-story of all time about the mysteries of Borkum and playgoers were disagreeably thrilled by the spectacle of an English householder, who had uttered sentiments in contradiction to those preferred by Lord Roberts and the National Service League, getting himself shot on his own dining-table by foreign invaders who bore an unmistakable resemblance to their German neighbours.

This growing mood, in which the public mind appeared to take an Anglo-German war for granted, presented Europe with a situation which the refinements of diplomacy were almost powerless to cure. The Kaiser made occasional attempts to reassure Great Britain; but as their admirable purpose was obscured by his customary infelicity, they frequently produced effects precisely contrary to those which he intended. A private letter, in which he sought to disabuse the mind of the First Lord of the Admiralty as to the alleged existence of a German menace by commenting with some freedom on English public men, was singularly unsuccessful, it eliciting no more than the prompt resignation of its recipient and a bleak intimation from his uncle Edward that direct correspondence between his ministers and foreign sovereigns "is a 'new departure.'" The publication of an interview announcing his persistent friendship with Great Britain, indicated by its exordium in which his English readers were pleasantly informed that they were "mad, mad as March hares" and particularly evidenced by the belated revelation of his considerate suggestions as to the best way to win the Boer War, was hardly more successful; and a subsequent outpouring in the same happy vein was hastily suppressed. An exchange of royal visits between London and Berlin preserved the decencies of international courtesy. But there was an air of unmistakable constraint about the whole proceeding, and the utterance of peaceful sentiments seemed more than usually forced. The world, perhaps excusably, was less interested in these blameless exercises than in the possible production of a 13.5-inch naval gun and the performances of the new Zeppelin and the appearance of machine-gun sections at the last German army manœuvres.

The sky was indubitably overcast; and King Edward needed all the vigour that he could derive from the bright air of Biarritz. But when he managed to get out again, his official correspondence was anything but cheerful. Mr. Asquith was at grips with his uncomfortable situation; and though the Budget passed the House of Lords at last, the future was obscure. The King was back in London now, and his customary round resumed. He was at the Opera within two hours of his return to town; and two days more sufficed him for a long string of audiences and the Royal Academy. Then he was off to the fresh air of Sandringham, where he insisted upon going for a damp and chilly walk. The consequences, when he got back to London, were extremely grave. He still received his callers; but the effort was unduly evident. "I shall not give in," he said to somebody; "I shall work to the end. Of what use is it to be alive if one cannot work?" And when his illness bore him down, he announced stubbornly that he proposed to fight it and that he should be about again in a day. But he smoked his last cigar on the next morning, heard the news that he had won another race at Kempton Park that afternoon, repeated firmly that he should not give in, and died that night, indomitably fond of life as he had lived.

The Prime Minister, who had snatched a short holiday at sea in the Admiralty yacht, was reached by a wireless message from the new King in the small hours of a May morning. As King George's reign was opening, Mr. Asquith went on deck. He was a little dazed; it was still night; and the first thing that he saw was "Halley's comet blazing in the sky. It was the only time, I believe, that any of us saw it during the voyage." But as the *Enchantress* laboured homeward through the Bay of Biscay on the morning of May 7, 1910, it hung there in the sky above them; and the new reign began.

NINETEEN
SEVENTEEN

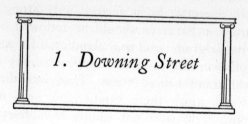

1. Downing Street

So this was england after two years and a half of war. The country was distinctly changed. It was no less England —possibly, indeed, a little more. But the place was noticeably different; and perhaps it was not quite the war that they had all foreseen so clearly.

True, there had been nothing very unexpected in the manner of its coming—a murder in the Balkans followed by an ultimatum, a brief interval of feverish diplomacy, and the dull reverberation across Europe of those orders to mobilise, after which there could be no turning back. It was the light-hearted Austrians that started it. Their intellect was never very strong; and the air of their delicious capital, which throbbed perpetually with the lilt and crash of their incomparable dance-music, was unfriendly to the more exacting forms of statesmanship. The Viennese, like their old Emperor, lived in their dreams, which had a slightly Oriental quality since Bismarck had dethroned Vienna from its European eminence and turned its outlook to the east. Their interests were mainly Balkan; and as the *Drang nach Osten* grew upon them, their policy enjoyed the mild excitements of a Balkan operetta. So it seemed only fitting that the double murder in Sarajevo should be followed by a stern vengeance on Belgrade; and they clamoured for an inexpensive triumph over Servia in the happy certainty that Germany would stand behind them. That was the decisive factor, without which there would have been no World War. But the Serbs were not wholly friendless, since the Russian mood was more spirited than it had been of late, as her embarrassments in the Far East receded and the revolutionary waves at home seemed to subside; and Russia was reluctant to permit the public degradation of a Slav state. Besides, another Austro-German triumph in the Balkans would be quite unbearable; and Count Berchtold could not be permitted to repeat Count Aehrenthal's success of 1909. This seemed to promise a three-cornered contest between Austria, Germany, and Russia; and for twelve days of agitated correspondence Sir Edward Grey fluttered, a well-meaning dove of peace, above the disputants. But it was manifest at an early stage that their alliance with the Russians would involve the French; and the dove was loudly importuned to alight upon the side indicated by the whole drift of British policy. There could not be the slightest doubt that Germany encouraged Austria in its defiance of the Russians and that, if it led to war, Germany would fight. This would bring in the French; and in that event Great Britain would have to make up its mind.

That process, oddly enough, was not so easy as it looked, since there was nothing in the nature of a binding military alliance to wheel the British into line. Ten years of Franco-British policy had led to nothing more explicit than a habit of co-operation; staff conversations on the shipment of the Expeditionary Force to France implied a promise that was never made; and the transfer of French naval forces to the

Mediterranean, which enabled England to concentrate on the North Sea and English Channel and left the northern coast of France without marine defences of its own, created nothing stronger than a mere debt of honour. It was all tragically embarrassing, and British ministers were reluctant to commit themselves to war with Germany until there was undisputable proof that Germany was the aggressor.

Meanwhile they multiplied their efforts to settle the original dispute before its radius extended to the whole Continent. Diplomacy had localised two Balkan wars in recent years; and there were grounds for hoping that, if discussion could only be prolonged, the latest controversy might be successfully adjusted. But there was no procedure to compel delay or to impose discussion of the issues under any form of law. The only law that reigned in Europe was that of self-preservation; and the mild efforts of diplomacy were gravely prejudiced by an uncomfortable sense that precious days were being lost. Diplomats were quickly elbowed out by General Staffs; armies began to mobilise; it became evident that there was to be a European war; and England faced its own dilemma. The Austrians were shelling Belgrade; but that was not a British *casus belli*. The Russians would be in East Prussia soon; but that could not be helped. If France were only left alone by Germany, they would avoid the fearful dislocation of war in Western Europe and Great Britain might escape its moral obligation to exclude the German Navy from the English Channel.

But Germany seemed disinclined to let anyone alone. A mood of desperation prevailed in Berlin. How could they draw back? The Emperor was trapped by his own heroics. This was the culmination of all his warlike speeches and theatrical diplomacy. For twenty years he had regaled the world with pounding charges of massed cavalry at the *Kaisermanöver* and sudden gestures in which shock tactics

[261]

were translated into terms of policy; and the *rôle* was too absorbing to be discarded suddenly. Besides, if they abandoned Austria, they had not a real ally in the world. So there was nothing for it: there would have to be a war, and the last hope in Berlin was that they might somehow persuade the British to stay neutral. True, the elusive Britons had steadfastly abstained in recent correspondence from commitments which would bind them to neutrality in a Franco-German war—as steadfastly as the Germans had abstained from slowing up the pace of their naval construction. But perhaps the British would not need much persuasion, if their attention was monopolised by the absorbing trivialities of civil war in Ireland.

The prospects, though, were hardly promising; and the German effort to detach Great Britain from the side of France was complicated by the emergence of a new interest in the incalculable British mind. If Germany fought France, Great Britain asked a trifle sharply whether Belgian territory would be respected. This was a little awkward, as France and Germany were both equally committed to a guarantee of the neutrality of Belgium; and its violation would put Germany completely in the wrong. That would be unfortunate, unless the disadvantages of this irregularity were amply compensated by the military gains which it made possible; and on the strictly military side it rather looked as though this would be so. For the Franco-German frontier was adequately fortified on the French side from Verdun to Belfort; but on the north, where Belgium intervened, France lay practically open to invasion. The German plan, noting this happy circumstance, proposed to march an army across Belgium into northern France without the least regard to Belgian rights and in a cheerful hope that nobody would mind. Unhappily Great Britain minded. This was a *casus belli* within the grasp of British comprehension. It was a simple issue, by which the elusive question of European right or wrong could be precisely tested; and the test was sharply embodied in a British ultimatum to Berlin, to which the German answer would determine England's attitude in the whole international dispute. Such niceties appeared unworthy in Berlin, where treaties whirled like feathers in the wind before a national necessity. It had become necessary to beat the French; the General Staff proposed to beat them by a march through Belgium; and when doubts were cast upon their right to conduct military operations anywhere they chose, a bewildered German Chancellor was left deploring the legalism of the British, who proposed to make war "just for a word—'neutrality'—just for a scrap of paper." That was the signal; and at midnight on August 4, 1914, the war began.

But was it quite the war that they had all foreseen? So far as concerned the German General Staff, whose forecast was perhaps the most coherent, events fulfilled their expectations for about six weeks. Belgium was duly invaded in accordance with their time-table; the fixed defences of Liège succumbed to their heavy guns; and their thrust went deep into northern France. But after that the unforeseen checked their advance, and the war was stabilised along a trench-line from the North Sea to the Swiss frontier. The French encountered unpremeditated elements still earlier in their career, since the sequence of events contemplated by 'Plan XVII' bore even less relation to reality than that envisaged by the plan bequeathed by the gifted (but happily deceased) Count von Schlieffen to the German army. For the Germans at least knew where they were going and went there; but the French, after an exciting fortnight of heavy fighting, failed to reach their first objectives and were condemned to a general retreat on the whole northern front. This circumstance involved their British allies in the unexpected almost from

[263]

the start. For if the Expeditionary Force fulfilled its authors' expectations by its prompt assembly, safe and secret shipment across the English Channel, and delivery at French railhead, its subsequent adventures bore the same relation to the sober programme outlined for it by judicious persons in the Committee of Imperial Defence as that borne by the more improbable of the *Arabian Nights* to the least exciting pages of the railway time-table. It had been expected to form the left of the Allied line (and it fulfilled the expectation nobly) ; but no one had expected that the line would be continuously moving backwards. The heroic episodes of the retreat from Mons were the first war-news with which Great Britain was regaled; and it found them slightly unassimilable. For this was not in the least like anything that anybody had expected; and even when the safety of Paris seemed to be comparatively assured by a victory on the Marne, there was a sad discrepancy between the military situation and the hopes with which the war had started.

This discrepancy was no less evident in other spheres. It was sfficiently exciting when the British Navy vanished in a mysterious air of sealed orders and unknown destinations to re-emerge, half-seen behind the northern mists, in inaccessible anchorages among the Orkneys. But there was a sad lack of maritime heroics to compensate spectators for the romantic exit of the Grand Fleet; and they were a little apt to take for granted the elimination of German sea-power, which had been promptly and silently achieved by British pressure. The menace of the High Seas Fleet, whose shadow had diverted the whole course of British policy, wavered and vanished like a dream. Its proud embodiment remained safe in harbour behind the German mine-fields, while detached units threw a few shells into English seaside resorts or maintained a hunted existence upon the outer seas. But there was no opportunity for spectacular performances by the British battle-fleets. Their victory (for they were completely victorious) was a triumph of potential force rather than of force demonstrated by the crash of British salvoes and the spectacle of sinking German ships; and the public mind learned to be satisfied with the lesser heroism of

> *Mines located in the fairway,*
> *Boats now working up the chain,*
> *Sweepers—Unity, Claribel, Assyrian, Stormcock, and Golden Gain.*

That, however, was quite unlike anything that anybody had anticipated—as dissimilar as "the same observation post, table, map, observer, and telephonist; the same always-hidden always-ready guns; and the same vexed foreshore of trenches, smoking and shaking, from Switzerland to the sea." This static warfare of unwearying blockade at sea and continuous bombardment along uninterrupted and stationary fronts on land was a complete surprise. It surprised the experts no less than the lay public, which had looked forward hopefully to an exciting spell of fleet-actions and open warfare. These excitements were reserved for secondary spheres; but in its main theatre the war continued to present a set of wholly unexpected features. For the paradox of trench-warfare confronted nations with an expenditure of ammunition wildly in excess of the most extravagant anticipations of their military experts and created problems of supply which transformed the whole face of industry. Industrial expansion became the road to victory. A war of engineers replaced the more romantic business which the public mind of Europe had expected; and there were other aspects in which it deviated gravely from the common expectation. For the Germans, always a little apt to confuse their national success with the unchallengeable will of God, abandoned those restraints with which the conscience of mankind had

[265]

sought to mitigate the horror of war and recklessly involved civilian lives in the operations of their aircraft and submarines, while their more enterprising scientists added poison gas to the unpleasing repertory of the world's arms. These influences and the dragging course of the whole contest deepened its bitterness; and as the angry, dreary years went by, the world settled down to something quite unlike the European war that European statesmen had foreseen so long.

Indeed, the statesmen found it no less difficult to recognise their new surroundings. The Germans' task was on the whole the simplest, since in their case the conduct of the war was relegated to professionals, and civilian ministers were left with duties which consisted largely of unwavering assertions that they were not doing things which they appeared to be or that, if appearances were too strong for them, the Allies had done it first. But Allied statesmanship was faced by more complicated tasks. After the opening diapason of eloquent invocations, by which public life was ennobled in the first weeks of war, it found itself wandering in a wholly unfamiliar world where few, if any, problems yielded to familiar treatment. Vast forces of popular opinion had to be directed, immense resources of collective energy conserved or canalised into fresh channels where they could serve the common purpose. It was no longer possible to solve a problem by the simple Parliamentary expedient of skilfully assembling a majority that would vote in favour of its solution. There was a peremptory call for action; and the administrative habits of a lifetime became inadequate under the new pressure. It grew evident at a fairly early stage that civilian ministers in France and England must retain ultimate control of military operations, since democratic constitutions loaded them with ultimate responsibility and there was nothing in the nature of a military caste qualified (as in Germany) by heredity and training to assume control once war had been declared. This faced them with a multiplicity of unfamiliar problems, half strategy and half economics; and even in the area confined by custom to civilian management the situation bristled with unpleasing novelties. In a simpler world the duties of diplomacy might have been expected to reach a minimum once war had been begun. But now Allied (and especially British) diplomacy was confronted by those rich and ramifying problems of neutrality which exhaust the patience of belligerents and provide congenial employment for the surplus energies of neutrals. Brusque solutions were inadmissible, because the leading neutral was the United States and it was essential to retain American sympathies for reasons of supply. This circumstance involved excursions into unrewarding dialectics and occasional restrictions on the free use of sea-power which left impulsive British patriots dissatisfied and exasperated sensitive Americans. In that debate the most hopeful factor from the Allied point of view lay in the simple circumstance that, while their alleged irregularities were largely technical and seemed to bear unfairly upon American property, German lapses from the strict rules of war were homicidal and involved American lives. But the whole problem was a grave and largely unforeseen addition to the responsibilities of British statesmen.

Not that their domestic situation was free from difficulty. A lightly poised majority had sufficed for Mr. Asquith's purposes in the years before the war; and when it came, an unexceptionable *casus belli* assured the nation's unanimity. His Government was loyally supported by the Conservatives in its irrevocable action; and the happy stroke of enlisting Lord Kitchener as Secretary of State for War emphasised its national character. But as the months went by and victory delayed, a natural impatience grew upon

[267]

those eminent Conservatives whom an accident of domestic politics had relegated to a passive *rôle* at a moment of supreme national importance. Their demand for a more active part was irresistible; and the Government was reconstructed on a Coalition basis, by which Mr. Asquith acquired a certain number of Conservative colleagues, while Lord Haldane was sacrificed to an imbecile suspicion that he had German sympathies and Mr. Churchill to a feeling that he was far too enterprising about the Dardanelles, and Mr. Lloyd George left the Treasury for a situation of greater freedom, though no less responsibility, at the new Ministry of Munitions. This party *condominium* presided with varying success over the conduct of the war. But it was less compact than homogeneous Cabinets recruited from a single party, and its component sections were unduly conscious of one another's imperfections. The Prime Minister's luminous intelligence, admirably fitted to perform arbitral functions in the judicious choice of policies when two or more alternatives could be lucidly presented by competent advocates, was slightly exceeded by the more brutal exigencies of supreme authority in time of war. His genius, indeed, was more judicial than executive. A cruel private loss slightly impaired his quality; and his authority began to suffer from a growing sense that the war was not being won as quickly as had been expected and that the nation (and even his own Cabinet) contained elements that were more capable of winning it.

The war, indeed, seemed to hang fire a little in 1916. The year had opened on the humiliation of the Dardanelles, where the defeated Allies drew off before the stubborn Turks, leaving the scarred Peninsula, the silent gullies, and the graves behind the empty trenches and the rusting wire. The great offensive on the Somme, from which so much had been expected, was the reverse of heartening; a grave defeat upon the Tigris and an Irish insurrection darkened the

scene; and the tragic loss of Lord Kitchener in a sunk cruiser
on his way to Russia was a depressing symbol. That impressive figure had been an emblem of the nation's effort in the
early months of war; and though much of its significance
had vanished, its sudden eclipse was a discouraging event.
Nor were the dark shadows of the picture lightened by the
first fleet-action of the war, fought in the haze of the North
Sea that summer. It was quite undeniable that the German
Navy had escaped destruction; and the public mind, accustomed to expect an exact repetition of Trafalgar, was
gravely disappointed. In the absence of technical instruction
it could hardly grasp that a fleet which broke and ran for its
own harbours was powerless to influence the issue of the
war at sea; and without the gift of prophecy it could not
foretell that long imprisonment in German ports would
end in disintegration, mutiny, and a complete surrender one
autumn day two years ahead, when all the German submarines came crawling into Harwich, and the next evening
when the High Seas Fleet lay captive in the Firth of Forth
and hauled down the German flag for the last time. But
these happy consequences were hidden from the popular intelligence, which received the news of Jutland with an uneasy
feeling that the German fleet had been encountered and had
got away, not without doing a somewhat disproportionate
amount of damage before it left.

That year the air was full of disappointment. An advance was checked in Palestine; Rumania, the last addition
to their forces, was eliminated within twelve weeks of joining the Allies; the defence of Verdun was, at best, a negative
success; and there was a growing sense of national discomfort, as the Allies failed to shake their enemies and even
reeled a little under German blows. In Great Britain this
feeling found expression in an increasing dissatisfaction
with Mr. Asquith's leadership. Always a little apt to under-

rate those forces which lay beyond the House of Commons, he was as completely misunderstood by them, since his unostentatious methods made few concessions to the emotional requirements of a nation labouring under great strain. For he was quite unable to discern that a prime requisite of the national morale depended no less on the appearance that its leader was trying hard to win the war than on the fact that he was actually doing so. But appearances were never Mr. Asquith's *forte;* and while the public eye was drawn increasingly to the winged shell that gleamed on the radiator of Mr. Lloyd George's car, indignant readers were reminded that the Prime Minister had once told somebody to "wait and see." The Cabinet's decisions were freely criticised (occasionally by his own colleagues) as dilatory; unfriendly whispers reached a larger public through impatient newspapers; and the consequences were inevitable. An internal controversy on the fruitful topic of administrative methods in the supreme direction of the war developed under skilful hands; a flurried week of argument and heated interviews between embarrassed colleagues and eager partisans resolved the Coalition into its component parts; and it was found that, whilst its Liberal ingredients retained their loyalty to Mr. Asquith, the Conservatives had transferred their allegiance to Mr. Lloyd George. It was a strange result, since there were far more items in the pre-war record of that Radical *sabreur* which Conservatives would find it hard to forgive than in the statelier annals of Mr. Asquith. But politics in time of war are a queer business; and by the end of 1916 Mr. Lloyd George found himself installed in office with Conservative support as the prospective saviour of his country.

The landscape which he surveyed from Downing Street that winter was not enlivening. The war in France was more than usually stationary; the war with Turkey consisted of a setback in Palestine, regrets in Mesopotamia, and bitter memories of the Dardanelles; there was a war of some kind in Macedonia, of which nobody quite understood the purpose; and the war at sea was slightly shadowed by the misgivings which had followed Jutland and the darker speculations stimulated by the unpleasant fact that German submarines were sinking Allied shipping faster every month. If that continued, Great Britain could not supply its Allies and its own armies indefinitely with war material and would eventually be unable to feed its civil population. This was a formidable prospect; and the situation was not improved by a public intimation that the Central Powers, "having given proof of their indestructible strength," were willing to negotiate for peace and by a more than usually pressing invitation from the President of the United States to specify precisely what each belligerent was fighting for. If anything was obvious, it was that scarcely any of the Allies' war-aims had yet been secured by force of arms. France, Belgium, Russia, Serbia, and Rumania had all been successfully invaded; and a settlement upon the basis of the military situation in January, 1917, was manifestly unacceptable. The night, it seemed, was at its darkest; and if the picture was to contain lighter elements, the new Prime Minister would have to bring them with him.

That was his *rôle*. A vague sense of relief in unofficial circles followed the change of government, and Mr. Lloyd George entered briskly on the vital duty of cheering up his countrymen. His powers in this respect had been hitherto confined to the more specialised performances of the Ministry of Munitions and a few eloquent pronouncements alternating between his loftier vein—"the great peaks we had forgotten, of Honour, Duty, Patriotism, and, clad in glittering white, the towering pinnacle of Sacrifice pointing like a rugged finger to Heaven"—and the less elevated (but no less inspiring) invocation of the 'knock-out blow,' which informed an interviewer that "it took England 20 years to defeat Napoleon, and the first 15 of those years were black with British defeat. It will not take 20 years to win this war, but whatever time is required, it will be done." That idiom was now translated into simple actions within the comprehension of the least imaginative of his fellow-countrymen. It was essential, if their effort was to be maintained, that they should realise their leader's new activity; and nothing could be better for the purpose than a good deal of advertised reorganisation. A War Cabinet was formed to take supreme direction, and a fair proportion of the problems which confronted it were relegated to new Ministries. Labour, Shipping, Food, and Pensions each received this hopeful treatment, which placed a new Right Honourable gentleman in charge, involved a vast increase of staff, and devastated the hotel accommodation of central London with no less than seven hundred tenancies of private property for public purposes. It was easy to remark that a fair proportion of the work of the new Ministries was being done before in less impressive styles and that a problem is not automatically solved by the creation of a Ministry of it. But with all its weaknesses this vast expansion of administrative services performed a valuable duty, since it impressed the nation with the scale and vigour of its own effort. That was the new Prime Minister's achievement. His direction of the war found little favour with professionals, who did their best to keep away from his electric contact. But the country, a little shriller now and noticeably more self-conscious, regained its confidence. His incomparable *verve* heartened a slightly jaded nation, which had grown a little numb beneath the blows of war; but now it tingled hopefully, as it observed its vast, articulated effort to achieve "a just and lasting peace. . . . First, the sanctity of treaties must be re-established; secondly, a territorial settlement must be secured based on the right of self-determination or the consent of the governed; and, lastly, we must seek by the creation of some international organisation to limit the burden of armaments and diminish the probability of war." That was the purpose of Great Britain after two years and a half of war. It was a vaster purpose than that for which the war had opened; but the war was vaster too.

2. Petrograd

THE THIRD WINTER of the war hung over Petrograd, and the pale sky looked down at the long avenues beside the frozen Neva. Its palaces still flanked the quays; its colonnades faced one another with their stiff dignity; its statuary pranced as usual upon its granite pedestals; and St. Peter and St. Paul still lifted a slim, gilded forefinger above the prison in their eternal warning. But Petrograd was not the same. For one thing, the Guard regiments were at the front. The barracks were still full of troops in Guard uniforms; but their occupants consisted largely of young soldiers crowded into city barracks that were full to overflowing. Their discipline was far from perfect, and it was not improved by persistent underfeeding in a Russian winter. Not that they were the only people who were underfed in Petrograd; for civilian shopping had almost been reduced to unrewarding vigils in interminable queues. The thin chimneys of the Putiloff works smoked more than ever; and the crowds still walked up and down the broad pavements of the Nevsky, watched by the police and the tall spire of the Admiralty that hung like a gold spectre in the pale winter sky above them. But authority seemed anything but spectral in Petrograd that winter. True, the Czar was at the front, and there was a good deal of promiscuous eloquence behind the fat pillars and self-conscious dignity of the Tauride Palace where the Duma sat. But the Czarina was only a dozen miles away at Czarskoye Selo, and she had told a British diplomat that "the Emperor, unfortunately, is weak; but I am not, and I intend to be firm." The handsome, thin-lipped lady held him to his task; and he was still Czar of All the Russias, although the Germans had invaded some of them.

Unhappily his armies seemed incapable of holding out much longer. That was the difficulty. For the military effort, which they had begun so hopefully when all the bands crashed out the anthem and the kneeling ranks were blessed by smiling, bearded priests in the first summer of the war and Rennenkampf swept gaily forward into East Prussia, seemed to be too much for the resources of the Russian Empire. The figures were immense, since thirteen millions of his subjects had been called to the colours, of whom two millions were dead and four millions—twice the population of his largest city—wounded. And what had they to show for it? An invaded country and the prospect of continuous defeat by the mere weight of German metal. The vast consumption of munitions far exceeded anything that Russian soldiers had expected or that their allies were capable of supplying. For Russia was not yet sufficiently industrial to meet the calls of modern warfare, and Russian manhood had fought doggedly with clubs and empty fists against the serried rifles of the German trenches in the unremitting crash of their artillery barrage and the steady tap of their machine-guns. That unequal contest could only have one end; and it looked unpleasantly as if the Russians might lose

[275]

the war. But if the Russian Empire lost the war, did that mean that it would cease to be an Empire? The unpleasant rhythm of Russian history seemed to impose a fatal alternation of defeat and revolution. Its pulse throbbed slowly through the century to that unchanging beat, and there seemed to be no escape from its rhythmical imperative. For the Crimean War had been followed by the concessions of Alexander II, the strain of victory over the Turks by the revolutionary movement in which he died, the Manchurian defeats by the revolution of 1905. Would German victories be followed by another revolution? That was the unpleasant riddle, to which the answer lay behind the house-fronts and barrack walls of Petrograd in the third winter of the war.

The answer was not quite so obvious as it might seem, since many of the elements of a successful revolution were absent from the Russian scene. In the revolutionary days of 1905 the number of workers taking part in political strikes had risen to 1,843,000; but the *tempo* of such activities was far slower in the war, since the figure fell to 156,000 in 1915 and 310,000 in 1916 and only mounted to 575,000 in the first two months of 1917. This scarcely indicated a mood of insurrection among the workers; and the men who might have raised it were not there to do their revolutionary work in factory meetings and crowded cellars on the Viborg side. Lenin was still in Switzerland, informing youthful Socialists a little sadly that "we of the older generation may not live to see the decisive battles of this coming revolution." That was how things looked from Zurich in January, 1917. He had returned to exile after his last disappointment in profound dejection, feeling "as if I had come here to lie down in my grave"; and it was a weary business waiting in Swiss lodgings for the revolution to begin. The days were tolerable, as he could spend them in the public library. But in the evenings at Geneva their bleak little room drove them to cinemas, from which they fled before the programme was half over to walk beside the lake and talk about the revolutionary day, whose dawn gleamed at the far end of every vista. The gleam was fainter now, and he began to doubt "whether I will live to see the next rise of the tide." But the existence of the tide itself could not be doubted, since it was prescribed by the irrefragable law of history revealed long ago to Marx on his secular Sinai. That faith supported him; and as the vision danced before his eyes in all its fairy brightness, the last of the romantics—a bald-headed man in a Swiss lodging-house—sat staring at his dream.

The slow routine of exile resumed them; and their little figures moved inconspicuously against the massive background of Switzerland, two microbes of strange potentialities in the European bloodstream. They read; they wrote; they argued endlessly with visitors; they moved to Paris where Lenin, always an absent-minded bicyclist, nearly ended his career in an unequal conflict with French motor-traffic; they sat in theatres studying the sociological significance of the performance and the audience's interruptions; they watched other people's lives (having practically none of their own) with the detachment of researchers; and they saw an unending procession of their fellow-revolutionaries, who wore drooping pince-nez that were never cleaned or emptied all the sugar in their soup or drank a little more than was good for them and then developed the most alarming nervous symptoms, in which violence alternated with visions of a sister who had been hanged. There is something a little touching in the queer existence of these fish out of water, who were convinced that they could teach the world to swim.

The outbreak of war found them in Austria, where their poverty was slightly mitigated by a small legacy from an aunt, who had been a school-teacher and left some ikons, a few silver spoons, and about £400. This welcome subsidy enabled them to live, although there was no deviation from the old austerity of life supported on nut-chocolate in penny bars and coffee out of cups with broken handles. Then he was back in Switzerland, addressing tiny meetings and confessing ruefully that an immediate Socialist revolution was hardly possible in Russia. His attitude towards the war was lucidly defined—to turn it into civil war at the first opportunity. That was his objective now, pursued through an interminable wilderness of angry little articles in obscure periodicals, that indicated the whole duty of a Marxist in time of war—"he criticises his government, he unmasks his bourgeoisie, he abuses his ministers"—and pointed to a rosy dawn in which "the proletariat, with arms in hand," was to achieve "a democratic revolution in Russia (democratic republic, eight-hour work-day, confiscation of landowners' lands)." That was the bright event to which the whole Marxian creation moved so far as Russia was concerned. If all went well, it might be followed by the greater glories of the world-revolution, when "the victorious proletariat of that country, having expropriated the capitalists and organised Socialist production at home, would rise against the rest of the capitalist world, attracting the oppressed classes of other countries, raising among them revolts against the capitalists, launching, in case of necessity, armed forces against the exploiting classes and their states." But that crusade must wait until there was a Socialist republic to go crusading. When it emerged, he was quite clear as to its constitution: "The political form of a society in which the proletariat is victorious, in which it has overthrown the bourgeoisie, will be a democratic republic, centralising ever more the forces of the proletariat of a given nation or nations in the struggle against the states which have not yet gone over to Socialism. It is impossible to annihilate classes without a dictatorship of the oppressed class, the proletariat."

That was the gleam he followed. But he was forced to follow it at long range, as Russia swerved towards defeat and the third winter of the war hung over Petrograd. He was not there to see the queues and feel the pulse of the Putiloff workers. The leaders of revolt were all spectators in distant seats—Lenin in Switzerland, Trotsky in New York, Dzerzhinsky at hard labour, Kameneff, Sverdloff, and Stalin in Siberia. If the Empire stumbled, there was nobody in Petrograd to trip it up; and if it fell, it must fall by its own weight. That contingency was not improbable, since no regime in history has carried a more massive load of folly than the Russian Empire in the first weeks of 1917. It had been administered by a succession of governments, for which the sole qualification appeared to be a standard of incompetence not hitherto attained in the management of human affairs and sometimes verging upon mental deficiency, though this requirement was occasionally waived in favour of extreme old age. A strange procession of 'transient and embarrassed phantoms' passed through the ministries, as the war deepened; and the pressure of the German armies was less deadly than the unsleeping efforts of their own incompetence. For nothing went where it was meant to go; supplies, where they existed, were disorganised with an unfailing touch; and the high temper of the nation, which had reached unprecedented levels of patriotic unity, was undermined with systematic skill that far transcended all the efforts of hostile propaganda. That disintegration was the unaided work of Russian administrators.

But the centre of the whole infection lay far above them, on the throne itself. The little fatalist that ruled them was more inert than ever in the hands of Providence; and now his fatalism had a more depressing tinge. For when the defeats began, he took command of all his armies with a dreadful feeling that an angry God was calling for a victim and that, if the Czar were only sacrificed, He might still save Russia. It was an act of noble abnegation; but a temper of disinterested suicide was an addition of doubtful value to the high command of the Russian armies. That, however, was his duty as the Czar saw it plain beyond all argument; and the imperial automaton went about his duties in the gathering gloom of the *Stavka*. His vision was no less distinct as to the course providentially laid down for him in the internal government of Russia. His Empress had thanked God that Russia was not constitutional, warned him against interfering persons, begged him to forget his gentle nature and to be an autocrat. Her daily letter breathed a passionate devotion and a simple-minded preference for government by God's anointed without unhallowed interference. Her faith surrounded him, multiplying sacred objects that carried the divine blessing and would bring him luck; and her mysticism was revolted by the thought of associating persons who were not sanctified by a divine mission in the sacred business of governing Russia. For the Czarina had no uncertainties. God's way was all too plain to her; and she conversed freely with God's messenger.

This holy man of excellent physique and somewhat intermittent piety was not her first experiment in the direction of the supernatural. Poor health combined with a supreme responsibility to render her unnaturally anxious to penetrate the future. It hung before them like a black curtain, and her eyes were always straining to see further into its dark folds. Would Russia prosper? Would she be the mother of a Czarevitch? These were the riddles that tormented her early years of marriage; and she reassured herself by strict religious observance and the consultation of highly

doubtful oracles. Her ritual degenerated swiftly into super-
stition, and her oracles were frankly magic. The mood grew
on her, until the granddaughter of Queen Victoria became
obsessed by the accumulation of holy pictures, with which
her room was plastered, and every known variety of *porte-
bonheur*. An heir was born at last. But the impenetrable
curtain hung before them still, since she was tortured by
uncertainty as to the future of her afflicted son. Could all
their care preserve that precious life for Russia? And if it
did, would Russia still be there for him to inherit? It was
somehow comforting to propitiate the unknown with mild
doses of domestic sorcery. She was convinced that if one
only acted properly under the right advice, the future would
give up its secret and become less frightening. In this
obscurity it was consoling to enjoy the friendship of a holy
man, who spoke to them direct from God and had a marvel-
lous effect upon the small Alexis. That miracle could not be
doubted, though how he produced it was Rasputin's hypnotic
secret. But after his miraculous performance how could
they ever part with the appointed healer of her ailing
son?

Besides, the anxious couple on their lonely eminence valued
him for his plain speech. It was so difficult for them to learn
the truth. But Rasputin would always tell them in his simple
words. He was a holy man, quite unafraid of earthly grandeur; and what he said could hardly fail to be the truth,
because it came direct from God. They seemed to be surrounded by smooth-spoken personages whose motives were
as doubtful as their policies were difficult to understand.
But Rasputin was always simple; he was their 'Friend,'
half mascot and half oracle. When he spoke, the lonely
couple in their English home, surrounded by a Court of
Baltic Germans, seemed to hear the authentic voice of Holy
Russia; and they relied with touching faith upon his oracles

spoken in the long beard beneath his strange, compelling eyes or imparted in those slightly Delphic telegrams which he preferred to the laborious business of handwriting. His views were always definite; his judgments upon candidates for office assessed their spiritual value without uncertainties; his devotion to the throne could not be doubted; he was quite clear what they should do; and since the course which he advised carried God's blessing, they generally did it. When the war came, they had been separated from him by an unlucky absence due to his convalescence from a knife-wound inflicted by a young Jewess in one of his less spiritual moods; and his telegraphic oracle, which shrewdly urged that war would be fatal to the dynasty, was unsupported by his personal appeal. So Rasputin was overruled, and Russia went to war.

The strange vacuum persisted round its pair of rulers; and their 'Friend' was the only piece of ordinary matter that managed to secure admission to that airless space. Indeed, he was almost too ordinary for his presence in their entourage to be congenial to normal Russians. For Russia was not unfamiliar with the vagaries of holy men from remote villages who alternated between a divine and a mundane intoxication; and when these frailties were combined with a high tariff for the sale of his official favours and association with highly questionable circles, his interposition between their subjects and the throne created an unbridgeable gulf. On the further side a lonely couple lived among their dreams and planned the future for their son or, when he was not quite so well, leaned together over the wicker back of the wheeled chair that carried all the hopes of Russia; while beyond the chasm a dull dissatisfaction spread, until few Russians could see much difference between Rasputin and the Empress or between the Empress, who tried so hard to be a Russian, and the Germans, whom they disliked with the increasing bitterness of military failure.

As the war dragged on from one disaster to another, there was a rising murmur, and persons of extreme respectability balanced the possibilities of a decisive change in the succession to the throne. The Czar was palpably inadequate, and the Czarina was still working on him to resist all tendencies towards the least improvement. Their 'Friend' was quite explicit on the subject, and her daily letter quoted his oracles with feverish reiteration. She begged her husband to be strong, to borrow strength from her if he had none of his own, to think of Baby, to remember that Russia loves to feel the whip, to be Peter the Great, Ivan the Terrible, and even Paul—the last an ill-judged reminder, as Paul had been quietly removed by his resentful subjects. And when the listless little man replied to her incitements with disarming candour that her poor old husband had no will, she multiplied her own about him, and the fierceness of her love supported him with its hysterical rigidity.

Events began to move. One winter evening at the end of 1916 Rasputin was gratified with an invitation to a great house in Petrograd. The town was under snow, and the holy man passed through the silent streets. When he arrived, his hosts were nervous, as they were unused to poisoning their guests and, if necessary, shooting them. But they discharged the unpleasant duty. So Rasputin was killed after a number of false starts unequalled in the long annals of unsuccessful homicide; and almost the last act of the Russian aristocracy was, characteristically enough, the most incompetent assassination in the whole of history. Late that night they stumbled out of the still house by the frozen canal with Rasputin's body. A waiting car drove them across the silent city to a distant bridge, where it was thrust beneath the ice. But even that was not the end, since it was recovered

[283]

from the river; and the Czar got back from the front in time for their 'Friend's' funeral. Now they were more alone than ever. His diary received its daily record of trivialities; they did puzzles after dinner with the same ardour which he had applied in the first autumn of the war to the absorbing pastime of sticking snapshots in back volumes of his journal. But the foreign diplomats that interviewed him in the first weeks of 1917 found a queer stiffness in his manner. He was without the slightest comprehension of the state of Russia; and when Sir George Buchanan nerved himself to beg him to regain his people's confidence, the Czar stared at him and asked if he meant that *they* were to regain *his* confidence. His passive trust in Providence exempted him from any form of thought. An angry God required a sacrifice, and he was numb with waiting for the blow to fall.

The Czar was back at Headquarters in the first week of March. The military prospect was less encouraging than ever; and his daily letter from Czarskoye Selo contained the customary mixture of fierce affection with incitements to be strong, to let his subjects feel the weight of his right hand, to remember that Slavs require a blend of love with firmness carried to the point of cruelty, and to note how many of her callers had remarked that what Russians needed was the knout. Their 'Friend' was in a better world; but the Czarina prayed with regularity beside his grave. Her eyes were tired with weeping; and her next letter brought the news that there was illness in the house. The children had developed measles. But that would make no difference unless they wished to leave Czarskoye Selo—and at that season of the year there was no reason why they should. Nor did an anxious mother forget to urge upon her husband the wisdom of hanging a tiresome deputy named Kerensky for a most improper speech and to remind him about writing to the King of England on the subject of Sir George Buchanan.

At Petrograd it had been snowing. The Putiloff chimneys were not smoking now, because the workpeople had been locked out. There were nearly half a million munition-workers in the capital, and owing to the ludicrous mismanagement of food supplies all of them were underfed. One Thursday (it was March 8) a good many of them came out on strike and spent a cheerful day in the inconsequent observance of Women's Day. There were a few red flags about and a mild flavour of sedition. That night a watchful searchlight on the Admiralty spire played down the long vista of the Nevsky; and on the next day the strikers' numbers were almost doubled, bringing out half the workers in the city. The Cossacks shewed a strange amiability in their dealings with the crowd. For though they had obeyed their officers so far as to ride into the throngs, they did not ride them down. The *nagaikas* were not whistling round civilian shoulders, because someone had forgotten to order them to bring their whips. They only carried lances; and what use were lances, unless it was a civil war? So they rode rather sheepishly among the crowds in single file, and the Cossack faces under the fur caps wore a friendly look. If they had had their whips, it might have been different. But as it was, they almost winked and positively let the demonstrators dive comfortably underneath their horses. After all, they were all Russians and they were all hungry. By Saturday the Cossacks were frankly siding with the crowd against the police. The strike was spreading; and the Czarina, with three cases of measles on her hands at Czarskoye Selo, was hoping that the Duma would not misbehave itself. It met on Sunday; and Sir George Buchanan, who had just got back from a week's leave in Finland (that harassed diplomat had no luck with his leave, having arranged to take some in 1914 in the unpropitious interval between the murder at Sarajevo and the Austrian ultimatum), found the city fairly quiet. But it was not quiet long. The Neva bridges were all closed by the police; but crowds of workmen from the Viborg side came swarming cheerfully across the river on the ice. There was some shooting, and the Duma was prorogued. (That night at Headquarters the Czar played dominoes.)

One company of Guards had mutinied on Sunday evening. On Monday, March 12, three regiments followed their example. For their imperfect discipline was quite unequal to the strain of firing on the crowds; and they preferred to march about the snowy streets, or join the hunt for machine-gunners whom the police had posted on the roofs, or drive about in motor-lorries with red flags all over them and two sailors lying on the mudguards and so many passengers with rifles bristling in their hands that the lorries looked like great hedgehogs. They tramped in solemn columns to the Duma, where they were addressed by excited politicians and swore eternal loyalty to something that they could not catch quite distinctly. As confusion gained upon the city, the area controlled by the authorities contracted swiftly, until the last defenders slipped out of the Winter Palace into the great building of the Admiralty and then went home. If Russia had a master now, it was the Duma, where agitated deputies who forgot to eat and drank quantities of tea in the intervals of shouting hoarsely at loyal deputations had erected something in the nature of a Provisional Government. For it was 1789 over again, with a happy air of brotherhood and broken chains. But the Russian monarchy faced its revolution without a Mirabeau to guide it. The Empress was still praying at Rasputin's grave (that day she sent the Czar a sacred fragment of his tomb); and in the night the Emperor started home by train.

[286]

Now he was in the trap, muttering that Moscow was still loyal and that, if all failed, he should abdicate and live quietly among his flowers at Livadia. The train clanked slowly across the winter landscape with the hunted Czar. He could not go further west, because there were the Germans; and he could not get back to Petrograd, because the mutineers were in the way. Every road seemed to be barred. But there was one way out: if he abdicated, they would let him go. They wanted him to abdicate. Petrograd had telegraphed to say so; the army commanders seemed to think so too; and he had no letters from Czarskoye Selo telling him not to. Someone was already on the way to shew him how it should be done; and a locomotive with a single coach came out from Petrograd to meet him. Then (it was Thursday, March 15) he was abdicating in his train among the uniforms at Pskoff. Before he signed the paper, he asked a doctor if his son was curable; and when the doctor shook his head, the Czar paused to think.

"That is what the Empress has long believed: I was not certain. . . . Since it is God's will, I shall not leave my poor child."

The Czar had spoken. Then he renounced the throne for himself and for his son as well. They had a cheerless dinner; and there were lights in the six windows of his railway coach. His throat was working painfully. Late in the night his train began to move again. He was no longer Emperor, but he must write his diary; and as he wrote, the four-wheel bogies clanked through the winter night.

3. Washington, D. C.

THE IMPACT of the war, which had numbed Europe into
an unthinking whirl of evenly-matched forces interrupted
here and there by the dull instincts of scared neutrals bent
upon self-preservation, had just the opposite effect on the
United States. For if Europe was past thinking, America
had ample leisure for reflection. That happy region lay
remote from the zone of conflict and saw nothing more of
the belligerents than a distant smear on the horizon from
a patrolling British cruiser or the smokeless funnels of the
German liners interned in the North River. But as the conflict deepened, it became steadily more sensitive to issues
which were not, to all appearances, its own immediate concern. For the modern world was gradually discovered to be
curiously interlocked. Invisible affiliations joined its most
widely separated units; a network of novel complications,
undreamt of by the simple-minded jurists of a earlier day,
entangled honest footsteps planted in the direction of a
sane (if slightly sanctimonious) detachment; and, in the
outcome, ineluctable events confirmed Macaulay's judgment

[288]

that, in order that one more King of Prussia might "rob a neighbour whom he had promised to defend, black men fought on the coast of Coromandel, and red men scalped each other by the Great Lakes of North America." Only this time they were not red, and they came to France to do their scalping.

When the storm broke over Europe, the official mind of the United States was mainly exercised by an unseasonable interruption of the tourist traffic, which flooded consulates with stranded travellers, lost luggage, and immobilised letters of credit. The issues of the war itself were exorcised so far as possible by diplomatic ritual. The State Department made the customary passes, and a proclamation of neutrality announced that the dispute was no concern of the United States. This done, the official mind assumed that slightly superior detachment which is the American form of self-control. But this reserve was not so easy for newspaper-readers assailed by daily headlines indicating lucidly that German armies had violated Belgium without undue tenderness in order to defeat the French, or for those citizens of German origin who saw the country of their birth at war with half the world, or in the Celtic twilight where Irishmen rehearsed their grievances and banked the age-long fires of resentment against England. The public sympathy was freely asked for either side. Appeals to aid the helpless victims of invasion challenged their generosity; and as the Germans had done most of the invading, these appeals were almost inevitably anti-German.

A further circumstance inclined them towards the Allies, as manufacturers shortly received vast Allied orders for American supplies. These passed across the ocean behind the shield of British sea-power, which kept the freedom of the seas for Allied shipping, while denying it (within the straining limits of the law) to goods designed for Germany.

A brisk series of debates ensued between Washington and the Allied capitals upon the ramifying problems of neutrality; and it became of high importance for the Allies to retain American sympathy, since it carried with it access to American supplies and credit. But it was of no less importance to the Germans. For if the United States could only be induced to raise objections to the uninterrupted use of British sea-power, the pressure upon Germany would be proportionately weakened and her prospects of success increased. By this embarrassing development the State Department was required to hold the scales with unimpeachable impartiality between both sets of belligerents, until the United States almost involuntarily became the conscience of the world. A happy accident of their domestic politics equipped them admirably for the *rôle,* since Woodrow Wilson happened to have been elected President two years before the war.

It is greatly to the credit of the American system that, unlike its European counterparts, it does not exclude men from public life on the bare suspicion of intellectual attainments. True, they must have something more to offer. But under suitable conditions even a college president might hope to serve the community of which he was a member; and what could have been more suitable than the conditions which prevailed in 1910? An aching void, inadequately filled by Mr. Bryan's throbbing eloquence, did duty for the Democratic leadership. Somebody would have to stand for President in 1912; and it was plainly to be hoped that he would combine a fair degree of party loyalty with views of a progressive shade and a distaste for the absurdities which Mr. Bryan talked about the currency upon the slightest provocation. Westerners were apt to feel that way about it; and as large numbers of their fellow-countrymen were still obstinately unconverted, shrewd Democratic eyes began to scrutinise the East for an heir presumptive. A lantern-jawed Professor of Jurisprudence and Politics was President of Princeton; and at an early stage an enterprising journalist indicated him to an after-dinner audience in New York as a likely President of the United States. But Colonel Harvey, whose colonelcy was of a strictly civil character, was no ordinary journalist. His political affiliations were rich and ramifying; he owned a magazine and moved with ease among the potentates with large cigars who ruled America from Wall Street; and when he indicated a future tenant of the White House, the news was highly interesting. But if his sponsor was unusual among contemporary journalists, Woodrow Wilson was not quite an ordinary college president. The course of academic life in the United States runs closer to the main stream of affairs than in the more secluded groves of other countries; and he had never hesitated to comment with freedom (though not always with that strict reserve that goes with personal ambitions) upon current politics. The object of the Colonel's choice received his prophecy with fitting modesty and continued to perform his academic duties, interspersed with public speeches of an elevating character; and when he was invited by the Democratic party managers in New Jersey to come out and run for Governor, he came and ran with a celerity and vehemence that quite surprised them. Professors were, it seemed, more vital than they had supposed; and though he had a disconcerting tendency to feel a warmer interest in measures than in men, there was plainly something to be said for launching this amazing amateur upon national politics.

That had been in 1910; and two years later, when the next Presidential election came round, he received the Democratic nomination after a vociferous and long-drawn Convention. The campaign of 1912 was the American equivalent of the transformation-scene enjoyed by British politics in 1906. A sense of change was in the air. "It was good form," as a survivor wrote, "to be a liberal. . . . Conservative lawyers, bankers, and men of affairs stepped out from their offices and lent their names to radical movements. . . . The younger generation was to achieve the things that had been denied my own. . . . The young people . . . hated injustice They had no questions about the soundness of American democracy. . . . They believed . . . that the truth would make us free." In that dawn the voice of Woodrow Wilson sounded an appropriate reveille. His "ardent but diffuse progressiveness" (as Mr. Roosevelt termed it a shade morosely with that excessive candour which reformers keep for one another) was the very spirit of the time; and in March, 1913, he found himself unpacking at the White House.

He was excusably a little breathless; and even when his breath returned, he surveyed his elevation with a queer detachment. He had always been a shade impersonal. Professors often are; and this promotion to an office upon which he had been lecturing for years inclined him to a strange duality. "The old kink in me is still there," he wrote. "Everything is persistently *impersonal*. I am administering a great office,—no doubt the greatest in the world, —but I do not seem to be identified with it: it is not me, and I am not it. I am only a commissioner, in charge of its apparatus, living in its offices, and taking upon myself its functions. This impersonality of my life is a very odd thing, and perhaps robs it of intensity, as it certainly does of pride and self-consciousness (and, maybe, of enjoyment) but at least prevents me from becoming a fool, and thinking myself *It!*" He merely tapped his typewriter in a new study, swallowed his breakfast of two eggs in orange-juice (as noted by an admiring British visitor) at a strange dining-table, and turned his mind to rather more immediate problems than those to which it was accustomed. That was all the difference.

But was it? True, he had passed his whole life in solving questions, and that was all that he was asked to do in Washington. Yet previously they had almost always been of an order with which he had long been familiar. But at the White House he was promptly faced with a thorny crop of problems that were entirely novel, since they grew beside the unfamiliar path of foreign policy. His interest in world affairs was of the slenderest. All his thinking had been done on the great issues of internal politics and government; his writings scarcely touched on other themes; and he shared none of Mr. Roosevelt's aptitude and eagerness to cast a lively shadow on world politics. On this side, at least, he knew his limitations. Did he not remark almost whimsically to someone before leaving Princeton for the White House that it would be the irony of fate if his Administration had to deal chiefly with foreign affairs? That irony befell him by the uncanny law under which reforming governments intent on home affairs are so frequently distracted by the harsh call of foreign politics. Had not M. Emile Ollivier proposed to ennoble 1870 with a new era of reform, and did not Mr. Asquith intend that Welsh Disestablishment and Home Rule for Ireland should bear the hopeful date of 1914?

The same melancholy accident diverted Mr. Wilson towards the uncharted seas of foreign policy. He faced the prospect manfully, since he had long realised that the United States could not avoid having one. For he judged their adolescent period of concentration on the fascinating processes of their own growth to be over; and he had written explicitly that "we have come to full maturity . . . And the day of our isolation is past." Indeed, his own Inaugural as President of Princeton informed his hearers with modest acquiescence that "a new age is before us in which, it would seem, we must lead the world," although there was no reference to world affairs in his Inaugural as President of the United States. But it could not be doubted that, if they were obtruded on his attention, they would be encountered in the same elevated tone. For in the absence of detailed knowledge or deeply-rooted predilections he would be apt to judge them by the simple principles of his morality. Wilson, the 'Presbyterian priest,' was nothing if not a moralist. His ethics were applied to practical affairs in a faint, improving echo of earlier calls to repentance; and he confronted politics in something of the attitude of an attenuated Gladstone. It followed that when he was called upon to navigate the strange seas of foreign policy, he steered by the unwinking light of his morality. For he was quite able to determine a moral issue when he saw one; and if he could only find the moral issue that underlay each international problem, he could quite easily resolve it. That was the Wilsonian method, which faced less spiritual adepts of diplomacy with something they had never met before.

This ethical interpretation of the world's affairs was boldly exemplified in his appointment of Mr. Bryan to be Secretary of State. Nobody supposed that Mr. Bryan could be trusted with anything so complicated as the currency. But the President committed world affairs into those slightly gesticulatory hands with perfect confidence, since world affairs were largely matters of morality; and none of those who doubted Mr. Bryan's head had ever doubted Mr. Bryan's heart. Indeed, the first intrusion of foreign policy was in conformity with Mr. Wilson's expectations, since Mexico passed into its seasonal ebullience and Washington had to determine what its attitude should be towards General Huerta. That was comparatively easy, since the moral issue was quite evident; and the ex-President of Princeton

it seemed, were cast among civilian colonels. A Texan with a private income and a consuming taste for politics, he had cultivated Wilson from the moment that his impending elevation became obvious; and when they met for the first time, the two middle-aged politicians talked for sixty minutes in a New York hotel and the Colonel in a glow recorded that "we had a perfectly bully time." After this austere initiation their meetings were repeated; and such confidences flowed between them that presently the Colonel asked the Governor with some emotion if he realised for how very short a time they had been acquainted, and the Governor replied in tones that Princeton rarely knew, "My dear friend, we have known one another always."

But though House had his uses as a friendly echo for a lonely man (Wilson had a rare gift for loneliness, which he was capable of feeling in a crowded life passed at the centre of a devoted family and was apt to mitigate by copious letter-writing to sympathetic ladies), he could not help the President to solve the riddle of the war. There was an engaging innocence about the Colonel's gambollings across the field of international affairs that in other circumstances might have been entertaining, since Austin, Texas, was a long way from Europe; and though the Colonel moved to New York, he never acquired a grasp of European issues comparable to his mastery of the finer shades of Congressional politics. The President was left to face the international dilemma in his customary solitude; and the typewriter tapped out his changing view, as the scene shifted.

It was less easy now to talk loftily about complete detachment, since the economics of neutrality were shepherding the United States steadily towards the Allies. The German claim to interrupt the flow of navigation towards Allied ports was inadmissible, because it was a threat to the main stream of American prosperity. That was the factor which

[297]

impelled an anti-German drift at Washington no less (and, in some quarters, rather more) than the senseless brutality of German methods. Mr. Lansing's ingenuity might indicate the imperfections of Allied jurisprudence. But the uncontrolled torpedo, which was Germany's last weapon, threatened the smoking chimneys of industrial America, as well as the sanctity of human life. That was, in the last analysis, the ruling fact, even simpler than those moral issues to which the President was so highly trained. But even on the moral issue the distracted Germans seemed to do their best to put, and keep, themselves completely in the wrong. The sinking of the *Lusitania* had all the simple crudity of child-murder. Their courtship of American opinion was a cave-man's wooing, conducted with incendiary bombs lovingly deposited in ships and factories and by the equally endearing comedy of preposterous incitements to the Mexicans to go to war with the United States in order to recover all the lands that they had lost in 1848. This was not the road to Mr. Wilson's sympathy; and on the moral side the President slowly came to view the Kaiser as a greater Huerta.

His problem was far simpler now; and as the first weeks of 1917 went by, the Germans solved it for him. For the brutal challenge of the submarine ended his doubts; and Wilson was soon sitting at his typewriter facing the odious prospect of war—of war that would inevitably make it difficult, if not impossible, to rebuild the peace of which he dreamed, of "a peace between equals . . . a peace the very principle of which is equality and a common participation in a common benefit." That was now his dream, as it had once been his desire to keep America above the conflict. But the Germans were too strong for him; and on an April night, as the spring rain streamed down on Washington, he led the United States into the war.

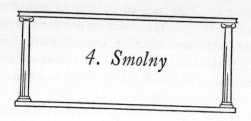

4. Smolny

SPRING came to Petrograd that year in a bright flowering of well-meaning eloquence. Even the departing Emperor was eloquent beyond his custom in the typewritten periods of his last appeal to every loyal son of Russia for a common effort to advance the country on the road to victory, prosperity and glory. His brother Michael, in whose favour he had abdicated, was promptly interviewed in Petrograd by ten gentlemen of well-tried eloquence, of whom he was addressed by five (since the new Russia suffered from no lack of spokesmen) with the immediate result that he abdicated in his turn and was rewarded by Kerensky with a metaphorical display of the first order. That pallid advocate, whose moment had arrived, was the most eloquent of all. His lean features and *staccato* utterance were a furore in the capital that spring; and his effects were heightened by a dramatic taste in costume, which inclined him to affect by turns a workman's blouse, field-service uniform, and naval jumpers in accordance with his hearers' varying requirements. Ladies in expensive seats thought with a little thrill that his pale mask was cruel-looking and were much relieved to find that he was not so cruel as he looked. For though the Russian Revolution had done some shooting in the streets and had a short way with policemen, it seemed domesticated now and was embodied in a Provisional Government with re-assuring manners, which dined at embassies and seemed to be quite sound about the war.

True, the royal family were prisoners at Czarskoye Selo. Passers-by stared through the railings and could see the Emperor moving about the grounds, discreetly followed by an officer. But they seemed quite happy. The Czar was sorting picture-postcards or shovelling snow or reading to them after dinner (they got through quite a lot of Conan Doyle, and he was studying Byzantine history). Besides, they would be leaving soon for England; and that would be the end of all their troubles. Indeed, they might have left already, if the children had not got measles. They might have left before the Government had time for second thoughts about them. But their indisposition left the Government with time to think; and its second thoughts were not so happy, since life was none too easy for those well-intentioned gentlemen. A lucky accident had raised them from the benches of the Duma. But besides the Duma there was the Soviet, a miscellaneous assembly with a large preponderance of soldiers ("grey army cloth," as Trotsky wrote, "became the general ground-tone of the Soviet") which chose to see itself as the direct embodiment of the revolution. This awkward dyarchy confronted the new Government with all the dangers of a parallel authority and faced it with a constant challenge to its revolutionary *bona fides,* which could not be met without a bold succession of revolutionary attitudes. In such a situation it was plainly difficult to let royal personages slip away to the felicity of life in England; and they remained prisoners behind the railings of Czarskoye Selo.

Their escorts were more interfering now; visitors were noticeably ruder; and somebody took the small boy's gun away from him. But the Czar, more philosophical than ever, sawed wood and bicycled about the grounds and kept his diary as usual. There was a marked improvement in the level of his reading; for he was studying a solid work by Kuropatkin on the problems of the Russian army, which he might have read with slightly more advantage before it had collapsed. He was sincerely anxious about his country's fate and worried by the lack of news about his mother. But these anxieties were not allowed to interfere with the Czar's enjoyment of his bicycle. For his detachment was uncanny. The circle of his interests had contracted to the pin-point of his daily life; and he was quite indifferent to his own captivity.

The same necessity for striking revolutionary attitudes which kept them at Czarskoye Selo impelled the issue of an Army order that destroyed the last remaining vestiges of discipline. The army was disintegrating fast. Before the revolution there had been more than a million deserters; and as discipline relaxed, the flow became a torrent. The countryside was flooded with returning villagers in uniform, who justified their absence from the front by the strength and emphasis of their political opinions and crowded every meeting with grey uniforms and the tramp of heavy boots. This process was completed by an order from the Soviet, which received subsequent approval from the Government, directing every military and naval unit in the capital to elect committees with control of all its arms and authority to hear appeals against its officers. Such tendencies reduced the armies at the front to a thin screen of public meetings, which was quite incapable of an offensive and could not be expected to resist the next forward movement by the Germans. For the revolution acted as a fatal solvent upon the Russian army, since revolutions (which have the power to create new armies) possess an awkward gift for dissolving old ones. The impetus of 1793 had sent France forward to victory; but had it come in the third year of a disastrous war, its consequences might not have been the same.

The paralysis of the navy was even more complete, since its political development was more advanced. Naval discipline was sterner and evoked a fiercer spirit of resentment among men living at the closer quarters of life at sea. Besides, the modern sailor was no longer a light-hearted mariner whose life was evenly distributed between going aloft and dancing hornpipes. Sea warfare was highly mechanised, and those floating boxes of tightly packed machinery employed a class of labour whose industrial development was far beyond the stage reached by the simple countrymen in uniform who knew quite enough to shoulder arms on shore. For there was not much that the Putiloff workers could teach the Baltic Fleet; and where Cronstadt hung low on the skyline beyond the beach at Peterhof the naval barracks housed an advanced academy of revolution. Their first outbreak, in which discipline was drowned in a flood of massacre, was terrible. The Russian fleet ceased to serve any military purpose; but in revenge the Russian sailor with his rifle and the long ribbons of his jaunty cap became a personage of grave political significance. His views were drastic; mutiny had pledged him to the revolution; and at the least alarm the streets of Petrograd were flooded with class-conscious mariners, whose naval duties sat more lightly on them than their political convictions.

But Russia was still in the war. This decomposing state with a seditious navy and a disintegrating army maintained its loyalty to the Allies. Brave declarations pledged it to persist in the despairing struggle; and a Russian front, however rickety, still faced the Germans. That was a serious consideration for the German high command, which watched with strained attention the preparations for a fresh Allied offensive in the west. For the moment the deft manœuvre of Ludendorff's retreat to the forbidding contours of the Hindenburg Line parried the blow. But it could not be doubted that one day the blow would fall; and when it did, the untouched man-power of the United States would lend it overwhelming weight. For that reason it was now essential for the Germans to conclude the struggle on the Russian front, to eliminate the reeling giant in the east, and to free the Austro-German forces for a final effort in the west. Light dawned upon the General Staff from a most unexpected quarter. For a Swiss Socialist applied to the German Minister at Berne for permits to ship Lenin and a carload of revolutionaries across Germany *en route* for Russia.

Lenin had received the first news of the revolution without undue enthusiasm. This, he felt, was a beginning; but it was emphatically not the end. For the bourgeoisie was in control. That would never do; and he continued to insist upon the need for "revolutionary propaganda, as heretofore, agitation and struggle for an *international* proletarian revolution and for the seizure of power by the 'Soviets of Workers' Deputies' . . . . Spread out! Rouse new sections! Awaken fresh initiative, form new organisations in every layer and *prove* to them that *peace* can come only with the armed Soviet of Workers' Deputies in power." That was the new revelation, for which there was the slenderest authority in Marxian Holy Writ. It was too bad that the revolution had occurred without assistance from the faithful. But as it had, the faithful must improve on it; and the new institution of the Soviet enabled them to go one better. Since the Provisional Government was still committed to the war and rested on the Duma, peace and the Soviet became his programme; and he burned to preach it on the streets of Petrograd. But he was still in Switzerland, dreaming of long-distance flights in phantom aeroplanes across Germany, across the battle-front to Russia. They even played with the notion of travelling as harmless neutrals with a Swedish passport. But he knew no Swedish; and when he suggested gravely that he might be deaf and dumb for the occasion, Krupskaya objected that he would inevitably fall asleep, dream about Mensheviks, and start to swear. The wild project was dismissed; but when it occurred to someone that his party might be exchanged for a few German prisoners of war in Russia, he leapt at the idea. For Lenin was quite prepared to do a deal with official Germany, if it would do a deal with him. So the Imperial Legation in Switzerland was formally approached. From their point of view the scheme had something to commend it, as there was a good deal to be said for introducing further elements of disintegration into Russia. The German mind had not shrunk from the stern duty of departing from the rules of war in the sacred cause of German victory; and the same cause would justify an attempt to relax the Russian war-effort by inoculating Russia with a few Bolshevist bacilli.

The strange agreement was concluded; and the Berne Legation accepted "this unique international treaty" (as Trotsky termed it) "between the editorial staff of a revolutionary paper and the Empire of the Hohenzollerns," by which a railway coach was to cross Germany in time of war. As the passengers were without valid passports, it would be exempted from all passport and customs formalities; and as the numbers of the excursion were strictly limited, it would take up no further passengers *en route*. All that was required of the grateful travellers was their undertaking to obtain the release of an equivalent number of German prisoners upon arrival at their destination. For once the German Government made a concession without obtaining payment in advance. But its kindly impulse was more than justified by the happy circumstance that the release of Lenin into Russian politics carried its own reward for German strategy; and it is pleasant to reflect that Communism owes its greatest debt to the German General Staff.

The train rumbled across Germany in the last week of March. Lenin was silent; but his fellow-travellers talked cheerful nonsense and ate larger meals than they had been accustomed to, whilst a small boy filled the whole carriage with his noise. They looked out of the windows at the German fields and noticed that there were few men about; and when they were shunted at Berlin, some German Socialists appeared. Then they were on the Baltic steamer; and when they got to Stockholm, someone made a speech. But Sweden was behind them now, and they were driving into Finland over the ice at Torneå. This was Russian territory at last, and they saw the familiar uniforms and the dilapidated rolling-stock they knew so well. The small boy was playing with a Russian soldier; and as the little stations of the north went by, one of the party hung out of the carriage window to shout, "Long live the world revolution"; but no one on the platform seemed to care. Lenin was arguing about the war with someone in a carriage full of soldiers, who stood on the seats to listen to the argument. His face was white and strained; for Petrograd was coming nearer, and they could not tell what Petrograd might hold. The safety of exile was far away; even the comparative security of Finland lay on the further side of a small stream, as the train clanked across a little bridge into Byelo-Ostroff; and at the frontier station, where some Bolsheviks appeared to welcome him, he asked if he would be arrested when he arrived.

It was after dark, when the first lights of Petrograd slid past his carriage windows and the train drew into the Finland Station with its dingy shed and discouraged iron pillars. The greasy boards of the platform were beneath his feet, and he could see a line of waiting soldiers. Was this his journey's end? Was he to be arrested here? An officer saluted and said something to him; and Lenin, who was unused to guards of honour, looked surprised, saluting in reply. A large bouquet appeared from somewhere; and holding it a little awkwardly the battered traveller walked hurriedly into a waiting-room, where he nearly ran into somebody who made a speech. He scarcely listened, as he stood there fumbling with his flowers; and his eyes wandered from the audience to the high ceiling of the room. For the place was unfamiliar to him, since it was the Czar's waiting-room. Then he made a little speech, pointedly addressed to his "dear comrades, soldiers, sailors, and workers," in honour of "the world-wide Socialist revolution." A band struck up the *Marseillaise* and (with less conviction) the more recently imported *Internationale*. There was a roar of cheering in the street outside; and somebody was helping him to climb on to an armoured car, from which he made another speech. Then they drove off in triumph through the Viborg side, with bands playing and Lenin on his armoured car and frequent halts for speeches to the crowds that stood in the glare of its headlight, to their headquarters which had been established with a pleasing irony in the flamboyant mansion where the Czar's favourite *ballerina* used to live. For that monstrosity of *art nouveau*, built in a distasteful shade of brown and backed by the bulbous domes and vivid colouring of an unlikely mosque which had strayed into Petrograd by some accident of imperial policy, now housed the Bolsheviks; and Ksheshinskaya's balcony was most convenient for addressing meetings in the street below.

The travellers sat down to an enormous tea, interrupted by more speeches from the balcony and a disquisition which alarmed the faithful. For discarding the revolution in its present stage, Lenin indicated vast and perilous horizons of revolutionary action, of a universal seizure of the land and straightforward government by the Soviet without the complications of a parliamentary republic or bourgeois democracy. He told them that he had expected to be taken straight from the train to the Fortress of St. Peter and St. Paul, which was just down the road, and added that his hopes of that event were not yet abandoned. Indeed, if he persisted, it seemed more than probable. For Lenin was determined to outbid the Government in revolutionary fervour, and his declaration on that April night was quite uncompromising. Across the river lights were burning in the Winter Palace, where the Provisional Government pursued its blameless way. But German cunning had released the forces of destruction; and Lenin's unresting energy challenged the Russian Revolution with a revolution of more profound significance. Three years before, as the first clouds of war were gathering, his sister had met Kerensky on a river-steamer. The two families were neighbours; indeed, Kerensky's father had been guardian to her brothers and sisters; and when they met on that summer evening in 1914, their talk ran on her exiled brother who was then far away in Austria. Kerensky told her not to worry, because war was coming and war would bring Lenin home. His forecast had been quite accurate; but Lenin's homecoming was not precisely what Kerensky had foreseen.

On the next day the prodigal stated his position to the Bolshevik members of the Soviet in terms which made no concession either to their intellects or to the Government. It was an angular and closely argued excommunication of the present rulers of Russia. His first sentences denounced "the triumph of the traitors to Socialism, the deception of the masses by the bourgeoisie" and attacked the war in its present form as an imperialistic adventure, which might be

[307]

sanctified or ended—he was not quite clear which—by a thorough-going proletarian revolution. The ingredients of that happy brew were then outlined—all power to the Soviets, a frank abandonment of the old ideal of a parliamentary republic, land confiscation, a workers' bank, and the substitution of armed workers for all soldiers, police, and public functionaries. As the result would look, if it looked like anything, a little like the Paris Commune and the ideals indicated by the title of the Russian Social Democratic Party were now manifestly out of date, he suggested that the faithful should take the name of Communists, reverting to a title that had once been applied to a vague group of Socialist precursors. This would enable them to take a lofty stand as simple primitives, whose doctrinal purity was uncontaminated by subsequent accretions to the faith and to confound the Government with a steady disapproval of its fall from grace. A long series of speeches, articles, and private talks hammered in the new ideals with metallic force; and the country settled down to an endless interlude of Russian talk, in which Kerensky grew more eloquent than ever, whilst Lenin answered harshly from Ksheshinskaya's balcony. Before the summer his forces were increased by the return of Trotsky, who brought with him all the showmanship of the revolution and had an unequalled way with soldiers. But in the spring of 1917 there were not more than 15,000 Bolsheviks in Petrograd and less than 80,000 in the whole of Russia. This was palpably no time for street-fighting at a disadvantage, since their unsentimental leader had a strong prejudice against unsuccessful risings; and his "high-powered peasant cunning" (as Trotsky called it) was soberly applied to multiplying the forces at his command before they could challenge the Provisional Government. The pavements of Petrograd were beneath his feet once more. He had returned with gusto from the theory of revolution to its practice, from the Swiss laboratory to the Russian crowds. But the transition left his grasp of cold reality quite unimpaired; and he was clear that there was nothing to be done until there were more Bolsheviks.

A premature explosion in July endangered all his work. The nation's mood was still unfriendly to a further instalment of disintegration. The armies at the front were even galvanised into some sort of movement; and Kerensky, in the ascendant now, was almost the whole Cabinet in his own person. The prisoners at Czarskoye Selo looked on approvingly, and the Czar's diary was highly complimentary about him. "This man," he wrote of his successor, "is decidedly in the right place at present; the more power he has, the better." For they had always entertained a vague notion that Russia might respond to a dictator. It had not been easy to discover one among his ministers; but the strange processes of revolution seemed to have produced a man capable of ruling Russia. True, Kerensky was unable to win the war for them. But that was too much for anybody to expect; and he was at least equal to dealing firmly with trouble on the streets of Petrograd. The Bolsheviks were checked, their leaders lucidly denounced as German agents; and Lenin, with someone else's passport and a wig, left hurriedly for Finland on the footplate of a locomotive. It was a swift reversal of his triumphal entry.

But his was not the only exit, since the Czar's presence on the outskirts of his late capital was slightly embarrassing. There was a certain element of risk in their continued residence in such proximity to disorderly and dangerous elements. Besides, his exile by the Government would be a reassuring gesture of republican propriety. So it was gently broken to the Czar that he was going to Siberia. He told Kerensky that he was not at all anxious, that they had faith in him, that if Kerensky said that it was necessary, he was

[309]

quite sure that it was so. Then they were packing for the long journey—all his photographs, the fifty volumes of his diary, Victor Hugo's *Ninety-three*, some Turgenieff, his wife's and mother's letters, *Sherlock Holmes*, Green's *Short History of the English People*, a good deal of Dumas, *War and Peace*, *The Scarlet Pimpernel* and its exciting sequel, *Anna Karenina*, a book by Maeterlinck, *The Garden of Allah*, and an extremely stupid anti-Semite forgery by which he was subsequently much impressed. On the whole, the Czar's selection was a fair sample of the books that were to be found in any English country-house, though it contrasted oddly with the libraries preferred by those of his own subjects who preceded him down the long road to Siberia. Their choice of reading had been a trifle more severe, since exile was the university in which they trained themselves for revolution. But the Czar was not in training for a new career. Their active life was over; and his acceptance of events was, as ever, quite unquestioning. On the last morning at Czarskoye Selo the dark curtain of their future seemed to open, and they passed beyond. They had packed overnight; and by the first light of a midsummer morning (he noted, with his odd precision, that the day was fine) the last Romanoff stepped through a French window out of his last palace. A car was waiting; all Czarskoye Selo lay in the early sunshine; there was some muddle at the station about their train; and as they started on the long journey to Siberia, leaving the gardens and the shaded balcony and all the ornaments they knew so well, the holy pictures in her bedroom, the frilled lampshades and framed photographs and the dashing picture by Detaille that hung downstairs, the Czarina was in tears.

That summer, as the royal family receded behind the endless distances towards Tobolsk and Lenin flitted about back-streets in Helsingfors, Russia was governed by Kerensky in an uneasy equilibrium. Now there were 200,000 Bolsheviks to challenge his authority. The army liquefied into an aimless surge of armed committee-men. They sang, made speeches, shot their officers, waved white flags, and traded freely with the Germans. The villages behind them swarmed with deserters, from whom the rural population was learning its first lessons in indiscipline. First they burned the trees and seized the land; and after that they burned the house. Books, bric-à-brac, blood stock, and model farms were all destroyed with fine impartiality by an enlightened peasantry, engaged in the confusing task of remodelling the Russian countryside nearer to its own image. The Government could do little more than make vague gestures of disapproval. Indeed, it was as much as it could do to maintain itself against the threat to its existence which came from the opposing quarter of the sky, embodied in the anæmic Bonapartism of General Korniloff. This was defeated by a combination of its own incompetence with the ability of the armed workers of the capital to defend themselves. The heartening experience gave them new confidence; but if Petrograd was capable of self-defence, it dawned upon it that it could replace the Government with something nearer to its taste.

Long months of Bolshevik persuasion were bearing fruit, as the Putiloff chimneys came up against the pearly autumn skies of 1917. Lenin was back in Petrograd without his beard; Kerensky, draped in the last fragments of authority, ruled Russia by excited telegrams from the big windows of the Winter Palace. But across the city the dull façade of Smolny, shouldering the bulbous domes and rich ornament of the Convent Church of which it was the organised negation, housed the Soviet. Politics became a duel between the two contrasted buildings, between the last echo of rococo elegance in Palace Square and the flat pediment and heavy-footed colonnades of Smolny. Late one night, after an endless session in a little flat, the die was cast. A clean-shaven Lenin, wearing a wig and spectacles, arrived with the proposal of an armed rising. They drank tea; they ate bread and sausage; they argued far into the night; and when they parted, Lenin had drafted something with a gnawed pencil on a sheet of paper torn from a child's notebook that changed the face of Russia.

The rest was swift. One November day the flaming Trotsky captured the Fortress of St. Peter and St. Paul with a single speech; a cruiser anchored off the Winter Palace and fired a shot that won almost the sole recorded victory of the Russian Navy, which had managed to defeat an admirable specimen of eighteenth-century architecture. Banks and post offices were seized with smooth efficiency; and Kerensky was left telegraphing helplessly for troops that never came. The army was indifferent, provided that it was not asked to fight; and the last phase became a duel between half-hearted Cossacks, some brave women in uniform, and a few scared politicians and on the other side the armed workers of the city, supported by their friends, the sailors. At the Winter Palace, where a few defenders waited behind barricades, there was no defence. Kerensky, with the Stars and Stripes fluttering on the radiator of his car, had gone off in search of reinforcements; and his foray ended on the bare slopes that climb out of the everlasting plain towards Gatchina, where stray footsteps echoed in the empty rooms of a deserted palace and the first saviour of his country faded into history, jauntily costumed as a Russian sailor. For the poetry of revolution had been defeated by its prose.

In Petrograd there was a little shooting on the quays. The sound drifted across the town to Smolny, where two weary men were lying side by side upon the floor. Trotsky was called out to speak in the big hall, where rows of delegates sat smoking. But Lenin waited until the moment came for him to speak. Then they saw the legendary man with the big head and little twinkling eyes. His aspect, even to his intimates, was unfamiliar, as he had shaved his beard, though it was growing once again. But this was Lenin, and that was the Soviet. He gripped the lectern; and as the cheering died away, they heard him say, "We shall now proceed to construct the Socialist order." It was a simple opening to an announcement of peace, land for the peasants, and a new Government of which he was the head. For Russia had a ruler once again; and Bolshevism had created a synthetic substitute for the Czar's authority. His long exile was over; Swiss lodgings and Finnish hide-outs lay far behind him now. "It makes one dizzy," as he said that morning; and as he said it, speaking in German, he made the sign of the cross before his face.

NINETEEN
NINETEEN

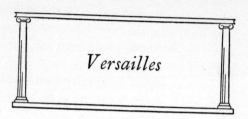

Versailles

It was past midsummer; and though the thunder of the war died on the distance, a shattered world still rocked to the long swell. The clouds hung low over a world of broken lives in which eight million men had died, of endless vistas of annihilation, towns without recognisable remains, the sea-floor littered with dead shipping, and a lunar landscape of inhuman surfaces where fields had been. Death, disease, and devastation stalked almost uncontrolled among the scared survivors with the crash still ringing in their ears, as they surveyed a world whose map was a delirium of fragmented empires. Russia had passed before the end was reached; and the disappearance of all organised resistance in the east encouraged Germany, whose powers were still unimpaired, to dictate a peace-treaty of meticulous brutality at Brest-Litovsk that stripped its helpless adversary of six provinces. Turkey was resolved into its elements; and Austria disintegrated almost without pressure into those national components which the Hapsburg nexus, now dissolved, had somehow contrived to hold together. The German Empire had been too much the creature of armed victory to survive defeat; and when its straining armies crumbled on the long line from the North Sea to Switzerland and its fleet mutinied in preference to a last encounter with the British Navy, the Teutonic edifice collapsed, its Emperor no more than the faint throb of a receding motor-engine in the direction of the Dutch frontier and its government a hurried rush of dazed and apologetic republicans.

That was the world whose outlines became dimly visible behind the storm-wrack of 1918. But the picture was not yet composed. It was still lacking in precision, although there was no shortage of eager hands to paint it, as the springtime of 1919 turned to summer and the Peace Conference still kept the delegates in Paris. They had been there for months. For it was not quite so easy to remake the world as it had looked a few weeks earlier to thoughtful gentlemen in libraries with maps before them. That discovery dawned painfully upon the President of the United States, who had crossed the ocean to apply the principles that he enunciated so unfalteringly from the White House. But as he negotiated the steep descent from theory to practice, from the sweeping aphorisms of his Fourteen Points to the precisely worded clauses of a peace-treaty, he discovered (as educationalists sometimes do) that it is considerably easier to impart than to apply instruction. The thoughtful silence of the White House was replaced by the crowded roar of Paris, where the markings on his maps came suddenly to life in the awkward form of eager deputations and excited advocates pleading feverishly for their racial prejudices or for the strict letter of diplomatic bargains, as he sat there listening politely with his fine head and sympathetic manner. He still had his principles, of course. But the worst of it was that they were hard to follow through the intervening jungle of detail. Mr. Wilson never lost his grasp of principle; but

[318]

there was so much detail in treaty-making; and, as another academic wrote of him with the disparagement that frequently moves learned men towards one another, "he could have preached a sermon on any of them or have addressed a stately prayer to the Almighty for their fulfilment; but he could not frame their concrete application to the actual state of Europe." Yet if Mr. Wilson could not, others could; and the business of treaty-making proceeded under his lofty inspiration.

The President had come to Europe with a weight of prestige far exceeding anything that his most convinced supporters in the United States had ever succeeded in imposing on their own countrymen. For American enthusiasms are tempered with a sane irreverence. The New World rarely keeps its face entirely straight about the exploits of its children; and Republicans were galled (and even Democrats found it a shade oppressive), when Europe greeted Mr. Wilson as a new Messiah. But that was how he seemed to Europe, where four years of war had debarred public men from the normal processes of cerebration. For Mr. Wilson positively thought. That was quite evident; and, what was more, his thought was lofty. This quality enthroned him in the public mind of Europe as a modern Moses, who enjoyed the singular advantage over his predecessor that he composed his own Commandments. Their luminous provisions, it was hoped, would guide the people through the wilderness of devastation which the war had left into a Land of Promise, where their dreams would all come true. That, indeed, had been his hope as well. But when the way was hard to find and he began to flag, his hands were stayed up on either side by his two companions, who were strange company for college presidents to keep. They were both lawyers, since France and England were more apt to choose their leaders from the law-courts than from the lecture-

room. But Mr. Lloyd George had far outgrown his old profession; and M. Clemenceau was more, much more than an
astringent lawyer-politician revelling in confrontations,
duels, acid witticisms, and exciting interpellations. For the
old man, with his unchanging mask and the gloved hands
perpetually clasped in front of him, was France itself, the
France of which "he felt" (as an observer wrote) "what
Pericles felt of Athens" and, like Clemenceau,

Broke to every known mischance, lifted over all
By the light sane joy of life, the buckler of the Gaul,
Furious in luxury, merciless in toil,
Terrible with strength that draws from her tireless soil.

That soil had already known the deadly pressure of invading German armies twice in his lifetime; and M. Clemenceau was fixed in his resolve that France should be made
safe for Frenchmen.

It was a modest aspiration compared with Mr. Wilson's
larger vision of a world made safe for his political ideals
as a democrat: but it would suffice for France—and for a
simple sense of justice. Mr. Lloyd George's views ranged
more widely with the more diffused interests and aspirations
of the British Empire of which, by a strange paradox, he
was now the incarnation; and he enforced them with that
"unerring, almost medium-like, sensibility to every one immediately round him . . . with six or seven senses not
available to ordinary men, judging character, motive, and
subconscious impulse, perceiving what each was thinking and
even what each was going to say next, and compounding
with telepathic instinct the argument or appeal best suited
to the vanity, weakness, or self-interest of his immediate
auditor." That was an unkind economist's shrewd diagnosis
of the Prime Minister. But human qualities are often un-

congenial to economics; and the unchanging colour of his mind was infinitely more significant than his rainbow method, with which it was richly overlaid. One of his ambassadors wrote later of that "invincible devotion to what he conceived to be the oppressed," which underlay the thinking of his whole career. For a steady bias against privilege was Mr. Lloyd George's strongest prejudice; and after a prolonged crusade on behalf of a variety of underdogs— "It has been all the same to me whether he was an underpaid agricultural labourer, a sick workman, an infirm and broken old man or woman, who had given their lives to the country, a poor slum-dweller, or a small nation harried by voracious Empires"—he found himself crusading in a war which he rightly believed to be a war for freedom and in the making of a peace which must take the form, if they were logical, of an emancipation.

To do them justice, that was precisely what it did, since the new frontiers of Europe embodied in the Treaty of Versailles and its subsidiaries left barely 3 per cent. of its population under foreign rule. Traced by those resourceful hands, a new state-system recorded the accomplished facts of 1918—the disintegration of the Austrian and Russian Empires into a series of new nationalities, the French recovery of Alsace-Lorraine, the German loss of colonies that German sea-power had been unable to retain, and the destruction of those weapons which Germany in desperation had systematically abused. The picture had its imperfections, since it was anything but easy to resurrect submerged nationalities without doing some violence to their surroundings. Besides, there was an undue tendency to overemphasise German ability to pay for all the wrong that German violence had done. But even that was comprehensible. For while the shattered skeletons of broken towns grinned nakedly from the French countryside, Germany was quite intact. A strict accounting in such circumstances might reasonably be expected to lead to wild arithmetic; and the peace-treaty was no more than a faithful reproduction of the world's mind in 1919.

But one portion of it was more, far more than that. For if the greater part of its provisions were a mere record of the situation which the war had left, there was one deliberate and conscious effort at a contribution to an ampler future, in which the lawless jungle of international relations in the pre-war world might be replaced by an ordered society embodied in a League of Nations. Many minds converged upon the new ideal; the President collaborated with English lawyers and South Africans; and when the Covenant was framed, it almost seemed that the Allies had beaten more than Germany, that they had positively beaten war itself.

That was the picture swiftly painted by busy hands in Paris, as the year turned to midsummer; and they had a gallery in which the picture could be hung with admirable effect. For the great mirrors at Versailles were waiting, still waiting in the long vista beneath the painted ceiling, where the bright surface of the glass had once reflected German uniforms and German swords and cheering German faces, as the sharp note of Bismarck's voice proclaimed a German Empire in the French king's palace. That had been nearly fifty years ago, when the great square before the Château was full of halted troops and a gay company filed up the palace stairs between the drawn swords of two rigid lines of *Cuirassiers* and the stiff silhouette of Germany passed cheerfully across the glass. But now the mirrors would not have long to wait, since there were troops outside the palace once again. All Versailles was filled with the faint blue of France; and as the company trooped up the palace stairs that afternoon (it was June 28, 1919), they passed between

[322]

the drawn swords of *Cuirassiers*. But this time they did not wear spiked helmets, since the dull gleam of their breast-plates was topped by the tall, horsehair-crested casques of Austerlitz and Rezonville. For France was waiting, had been waiting there for nearly fifty years; and the great mirrors in King Louis' gallery had Germans to reflect once more that afternoon.

This time the Germans (there were two of them) were not in uniform. But two frock-coated men waited among the smiles and roses of the Nattiers until somebody told them to come in. Then they walked into a corner of the great gallery and sat in comfortable obscurity between Japan and Uruguay. The peace-treaty lay on a table; and when M. Clemenceau waved his gloved hand towards it, they left their places, drew fountain-pens (they had been more than half afraid of some distasteful trick about the pens, of writing implements to be provided by the gleeful population of Alsace-Lorraine), and signed for Germany. Mr. Wilson was the next to sign, followed by the British delegates; and then the French. All the world was signing now, and everybody talked at once, until a Bolivian walked over to the silent Germans and asked them for their autographs, followed by two Canadian enthusiasts for souvenirs. Outside the guns began to thunder out salutes in the summer air; the fountains on the terrace leapt in the sunshine; and in the Galerie des Glaces the watching Conference saw two black-coated Germans pass once again across the mirrors.

NINETEEN
TWENTY

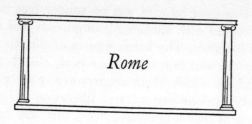

Rome

O F ALL THE EXQUISITE and awe-inspiring objects of the Italian countryside, its inhabitants had been, since their emancipation, by far the least impressive. For that stupendous aggregation of dignity and loveliness relegated them to the frankly secondary *rôle* of figures in the fore-ground of an incomparable landscape; and the eye took so much pleasure in the landscape that it forbore to dwell upon the figures. They were not asked to be impressive, because that was done for them by the background; and it was so indisputable that they had a past that it was almost an impertinence to wonder if they had a future.

So long as they had been understood to groan beneath a foreign and even (in Naples and the Romagna) a native tyrant's heel, a certain wistful charm hung round them. Misgovernment rewards its victims by making them appear romantic, lending to the Russian *moujik* or the Roman *pifferaro* pictorial attractions which evaporate as soon as the same individual recurs as a cloth-capped worker on a collective farm or a citizen of the United States. That is, per-

haps, the price men pay for freedom; and the Italians paid
it in full. For their country was no sooner free than its inhabitants ceased with alarming promptitude and thorough-
ness to be romantic. The heroic figures of the *Risorgimento*
faded into the vast canvas of their past, absorbed into the
background by which their countrymen were perpetually
dwarfed. Even their two wars of liberation were not quite
so romantic as they might have been, since the first proved
upon examination to have been won for them by France and
the second by Prussia. These services went unrequited, since
the grateful beneficiaries of Napoleon III rewarded him for
making war against the Austrians on their behalf by main-
taining a severe neutrality in his death-struggle with Germany and afterwards repaid the Prussians by intervening
in a later war on the opposing side. For the Italians were
strictly unromantic in affairs. Their politics became an unimpressive variant upon the normal Continental model, and
their international appearances were almost uniformly ineffective. An ill-judged experiment in empire-building covered them with public shame, when the untutored Abys-
sinians were able to repel an Italian invasion with ignominy;
and their forcible extrusion of the Turks from Tripoli was
not much more impressive. In diplomacy their country
ranked as a member of the Triple Alliance; but if the truth
were told, Italy was generally felt to be a Great Power only
by courtesy.

This slight inferiority was scarcely modified by their proceedings in the course of the World War. Its outbreak
found them reluctant to take sides with either group in spite
of the enticing circumstance that they were allied to one and
highly friendly with the other. But the Italian attitude remained severely rational (in striking contradiction of the
popular belief in ardent and impulsive Latins) until the relative advantages of joining either side had been precisely

ascertained. Since the Allies could plainly offer them more Austrian territory than Austria was willing to concede, their choice was manifest; and nine months after the outbreak of war the Italian tricolour fluttered among the Allied flags.

Their intervention, which took the highly exacting form of mountain warfare in an Alpine area, was largely unproductive in a military sense, although the casualties were heavy and their operations detained considerable numbers of Austrians from other battle-fronts. But in 1917 their slow progress was arrested by an Austro-German blow at Caporetto, in which they lost a quarter of a million prisoners and were swept far behind their own frontier. This humiliation was redeemed with Anglo-French assistance by a renewed advance in the last fortnight of the war. But though the war was won, it was impossible to say that it had raised Italian prestige. The Peace Conference reflected this eclipse; and Mr. Wilson scrutinised without enthusiasm the terms of the Italian bargain with the Allies. Their territorial gains were ample, and Italy resumed the spreading confines of *Italia irredenta*. But Italian appetites were stimulated by the spectacle of a world in which so many frontiers seemed to be so fluid; and as the war was safely over, Italy became extremely warlike.

This development coincided with an exciting reconstruction of their internal order. Democratic government, always a shade precarious in Latin countries, soon proved itself unequal to the effort of directing Italy through the rough waters of the post-war ferment. A touch of Bolshevist infection raised Italian temperatures to a dangerous height; and an antidote was found in the picturesque, though no less violent, proceedings of Benito Mussolini's *Fascio di Combattimento*. This eager publicist, named by an enthusiastic parent after a Mexican republican, had run in less than twenty years through the whole revolutionary gamut. Starting life among the Socialists, he served a brisk apprenticeship of agitation and imprisonment. His advocacy of opinions that failed to win majorities inspired him with a strong distaste for Parliamentary methods, to which Sorel's philosophy of Syndicalism seemed to provide a sound (if not strictly Marxian) alternative. But the pale goddesses of international Socialism failed to satisfy his growing patriotic sense; and his evolution was accelerated by the war, during which his drift from orthodoxy towards patriotism became manifest. His violence was now transferred to the expression of patriotic views. A *"Fascio* of Revolutionary Action" was formed to work for intervention on the side of the Allies and, by a pleasing irony, the first *Fascisti* campaigned against autocracy.

The flux of post-war politics evoked a repetition of his method, and once more a *Fascio di Combattimento* was formed. But this time its objectives were strictly national. For Mussolini had now evolved a patriotic form of Syndicalism, in which Sorel was flavoured with a strong admixture of D'Annunzio. That was the creed, half patriotic and half anti-Communist, in which black-shirted men, after an interlude of strike-breaking and faction fights, marched thousands strong on Rome, installed their chief in office under the thin shelter of the monarchy, and began the reign of Fascism. For the first time in European history a revolution of the Right had been effected with the apparatus associated with revolutions of the Left. That was the distinctive quality of Fascism. Like the Communists in Russia, Mussolini installed the dictatorship of an armed party; and Italy, where arms were held in high respect, enjoyed the experiment. Most Europeans were habituated by the war to state omnipotence; and Mussolini had managed to remake the state after their own image. It promised an exciting age of rousing spectacles, of public works, and of bright uniforms replacing the drab costume of democracy. It was incontestably Italian; and although there was a free employment of Roman terminology, Italy was heartened by a sense that it was free at last from that immense and overwhelming past which Marinetti and the Futurists found so discouraging. But other forms of freedom were less readily discernible, though this circumstance was not unduly distressing to large numbers of Italians whose acquaintance with liberty had, after all, been brief. To European eyes Italy receded once again beneath a modernised example of those tyrannies with which it was so long familiar; and the splendid gesture of the *Duce* failed to awe more sceptical observers. For when he visited an Allied capital that year with the full panoply of iron mouth and rolling eye, Mr. Asquith asked the Prime Minister what he thought of Mussolini. "A lunatic," said Mr. Bonar Law.

NINETEEN
THIRTY–THREE

1. Berlin, NW.

A TONGUE OF FLAME crept up the heavy curtain by the door of the refreshment-room, and in the darkness a strange figure flitted silently across the floor towards the pale rectangle of the broken window by which it had climbed in. In the draught near the window something was still sputtering on a table, and the intruder stood there for an instant fumbling with the window-curtain. Then he vanished into the dark building, ran across a lobby, and found himself confronting the pale marble bulk of Kaiser Wilhelm I. That noble effigy stood glimmering uncertainly in the dim light of a glass roof; but a brief inspection satisfied its latest visitor, since Pfuhl's *chef d'œuvre* had nothing in the least inflammable about it. His subsequent proceedings, if the story which he was reported to have told to the police could be believed, were no less creditable to his ingenuity and physical resource than to his narrative ability, which was replaced at later stages of his singular career by monosyllabic answers in an unintelligible blend of Dutch and German. For this shock-headed labourer with defective eyesight and a foolish laugh was stated (and believed by the police) to have occupied the next eighteen minutes in the empty rooms of a dark building in a foreign capital, which he had never visited before, in ways that would have done the highest credit to a syndicate of trained incendiaries with a more adequate equipment than a single packet of fire-lighters and an intimate acquaintance with its combustible possibilities. It was supposed that, after stripping to the waist he set fire to his shirt, returned to the refreshment-room, entered a pantry, knew by some divination where they kept the linen, found a tablecloth, and lit it with his burning underwear. Then he ran downstairs, kicked in a glass door without injury to toes that were almost protruding from his boots, and was preserved by the same magic from a single scratch in crawling through the broken pane. Encouraged by this miracle, he smashed another pane of glass downstairs, set fire to some towels, and trailed them after him. Returning to the upper floor, he found himself once more confronted by the marble Emperor whom nothing could ignite. But his discarded clothes were lying on the floor of the dim gallery; and presently the strange, half-naked figure with a blazing jacket in its hand appeared in the great semicircle of the Reichstag. It stood where German Chancellors had stood to speak for nearly forty years; and the last occupant of the tribune was Marinus van der Lubbe busily engaged in setting fire to a curtain. This modest conflagration fired the hall with a rapidity and an impressive detonation that were hardly explicable without further miracles or the adventitious aid of celluloid in strips and liquid chemicals unknown to van der Lubbe. But while the Chamber filled mysteriously with a burning haze, that amateur incendiary was setting fire to a leather sofa; and as he ran into the arms of his pursuers, an explosion sent the Reichstag up in flames.

[336]

It was a crowded evening; and the new Minister of the Interior, who drove up in his car eight minutes later, was instantly convinced that it was all the work of Communists. He added that he wished the rest of the world had seen it as clearly; but other people were not always equal to Captain Göring's mental processes. It was not quite so easy for the world to understand precisely why the Communists should choose to burn down the Reichstag six days before a General Election in which they had every prospect of adding to their strength on the benches of the doomed building. For they had increased their poll quite steadily in recent years; and even Communists were hardly likely to overturn the Parliamentary chess-board while the game was going in their favour. Besides, it was a little difficult to lay a finger on the practical utility of that amazing conflagration. What purpose was it designed to serve? A startled public was informed that it was to have been the signal for a Communist rising. But though the signal was duly given, no rising followed. The Communists, it seemed, were unresponsive to their own instructions; and their leader was so negligent as to be having supper in a public place at the decisive moment. When a waiter told him of the fire, he did not leap to revolutionary action, but took a tram and positively went to have a look at it. Then he played a quiet game of Skat with someone in a café and went to bed—strange conduct for a leader of revolt.

But other persons found the signal more inspiring, since by a pleasing chance the Nazi trinity were in Berlin. Though polling-day was imminent, no election meeting had been fixed on February 27 for Captain Göring, Dr. Goebbels, or Herr Hitler; and all three were quickly on the spot. The Captain's instinct told him that Communists had been at work; and Hitler, who was rarely grateful to the Communists, piously informed an interested bystander that

[337]

"this is a God-given signal! If this fire, as I believe, turns out to be the handiwork of Communists, then there is nothing that shall stop us from crushing out this murder pest with an iron fist." He added that his happy interlocutor was privileged to witness the beginning of a great new epoch in German history. "This fire," he said, "is the beginning"; and he spoke the truth.

For that surprising evening saw the birth of his supreme authority; and Adolf Hitler was the grateful beneficiary of the Reichstag fire. Unlike the Communists, his party had been losing strength; but the sudden shock restored its prospects, and it rose like a phœnix from the ashes of the Reichstag. Indeed, the signal upon which the revolutionaries so strangely failed to act was acted on with such rapidity by the saviours of society that it might almost have been their own. For that questionable conflagration was followed by innumerable arrests and an electoral majority that authorised the National Socialists to save Germany from anything and anybody; and as they were unarmed, it was thought best to save her from the Jews.

Half terrorised and half consenting, the German mind collapsed into hysteria; and the repulsive antics of its latest masters were substituted for the ordered processes of government. The German gift for politics was never strong. Their attempt to reproduce the Revolution of 1848 beyond the Rhine had been half-hearted and grotesque; and Russian models had no more success, when followed in the post-war years by Berlin Spartacists or the Munich Soviet. The public mind was far too deeply saddened by the war for rational reflections; and as the years went by, it came increasingly to seek consolation in a comforting belief that Germany had not been beaten. True, she had not won the war. But that, they argued, was the consequence of a momentary paralysis of her armed forces attributable to the base activities of traitors, Socialists, and Jews. Drugged by this fantasy, her patriotic pulse began to throb again; and all the old beliefs revived. The voices that had whispered to excited lecturers in pre-war classrooms buzzed in their ears once more. The strong Pan-German faith of Treitschke, Bernhardi's *Weltmacht oder Niedergang* and, faint and far, the voice of Nietzsche praising force and the blonde *Übermensch* resumed their lullaby, singing the German intellect to sleep. The melody was slightly modernised and provided with a new libretto by the endless ruminations of Oswald Spengler, who emerged from a vast sea of amateurish erudition with the happy sense of having written *"the* philosophy of our time" and answered the riddle of the ages by a freer use of historical analogies than would always bear examination by less impulsive minds. But that excited *Oberlehrer* was unfriendly to the excessive use of the intelligence, since it appertained to "the parasitical city-dweller, traditionless, utterly matter-of-fact, religionless, clever, unfruitful, deeply contemptuous of the countryman, and especially of that highest form of countryman, the country gentleman." This apotheosis of the Prussian *Junker* was supported by a formidable apparatus of miscellaneous information, in which the author's fancy played at large over the face of history, appropriating any creditable achievements to the German genius and leaving Asiatic influence to take the blame for anything that did not chance to meet with his approval.

The resulting thesis bore a marked resemblance to the eccentric lucubrations of Houston Chamberlain, who had entertained the pre-war generation by detecting Teutonic features in types so far apart as Jesus Christ and Dante. A fevered racialism was implanted in the German mind by the unhappy circumstance of having come into the world a little late as a Great Power. Long centuries of history convinced the French that they were Frenchmen and that it was a satisfying thing to be. But Germans felt no such assurance, since the brief annals of United Germany had begun no further back than Bismarck in their own fathers' lifetime. It almost seemed that, if they were not careful, they might revert to the comparatively humble rank of Saxons, Mecklenburgers, or Bavarians with the inferiority attaching to membership of inconsiderable states; and they combated this dreaded possibility with a desperate insistence upon their nationality, which ranged far beyond the facts of German history into a *hinterland* of highly dubious ethnology. When this could be combined with a philosophy that banned the urban worker and the Jew (who were both lamentably apt to vote for Socialists), its popularity was quite assured with those discouraged layers of society which defeat and the Republic had eclipsed. For after the catastrophe, severely aggravated by injudicious and avoidable manipulations of the German currency, the country was full of broken gentlemen and of others, no less broken, who could be described with less certainty as gentlemen. This sediment was wholly out of sympathy with the halfhearted experiment of German democracy and grasped at an alternative philosophy that seemed to satisfy its selfesteem. They gravitated towards groups devoted to furtive patriotic action and stimulated by a taste for their own racial origins, which sometimes flowered in such eccentricities as a deliberate return to Wotan and the primeval figures of the pagan North in preference to Christianity by reason of the latter's questionable association with the East and an unsatisfactory war-record.

But these Wagnerian experiments were less significant than their political activities, which culminated in the singular career of Adolf Hitler. An Austrian by birth, he became feverishly German by conviction; and his racial consciousness was gravely offended by the failure of his Jewish fellow-subjects to conform to the mysterious requirements of what he supposed to be the German race. Besides, there was a lamentable lack of uniformity about the population of Vienna, inherent in the presence of Czech, Polish, Magyar, and Croatian subjects of the Hapsburg Empire; and he found Munich more congenial. This *hegira* involved him in war-service as a volunteer in a German unit; and he emerged from the catastrophe as a Bavarian ex-serviceman addicted to extreme opinions. The unrestful sea of post-war politics invited him, and he plunged happily into those troubled waters with an equipment that consisted of unusual powers of public speech, a neurotic taste for extreme virility, and a fanatical distaste for democrats, Jews, Socialists, and anything that was not demonstrably German. This stock-in-trade was not particularly marketable in the first years of the Republic; and in its early stages the career of the National Socialist Party was obscure and unrewarding. But as German politics degenerated and street-fighting became the normal form of public controversy, it gained on its competitors. Russian Communists and Italian Fascists had already shown the way to the dictatorship of an armed party; and his brown-shirted bravoes gradually won attention. Their creed was an exaggeration of the Germanism that prevailed in Opposition circles, and a fanatical abhorrence of that Communism with which the German General Staff had so deftly impregnated Russia in 1917; and the public violence of their proceedings was less shocking to Teutonic feelings than to more experienced democracies. The whirlpool of political events floated him into office. But until the evening of the Reichstag fire he was no more than a mere office-holder. Twelve hours later he was the autocrat of Germany; and that dubious event produced a form of government that combined a political method borrowed from the Communists with hectic patriotism and a fair share of collectivist ideals.

The Nazi monarchy (for it was nothing less) soon set about to reassure the shrinking German mind as to the international significance of Germany. This was achieved by the official adoption of a philosophy of force and by strenuous reiterations of the German claim to disregard the peace-treaty, as well as of the inalienable German right to anything that German destiny seemed to require. Vigorous rearmament and a vociferous repudiation of the world's attempt to substitute the rule of law in international affairs for the survival of the fittest rendered Germany once more an object of alarm in Europe, as German youth prepared itself quite openly for war (and very little else) and German womanhood was relegated to the secondary *rôle* of tribal womanhood in war-time. These exercises turned the eyes of Europe with growing apprehension towards Berlin; and though the last experiment of the same nature by Kaiser Wilhelm was not encouraging in its results, Germany recovered its long-lost confidence, and Germans were prepared to forgive the regime its more obvious shortcomings in return for that achievement. Like Communism, it had enthroned a single party in control of the whole nation; and it maintained itself by a vast exercise of propaganda, by ceaseless broadcasting and popular parades and an enormous parody of the processes of democracy in plebiscites and forced elections. For armed demagogy is rather a disease to which democracies are subject than an alternative and distinct system of government. The recorded symptoms are a party tyranny and a complete elimination of freedom, a prolongation of the war-time omnipotence of the state, and a systematic concentration on the mind of youth. But as all diseases have their cycles, democracy may yet outgrow this strange corruption of itself.

BERLIN, NW.

The world beyond the German frontier was promptly faced with an armed resurrection of the old Germany and a harsh restatement (in instalments) of those ideals which they had laboured to suppress in the World War. The nobler, no less than the more questionable, aspects of the European settlement of 1919 were directly challenged; and a world at peace became almost at once a world in uneasy argument with war-makers.

2. Washington, D. C.

WOULD THE DEPRESSION never end? It had all come so suddenly in the disastrous Fall of 1929, when stock prices showed a complete unconsciousness of Professor Irving Fisher's recently expressed opinion that they had reached "what looks like a permanently high plateau" by dropping nearly out of sight over a precipice of which nobody could see the bottom. The Fall of Man was nothing to it; and they fell with a Miltonic splendour and rather more than Lucifer's rapidity, as

> *from morn*
> *To noon he fell, from noon to dewy eve,*
> *A summer's day, and with the setting sun*
> *Dropt from the zenith, like a falling star.*

The racing tape-machines lagged far behind the market, which incontinently crumpled up in spite of Mr. Mitchell's diagnosis that the National City Bank of New York knew of nothing fundamentally wrong with it. Indeed, it dropped so far that it appeared to be resolved upon exploring its own fundamentals, ignoring Mr. Lamont's gallant explanation that these untoward events were due to a "technical condition of the market," which somehow seemed inadequate to the alarming circumstance that no less than twelve million shares changed hands that day. That was on Thursday, October 24. But five days later sales had mounted to sixteen millions and prices vanished out of sight, taking innumerable hopes, ambitions, savings, enterprises, and careers with them. The whole of the United States—large operators, window-cleaners, business men, clerks in department stores, waitresses, and boot-blacks—had backed the stock market to win. The steady march of richly publicised prosperity encouraged them to wager all they had earned or (better still) could borrow that the country would still grow more prosperous. It looked as though it would. With Mr. Coolidge at the helm and high-power salesmanship vociferating its appeals to purchase luxuries they could not pay for and bonds they did not understand, it was so tempting to sit back and have their fortunes made by the unalterable destiny of the United States. The prophets were unanimous. New industries sprang up on every hand and blossomed like the rose. Automobiles swarmed on the new highways; motion-pictures flickered all day long, while their electrics flashed at every street-corner; and radio sang, whistled, syncopated, preached, hallooed, and droned its way into innumerable homes. Stock values soared in sympathy with this tropical proliferation of new enterprises; and it seemed so simple to acquire a share in it by falling into step beside the magnates in their easy march towards a golden dawn.

That was the happy mood of the United States, when Mr. Coolidge sat primly in the White House and Mr. Wilson's life drained silently away in a quiet house on S Street, from which he watched the wreck of all his hopes

[345]

and the repudiation of the word that he had pledged in Paris by the withdrawal of his countrymen from practical participation in the world's affairs. It was his tragedy, and Europe's too. But the Republicans were in control once more; and the United States in the gay decade of prosperity were disinclined to dwell on tragedies. Their ears were not attuned to minor airs. Indeed, there was no need for them to hear any, with values soaring and new automobiles pullulating and a carnival of real estate in Florida and the swift rise of Hollywood to world-power. A gay community, devoting rather more of its activities to the pursuit of happiness than to an academic liberty which unreasonable persons like the Bolsheviks might use to interfere with the life-giving flow of business, enjoyed itself immensely. Their outlook had become frankly local once again; and they saw Europe, where the lean shadow of Mr. Wilson had once been cast so impressively, as a mere playground in which their dollars bought more of the local currency than was entirely good for them and guileful aliens displayed an unaccountable reluctance to repay that generous, if strictly temporary, accommodation which had been the foremost contribution of the United States towards a common cause. The cause, however, was no longer common; and an air of virtuous detachment brooded once again over American policy. For the United States had more and better things at home to think of. If their eyes ever strayed beyond their borders now, it was in the opposite direction, where the unearthly silhouettes favoured by Japanese naval designers manœuvred in the low Pacific mist. But they were not greatly interested by anything outside the United States; and the carnival of their prosperity continued until the October day in 1929, on which the bottom of the stock market astonished everyone by falling out.

That calamity was the first link in a long chain of interlocked disasters, whose melancholy and successive impact reverberated with the depressing sequence of a line of shunting freight-cars. For as the ruined speculators ceased to order goods for which they could no longer hope to pay, tradesmen were left without their customers, and manufacturers discovered suddenly that there was not the slightest reason why they should go on manufacturing. Those simple facts, combined with the unhappy circumstance that foreign countries could not afford to buy high-priced American products, evoked the universal shadow which crept over the United States; and the depression had arrived.

It had all come so suddenly; but, to all appearances, there was no reason why it should ever go. Well-meaning persons made vague passes at it. Mr. Hoover was convinced at intervals that confidence had been restored; and business leaders exhausted the vocabulary of hope. But nobody believed them now; and hope was still deferred and hearts were sick, when a despairing country turned once more towards the Democrats. It was not altogether clear what they could do. But Mr. Franklin Roosevelt seemed full of bright, though somewhat undefined, expedients, collectively described as a 'New Deal'; and Washington was waiting hopefully in 1933 for the performance to begin.

It was deferred, with fatal consequences, by those provisions of the Constitution which moved a disrespectful British visitor to term it the one genuine antique in the United States. For in the interval prescribed by eighteenth-century deliberation in order to permit the post-chaises and berlines of legislators to reach Washington from outlying points, the whole economic fabric of the United States collapsed. Bank-failures were already frequent over those eccentric areas of banking in which anyone with cash enough to pay a sign-painter could start a local bank; and the paralysis of motor-manufacturing had closed the doors of every bank in Detroit. But these were special cases; and there seemed no compelling reason why the distemper should extend, until the wild stampede of the last week that Mr. Hoover spent at the White House. Excited Governors began to gratify reporters with midnight conferences of bank presidents; and, conscious of their duty, the reporters passed on the excitement. Scared depositors opened their newspapers to read that the trustees of all their money had been closeted with the authorities; and as their trust in bankers was now strictly limited, it was not long before quiet crowds assembled on the pavements outside down-town banks to look at the armed guards, who stood behind the door in leather coats fingering their automatics and watching the cashiers shuffle their property across the counter to fortunate depositors. That was how the runs began, because nobody could trust a banker, since they had come to think of bankers as individuals who made question-able fortunes by lending other people's money on inadequate security in the intervals of selling worthless bonds to their confiding customers; and there was no one else for them to trust under a Constitution which decreed a fatal inter-regnum between the effective term of one President and the installation of the next.

Then Mr. Roosevelt smiled his way into the White House one gusty afternoon in March, 1933; and the new reign began. Its first accompaniment was the melancholy sound of closing banks. But no one seemed to mind, because it had occurred to some genius to call it a bank holiday; and there was a fine disposition to help one another through an uncomfortable episode, after which the Presidential miracles could begin. But would they? There were no misgivings at Washington that spring, and a devoted Congress proclaimed its loyalty as loudly as a Restoration Parliament. The air was full of new proposals and of unfamiliar faces, freely identified as members of Mr. Roosevelt's 'Brain Trust,' that happy band of rare spirits who positively thought about affairs. Their thought, indeed, was rarely turned towards the growing turmoil of the world beyond the United States, where Europe seemed to be reverting swiftly to its ancient self—the Germans to a tight-skinned oligarchy of men in uniform and the Russians to their ancestral ikon-worship, with the sole distinction that their ikons were now sacred pictures of Communist divinities. There was a respectful feeling for Great Britain, which had somehow contrived to weather such a storm as was now rocking the United States. But their minds were busy with their own problems, with the haunting riddle of the vast stoppage of production and the best method (if there was one) of controlling those immense economic units by which their lives were almost wholly shadowed since the transformation of the United States by joint-stock companies. The White House was to supersede Wall Street once again in the government of the United States; and Mr. Roosevelt, it was almost universally believed, would find a way. National discipline had been miraculously recovered; and the next item was to deal boldly with the depression. They felt sure that it could be done by legislation; and as they waited for the performance to begin, they turned hopefully towards the iron dome at Washington.

NINETEEN
THIRTY–SIX

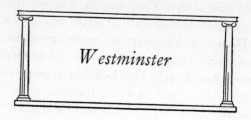

Westminster

ALL THE FACES in Trafalgar Square that winter afternoon looked eastwards, because that was where they would be coming from. Line after line of staring faces, packed in the roadway and piled round the plinth of the great column, turned towards the Strand and waited for the King to come. It seemed strange to be waiting for him there in the cold, because it was not long since they had stood in the same place to see him drive along the Strand through the spring sunshine to St. Paul's. That had been only a few months ago, when they were packed in cheerful rows behind the soldiers and passed the time listening to bands and watching cars go by with sudden glimpses of embroidered chests and epauletted shoulders bound for the Cathedral. They had stood there singing in the sunshine; and as they lined the gravelled roadway, the passing traffic gradually rose in quality and the crowd's note mounted to a cheerful roar. More cars, the Speaker's coach behind its ambling dray-horses, and an open carriage with the Prime Minister dressed for once in the bright plumage of his office and discarding the more uneventful aspect with which Mr. Ramsay MacDonald had stolen Tory hearts. He sat there smiling gaily with an unaccustomed air of nautical magnificence, followed by Dominion Premiers in more carriages and quite unaware of their happy tendency to acknowledge a fair proportion of his cheers. For London crowds are slow to recognise new faces; and as a comfortable glow of evening began to settle upon Mr. MacDonald's slightly circuitous career, the London streets were just beginning to know what he looked like. Then the royalties commenced; and two small Princesses in pink bonnets followed by a smiling couple, not long returned from honeymoon, took the long roar of cheering down the Strand. More Lifeguards, and the loudest cheer the day had yet produced brought on the best-known of all English Princes, looking a little lost in an enormous bearskin. Then they left off searching for individuals to cheer, and settled down to a brief processional interlude of mounted troops and full-dress uniforms, of trim Hussars and Lancer pennons dancing by, and the gleam, clank, and jingle of the guns, until the whole width of the roadway filled with the white torrent of a Sovereign's escort of Lifeguards. After them two happy figures in an open carriage behind the walking creams moved slowly through the friendly roar, and his people saw King George drive through the sunshine to St. Paul's.

It seemed such a short while ago that it was strange to stand there in the winter afternoon waiting for him to pass again. His Jubilee, launched almost tentatively as something in the nature of a family occasion designed to celebrate a private anniversary, had far outgrown its modest origins. The warmth of feeling, which packed the roaring streets that morning and sent cheerful multitudes to beat in waves against the palace railings night after night in friendly insistence upon a distant view of royal heads on a far-off balcony, came as a complete surprise. Yet it was not surprising that a generation which had lived through so much with him—the war, the troubled years of aftermath, the long depression, and the slow march towards recovery—combined to honour a survivor of unquestionable gallantry and, in honouring the King, to celebrate their own achievement.

There was nothing arrogant about their celebration, no flavour of the old delight in far-flung battle-lines. The taste of victory was only one degree less bitter than the flavour of defeat. But England felt that summer that it had somehow managed to live through an awkward stage in its long history. The German challenge had been faced and answered; and the strange amalgam of the Empire had survived the test, whilst its readjustment indicated the uncanny British aptitude for retaining nearly all the substance by a judicious sacrifice of those shadows to which peoples of more formal mind attach so much importance. Their own form of government was, they were happy to observe, unmodified in a world which had unlearnt so many democratic lessons that its English teachers began to wonder in their weaker moments whether they were right after all. They were inclined to think so, because there was not much in their own experience since the war ended to suggest that they were wrong so far as England was concerned. For the country had abstained from those experiments which other nations seemed to find so heartening; and its mental balance, no less than its material well-being, compared favourably with those prevailing on the Continent.

It had discarded the brisk experiment of Mr. Lloyd George's war-time dictatorship with a relief and promptitude that came ungenerously near to ingratitude. It had swung sharply away from the class heroics of the General Strike in the cold springtime of 1926. That was a blurred

and accidental composite of Trade Union officiousness, of
happy memories of settlements imposed in time of war upon
distracted ministers after much photographing on the door-
step of 10 Downing Street, of vague appetites for power
that seemed difficult of attainment by Parliamentary
methods, of a rash decision to try a pre-war weapon on a
war-hardened public. It failed because the post-war citizen
was less easily alarmed than his predecessors. If his trains
were stopped, he sat down on a bag to wait until somebody
came along and gave him a lift. If his newspapers failed
to arrive, he listened to the news by wireless. If his milk
was rationed, that was something that he had known before. Besides, the spear-head of the General Strike was its
attempt to immobilise the nation; and it failed because the
nation had learnt to drive a car. Petrol, in fine, defeated
steam; the common man defeated the aristocracy of Labour;
and England returned to the familiar routine of governing
itself by arithmetical majorities, of counting heads in preference to the more exciting Continental method of breaking
them.

A similar decorum attended its strong Conservative re-
vulsion five years later, when the cheerful spending of a
Labour Government was sharply arrested. Other nations,
faced by unpleasant economic situations, tended to the
higher forms of public drama. But Great Britain was
lamentably undramatic. The best that it could do in 1931
was a few hurried conferences of party leaders and a swift
change of government, followed by a General Election of
slightly overheated patriotism. Yet even that was deprived
of nearly all its drama by the unheroic circumstance that
Mr. MacDonald was willing to oblige by acting as his own
successor; and what tragedy could hope to cause a thrill, if
the same actor insisted upon playing hero as well as villain?

The simple processes of Parliamentary politics resumed,

with the sole difference that Opposition speakers now denounced a National instead of a Conservative Government. That was the nearest England came to the strange contagion of dictatorship, by which the stature of more backward races was stunted. The skies of nearly half the world had darkened beneath the beating wings of revolution, and they were still dark with tyranny. But, through it all, the British mind remained as incapable as ever of absorbing those explosive generalities that exercised a fatal fascination upon more receptive Continental intellects. A harsh distemper had replaced democracy in regions where it was not yet acclimatised with the most unappetising form of despotism. For beginners at the exacting art of self-government, substituting armed force for less exciting methods of establishing the general will, succumbed to tyrannies which were imperfectly disguised with demagogic showmanship. The wheel had come full circle; and in those countries, which had been shadowed a hundred years before by Metternich's police and the soft tread of Papal *sbirri,* the heavy step of despotism had resumed its sentry-go. But that was, after all, only a small part of the world; and free government retained its strongholds. France and the north were free; Spain stumbled into freedom; free men ruled all the world beyond the ocean; and Englishmen, untouched by the infection, retained their preference for democratic government, pausing that summer to survey their own performance without undue dissatisfaction. It had been achieved without the unhealthy discipline of organised hysteria; and they took pride in crowding voluntarily into the London streets to cheer a king of whom they were not in the least afraid.

An unaccustomed levity coloured their jubilation, and a warm May night afforded the unusual spectacle of Englishmen dancing in the streets, seated along kerbs in earnest conversation, wearing paper caps, and perched in cheerful tiers round the Piccadilly fountain to watch the dancing in the Circus, where gay pedestrians were celebrating the total absence of wheeled traffic as well as their sovereign's Jubilee. They were all genuinely grateful to him for the bright occasion. Besides, the last of all inventions annually brought the royal voice to their dinner-tables; and that miracle, by which the King of England regularly rounded off their Christmas dinner with a friendly word of elderly benevolence, had multiplied his contacts by millions. It made them feel as if he knew them all; and its kindly echo hung in their memories as they stood waiting in the cold for him to pass again.

All the faces in the square turned suddenly towards the Strand. This time there were no bands, no lines of soldiers along the street, nothing more to see than five policemen riding up the Strand before a draped gun-carriage and five bare-headed men walking hurriedly behind it. They walked quickly through the silence to keep up with the horses; and as they passed, the watching streets saw the new King go by. They had already learnt to know him better than they knew any of his subjects; and twenty years of active life had taught him almost all that there was to be known of them. For men of twice his age were lucky if they had seen half as much as his experience had crowded into a short lifetime; and they saw him hurry past, bare-headed and fair-haired. The strange little *cortège* passed quickly, crossed a corner of the square, and was gone. The light was failing as the gun-carriage went by on its way down to Westminster, where rigid men stood with bowed heads and arms, reversed to guard a king they could no longer serve; and the light faded from the sky.

Night fell on Europe, as the lights leapt out along the London streets. Beyond the Channel a bright tracery of lights showed Paris; lights were burning late in German factories; strong lights glared on the barbed wire and striped barriers of guarded frontiers; and further to the east dim pools of light showed in the empty squares of Leningrad. Beyond the ocean, as the winter light died from the sky above America, all the spangled avenues of the United States gleamed brightly, and the bright glare of headlights swept along their endless roads from sea to sea, racing the lighted windows of expresses as they moved across black distances; and while the world of 1936 lay waiting for the dawn, lights hurried through the night sky. The hours passed slowly in the great Hall at Westminster, where men stood stiffly with bowed heads beneath the tall flambeaux. But as the winter light crept through the quiet windows, the dawn came through the London trees again and the first light of a new day swept round the world.

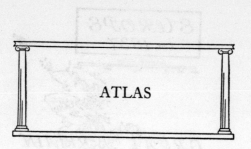

ATLAS

EUROPE
in 1837

English Miles

Finland

Helsingfors Cronstadt
St.Petersburg

RUSSIA

A
Poland

Galicia

AUSTRIAN
HUNGARY

EMPIRE Transylvania
Moldavia

Wallachia
Crimea
Sevastopol

Bulgaria
Montenegro
lia
Albania Constantinople

E M P I R E

Morea Smyrna
Athens

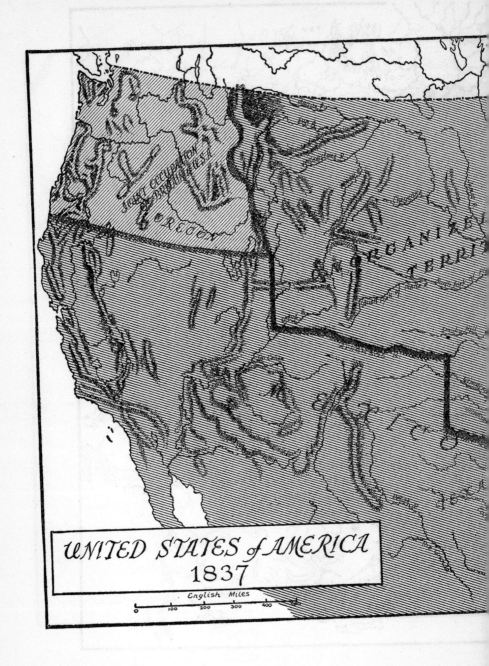

JOINT OCCUPATION OR BRITISH & U.S.

OREGON

UNORGANIZED TERRI

UNITED STATES of AMERICA
1837

English Miles
0   100   200   300   400

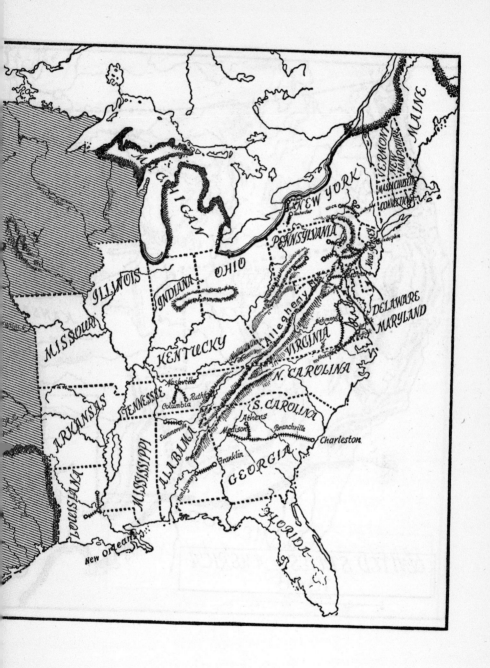

UNITED STATES of AMERICA
1848

English Miles

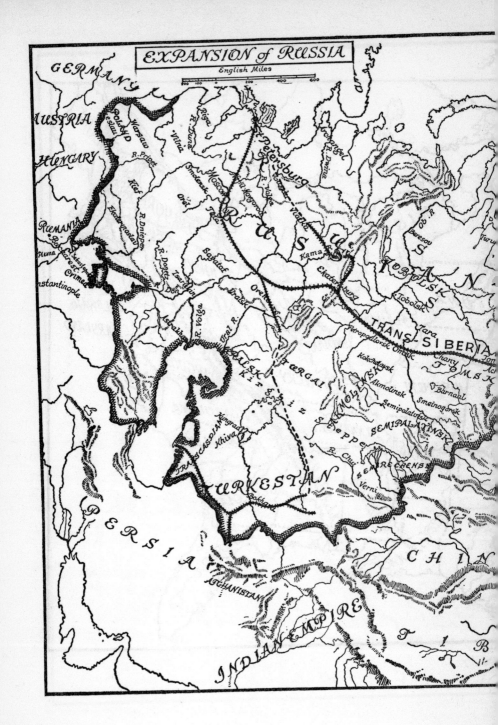

EXPANSION of RUSSIA

English Miles

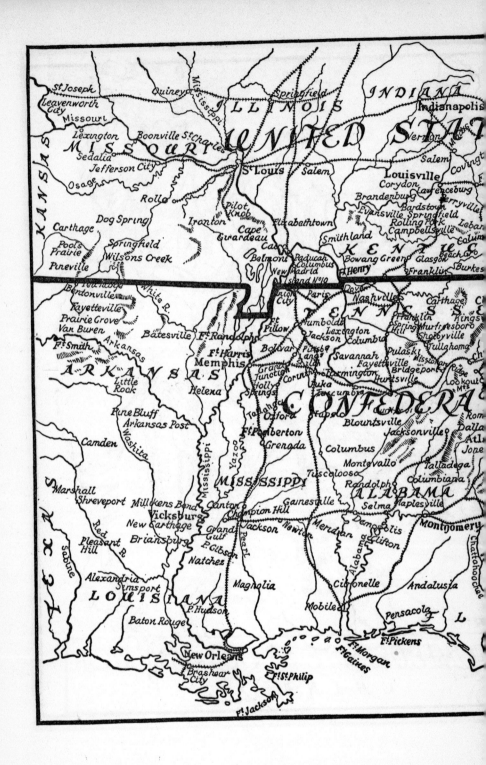

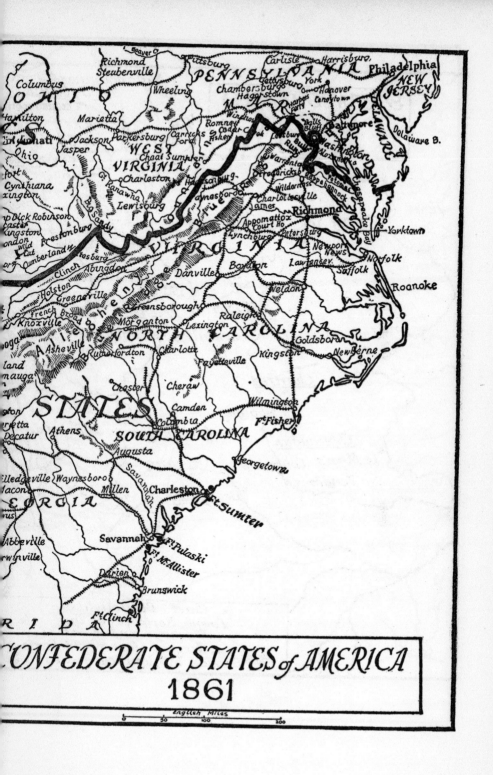

CONFEDERATE STATES of AMERICA
1861

English Miles
0   50   100   200

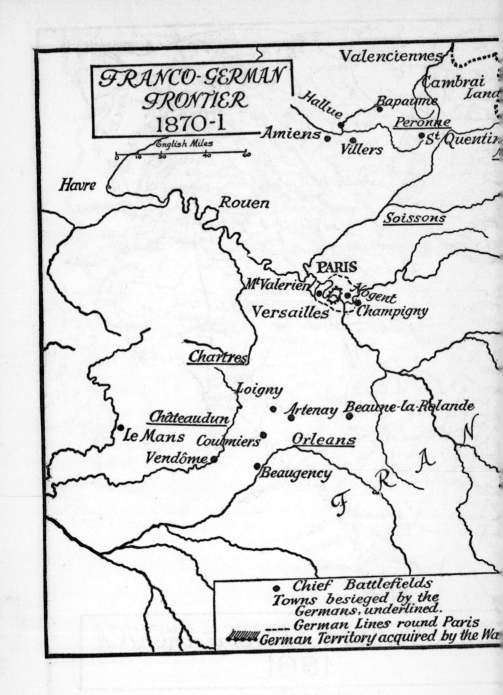

FRANCO-GERMAN
FRONTIER
1870-1

English Miles
0 10 20 40 60

Valenciennes

Cambrai
Land

Hallue
Bapaume

Peronne

Amiens
St Quentin

Villers

Havre

Rouen

Soissons

PARIS

Mt Valerien
Nogent

Versailles
Champigny

Chartres

Loigny

Artenay Beaune-la-Rolande

Châteaudun

Le Mans Coulmiers Orleans

Vendôme

Beaugency

F
R
A
N

● Chief Battlefields
Towns besieged by the
Germans, underlined.
---- German Lines round Paris
German Territory acquired by the War

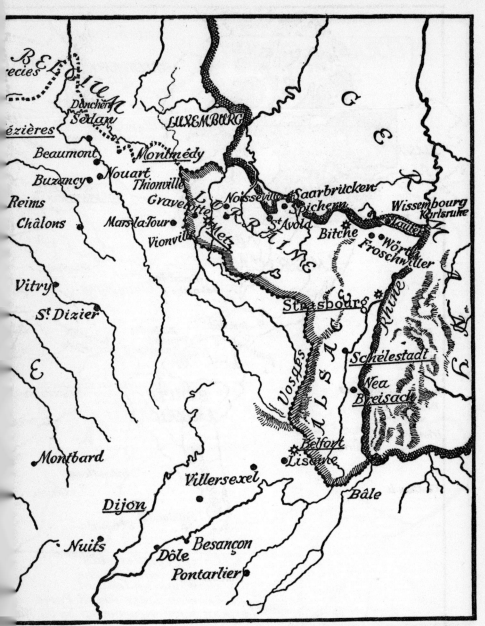

After Muir and Philip (Philip's Historical Atlas, Mediaeval and Modern)

GREENLAND

ALASKA

Dominion of
NORTH CANADA

Vancouver

AMERICA

Orkneys
Shetlands

UNITED
KINGDOM

Gibraltar

• Bermuda
Bakamas

Jamaica

Honduras

Barbados
Trinidad
Georgetown

Bathurst
Sierra
Leone

Cape Coast

• Palmyra

Christmas I

Penrhyn
Vostok

Marquesas

Friendly Is.

Pitcairn

• Chatham Is.

SOUTH
AMERICA

ARGENTINA

Falkland Is.

• Ascension

• St. Helena

Tristan d'Acunha

Gough

Sth Georgia

Sandwich Is.

S. Shetland

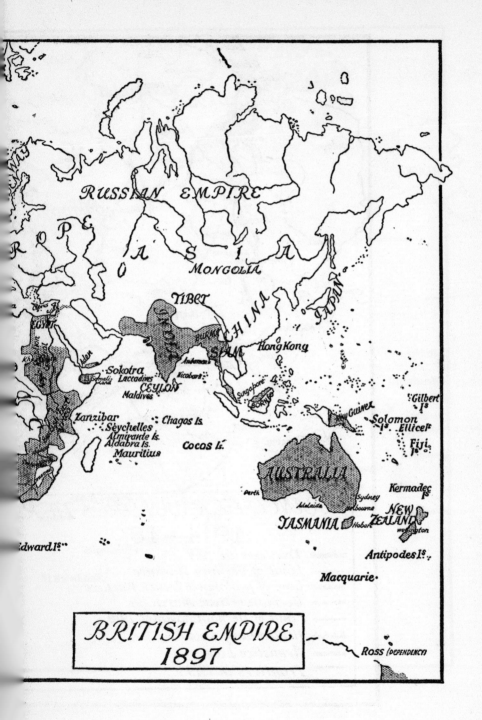

RUSSIAN EMPIRE

E
U
R
O
P
E

A S I A

MONGOLIA

TIBET

CHINA

JAPAN

INDIA

BURMA

SIAM

Hong Kong

EGYPT

Cyprus

Aden

Somali
Land

Sokotra

Laccadives

Andamans

Nicobars

CEYLON

Maldives

Singapore

BORNEO

New Guinea

Gilbert
Is.

Zanzibar

Seychelles

Chagos Is.

Solomon
Is.

Ellice Is.

Almirante Is.

Aldabra Is.

Mauritius

Cocos Is.

Fiji
Is.

AUSTRALIA

Perth

Kermadec
Is.

Adelaide

Sydney

Melbourne

NEW
ZEALAND

Wellington

TASMANIA

Hobart

Edward Is.

Antipodes Is.

Macquarie

BRITISH EMPIRE
1897

ROSS (DEPENDENCY)

FRANCO-GERMAN FRONTIER
1914 – 18

〰〰〰	Frontiers in 1914
------	Limit of German Advance
▬▬▬	Line of prolonged Trench Warfare
▬ ▬ ▬	German retreat March 1917
▬▬▬	Limit of German Advance 1918
▲▲▲▲	Hindenburg Line
⊞⊞⊞⊞	Armistice Line
- - - -	Frontiers in 1919

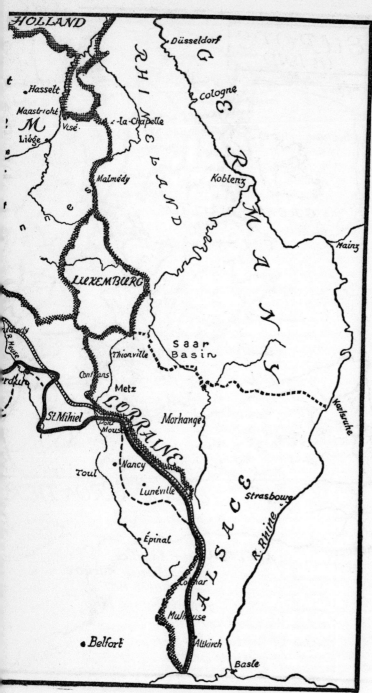

HOLLAND

Düsseldorf

Cologne

GERMANY

Hasselt

Maastricht

Liége · Visé

Aix-la-Chapelle

Malmédy

Koblenz

RHINELAND

Mainz

LUXEMBURG

Saar
Basin

Thionville

Karlsruhe

Confans

Metz

Verdun

St. Mihiel

Don
Mousso

Morhange

LORRAINE

Toul

Nancy

Lunéville

Strasbourg

Épinal

ALSACE

R. Rhine

Colmar

Mulhouse

Belfort

Altkirch

Basle

After Muir and Philip (Philip's Historical Atlas, Mediaeval and Modern)

EUROPE in 1919

English Miles

AUTHORITIES

Authorities

1837

1. Dawn. Sunrise in London on June 20, 1837, was at 3.42 a.m. Archbishop Howley and Lord Conyngham left Windsor Castle immediately after the death of William IV, which took place at 2.12 a.m. (*Girlhood of Queen Victoria*, i, 196) or 2.20 a.m. (C. C. F. Greville's *Journals of the Reigns of George IV and William IV*, iii, 406).

F. H. Skrine's *Expansion of Russia* (1915) contains a useful summary of Russian history, which may be supplemented from the Communist standpoint by M. N. Pokrovsky's *Brief History of Russia* (1933). Austria and Central Europe may be reconstructed from vol. vi of Prince Metternich's *Mémoires Documents et Ecrits Divers* (1883); and the facts are summarised in vol. i of Sir A. W. Ward's *Germany, 1815–1890* (1916). The situation of France is presented in outline by P. de la Gorce in *Louis Philippe* (1931). H. Butler Clarke's *Modern Spain* (1906) is an invaluable summary.

The United States in 1837 are outlined in vol. v of E. Channing's *History of the United States* (1930) and the authorities there cited.

2. Kensington. Details of the official messengers' arrival are to be found in Miss Wynn's *Diaries of a Lady of Quality* (1864). The Queen's own account of her accession is in *The Girlhood of Queen Victoria* (1912), i, 195–8, and her correspondence with King Leopold in vol. i of *The Letters of Queen Victoria* (1907). There is a useful summary of events in vol. iii of *Dictionary of National Biography:*

Supplement (1901), s.v. *Victoria,* and details in C. C. F. Greville's *Journals,* iii, 406–8, W. F. Monypenny's *Life of Disraeli,* i, 371, B. Disraeli's *Sybil,* i, cap. 6, and L. Strachey's *Queen Victoria* (1921).

The realities of English life are summarised in J. H. Clapham's *Economic History of Modern Britain: the Early Railway Age* (1926).

3. *Washington, D. C.* The leading figures and features of the Panic of 1837 may be studied in vol. v of E. Channing's *History of the United States,* vol. iv of Woodrow Wilson's *History of the American People* (1902), and E. M. Shepard's *Martin Van Buren* (1890); and details in vol. iii of J. G. Wilson's *Memorial History of the City of New York* (1893) and Henry James's *The American Scene* (1907) and *A Small Boy and Others* (1913).

Underlying factors are analysed in F. J. Turner's *The Frontier in American History* (1920), F. L. Paxson's *History of the American Frontier* (1924), and J. T. Adams' *Epic of America* (1932). Details of Louis Napoleon's visit are to be found in vol. ii of B. Jerrold's *Life of Napoleon III* (1875), F. H. Cheetham's *Louis Napoleon and the Genesis of the Second Empire* (1909), and *The Second Empire* (1922) by the present writer.

1848

1. *Windsor Castle.* The Queen's development may be studied in vol. ii of *The Girlhood of Queen Victoria* and vols. i and ii of *The Letters of Queen Victoria,* analysed in L. Strachey, *op. cit.,* and *Palmerston* (1926) and *The Queen and Mr. Gladstone* (1933) by the present writer; details in vols. i and ii of Sir T. Martin's *Life of the Prince Consort* (1875–6), *The Principal Speeches and Addresses of H.R.H. the Prince Consort* (1862), and Queen Victoria's *Leaves from the Journal of Our Life in the Highlands* (1868).

The methods and influence of Dr. Arnold are described in A. P. Stanley's *Life and Correspondence of Dr. Arnold* (1844), T. Hughes' *Tom Brown's School Days* (1857) and *The Manliness of Christ* (1894), and the present writer's *Bonnet and Shawl* (1928), s.v. *Mary Arnold.*

2. *Mexico City.* The facts as to this extension of the United States are to be found in outline in vol. v of E. Channing's *History of the United States* and F. L. Paxson's *History of the American Frontier,* and in detail in vol. ii of G. L. Rives' *United States and Mexico: 1821–1848* (1913); analysis in F. J. Turner's *Frontier in American History* and J. T. Adams' *Epic of America.*

The Mormon episode is well summarised in L. E. Young's *Founding of Utah* (1924).

AUTHORITIES

3. *Paris.* The events of 1848 are summarised in vol. i of P. de la Gorce's *Histoire de la Seconde République Française* (1887); details in Victor Hugo's *Choses Vues* (1887).

4. *Continental.* The European revolutions outside France are narrated briefly in vol. i of Sir A. W. Ward's *Germany, 1815–1890,* summarised in his chapters of vol. xi of *Cambridge Modern History* (1909), and G. M. Trevelyan's *Garibaldi's Defence of the Roman Republic* (1907), supplemented by C. E. Maurice's *Revolutionary Movement of 1848–9 in Italy, Austria-Hungary, and Germany* (1887); details in E. H. Carr's *Karl Marx* (1934) and vol. viii of Prince Metternich's *Mémoires Documents et Ecrits Divers* (1884).

5. *Kennington Common.* The anecdote of Louis Napoleon is found, with slight variations, in G. H. Putnam's *George Palmer Putnam* (1912) and F. A. Simpson's *Rise of Louis Napoleon* (1909); further details in F. H. Cheetham's *Louis Napoleon and the Genesis of the Second Empire* and the present writer's *Second Empire.*

Details of events in London are in vol. ii of Sir H. Maxwell's *Life of Wellington* (1899), vol. i of J. A. Froude's *Thomas Carlyle: a History of His Life in London* (1884), vol. ii of Sir T. Martin's *Life of the Prince Consort,* vol. i of E. Ashley's *Life of Viscount Palmerston, 1846–1865* (1876), vol. ii of Lady Airlie's *Lady Palmerston* (1922), and vol. ii of *The Letters of Queen Victoria.*

A survey of the movement is in J. L. and B. Hammond's *Age of the Chartists, 1832–1854* (1930), and vol. i of J. H. Clapham's *Economic History of Modern Britain* summarises the underlying facts.

6. *Paris, II.* The facts as to the June outbreak are summarised by P. de la Gorce in vol. i of his *Seconde République* and observed at first hand by Victor Hugo in *Choses Vues.*

7. *Chicago, Ill.* Facts in F. H. Spearman's *Strategy of Great Railroads* (1904) and E. L. Masters' *Tale of Chicago* (1933).

1861

1. *St. Petersburg.* The Czar's Rescript of Emancipation was signed at St. Petersburg on February 19/March 3, 1861, when the Court was in residence at the Winter Palace.

F. H. Skrine's *Expansion of Russia* is a useful summary, supplemented by vol. iii of P. Milioukov's *Histoire de Russie* (1933) and vol. i of M. N. Pokrovsky's *Brief History of Russia;* details in S. Graham's *Alexander II* (1935).

2. *Charleston, S. C.* The narrative is mainly founded on the balanced summary in vol. vi of E. Channing's *History of the United States;* analysis in J. T. Adams' *America's Tragedy* (1934) and *Epic of America,* and vol. ii of C. A. and M. R. Beard's *Rise of American Civilization* (1927); and details in St. J. Ravenel's *Charleston* (1929).

The most practical military narrative of the war is *A History of the Civil War in the United States* (1905), by W. B. Wood and J. E. Edmonds.

3. *Osborne.* The Queen's mind is fully revealed in vol. iii and vol. i (Second Series) of *The Letters of Queen Victoria* and vol. i of the present writer's *The Queen and Mr. Gladstone* (1933); further analysis in L. Strachey's *Queen Victoria;* additional material in vol. ii of *The Later Correspondence of Lord John Russell* (1925) and vol. v of Sir T. Martin's *Life of the Prince Consort* (1880).

Internal politics in vol. ii of J. Morley's *Life of Gladstone* (1903) and the present writer's *Palmerston* (1926) and *Gladstone and Palmerston* (1928); European politics in P. de la Gorce's *Histoire du Second Empire* (1903), vol. iii of E. Bourgeois' *Manuel Historique de Politique Étrangère* (1909), and C. Seignobos' *Histoire Politique de l'Europe Contemporaine* (1908); supplemented by *The Second Empire* by the present writer and vol. ii of E. Ashley's *Life of Viscount Palmerston: 1846–1865* (1876); Anglo-American relations in E. D. Adams' *Great Britain and the American Civil War* (1925) and vol. i of Lord Newton's *Lord Lyons* (1913).

1871

Versailles. The operations and aspect of the Franco-German War are summarised from the French point of view in Lt.-Col. Rousset's *Histoire Générale de la Guerre Franco-Allemande* (1912) and from the German point of view in Major-General J. F. Maurice's *Franco-German War* (1899), translated from the German text of C. v. d. Goltz, J. v. Pflugk-Harttung, and others; additional material in A. Dayot's *Second Empire* and *L'Invasion, Le Siège, La Commune.* Details of the German occupation in A. von Werner's *Versailles and Head-Quarters* in Maurice's compilation, A. Duquet's *Paris: La Capitulation et l'Entrée des Allemands* (1899), and the anonymous *Bismarck in Versailles: Erinnerungen an Versailles, 1870–1871* (1886).

The creation of the German Empire is outlined in J. W. Headlam's *Bismarck and the Foundation of the German Empire* (1904), J. Klaczko's *Deux Chanceliers: le Prince Gortchakof et le Prince de Bismarck* (1877), and G. Roloff's chapter in vol. xi of *Cambridge Modern History,* and summarised by the present writer in *The Second Empire.*

The physiognomy of Paris during and after the siege is incomparably rendered in vol. iv of the *Journal des Goncourt* (1892). The ensuing diplomacy is narrated in T. Flathe's *Political History of the War*, in J. F. Maurice's compilation and vol. ii of A. Sorel's *Histoire Diplomatique de la Guerre Franco-Allemande* (1875); details in Comte d'Hérisson's *Journal of a Staff Officer in Paris* (1885). The German entry into Paris is recorded in A. Duquet's narrative and A. Dayot's illustrations; and the Marxian view of the Commune is to be found in E. H. Carr's *Karl Marx* and *The Correspondence of Marx and Engels* (1934).

1881

1. *Winter Palace.* Facts in S. Graham's *Alexander II*, F. H. Skrine's *Expansion of Russia*, vol. iii of P. Milioukov's *Histoire de Russie*, and vol. i of M. N. Pokrovsky's *Brief History of Russia;* detail, in vol. i of Sir S. Lee's *King Edward VII* (1925).

2. *Marlborough House.* The career of the Prince of Wales is recorded in vol. i of Sir S. Lee's *King Edward VII;* details in H. C. Burdett's *Prince, Princess, and People* (1890) and *The Queen and Mr. Gladstone* by the present writer; social detail in *Fifty Years: Memories and Contrasts, 1882–1932* (1932), vol. i of R. H. Gretton's *Modern History of the English People* (1913), and Max Beerbohm's *1880* in his *Works* (1896); home politics in vol. vi of G. E. Buckle's *Life of Disraeli* (1920).

3. *Buffalo, N. Y.* The rise and methods of the Standard Oil Company are presented from an unfavourable angle in I. M. Tarbell's *History of the Standard Oil Company* (1905); general comment in vol. ii of C. A. and M. R. Beard's *Rise of American Civilization;* railroad history in J. Moody's *Railroad Builders* (1919) and R. G. MacBeth's *Romance of the Canadian Pacific Railway* (1924).

1897

St. Paul's. Sir H. Maxwell's *Sixty Years a Queen* (1897) contains a full record of the Diamond Jubilee celebrations with a retrospect of Queen Victoria's reign in the mood of 1897, which may be supplemented by H. W. Lucy's *Diary of the Unionist Parliament, 1895–1900* (1901), and R. Kipling's *Barrack-Room Ballads* (1892), *The Seven Seas* (1896), and *The Five Nations* (1903). The Queen's personal record is in vol. iii (Third Series) of *The Letters of Queen Victoria.*

The first Jubilee is recorded in vol. i (Third Series) of *The Letters of Queen Victoria* and the intervening history in vol. i of R. H. Gretton's *Modern History of the English People,* vol. iii of J. Morley's *Life of Gladstone,* and H. W. Lucy's *Diary of the Salisbury Parliament, 1886–1892* (1892), supplemented by vol. ii of *The Queen and Mr. Gladstone* by the present writer.

The growth of imperialism may be studied in Ramsay Muir's *Expansion of Europe* (1922) and *Short History of the British Commonwealth,* vol. ii (1922), supplemented by Sir J. Seeley's *Expansion of England* (1883) and vol. iii of J. L. Garvin's *Life of Joseph Chamberlain* (1934).

1901

St. James's. The circumstances of King Edward's accession are recorded in vols. i and ii of Sir S. Lee's *King Edward VII* and vol. i of Sir A. Fitzroy's *Memoirs* (1925).

The preliminaries of the South African War are to be found in vol. iii of J. L. Garvin's *Life of Joseph Chamberlain* and an adequate contemporary narrative of its course in A. Conan Doyle's *Great Boer War* (1900); home politics in vol. ii of the Marquess of Crewe's *Lord Rosebery* (1931).

1905

1. *Winter Palace Square.* The Russian revolution of 1905 is recorded in vol. iii of P. Milioukov's *Histoire de Russie* and vol. ii of M. N. Pokrovsky's *Brief History of Russia;* political details in S. P. Turin's *From Peter the Great to Lenin: a History of the Russian Labour Movement* (1935); personal details as to Nicholas II in *Archives Secrètes de l'Empereur Nicolas II* (1928), *Journal Intime de Nicolas II* (1934), *Lettres de l'Impératrice Alexandra Feodorovna à l'Empereur Nicolas II* (1925), M. Paléologue's *Russie des Tsars pendant la Grande Guerre* (1922), and vol. ii of *Journals and Letters of Reginald, Viscount Esher* (1934). Russian aims in the Far East are summarised in F. H. Skrine's *Expansion of Russia* and the Russo-Japanese War in vol. ii of J. and C. Vial's *Histoire Abrégée des Campagnes Modernes* (1910) and Sir I. Hamilton's *Staff Officer's Scrap-Book* (1906). Revolutionary life and thought may be studied in vol. i of N. Krupskaya's *Memories of Lenin* (1930), L. Trotsky's *My Life* (1930) and *Lenin* (1925), R. Fox's *Lenin* (1933), vol. i of W. H. Chamberlin's *Russian Revolution* (1935), and the translated volumes of Lenin's *Collected Works.*

2. *Tangier.* Details of the Kaiser's visit are in vol. iii of *British Documents on the Origins of the War* (1928), M. Paléologue's *Un Grand Tournant de la Politique Mondiale: 1904–1906* (1934), and vol. iii of Prince von Bülow's *Memoirs* (1931) which contain the fullest, though not always the most truthful, picture of Imperial Germany. E. Ludwig's

AUTHORITIES

Kaiser Wilhelm II (1926) is a penetrating, if unsympathetic, study of the Emperor, which may be supplemented by Sir F. Lascelles' analysis in pp. 434–8 of *British Documents,* vol. iii, and the caricatures reproduced in J. Grand-Carteret's *Lui* (1905). His relations with Edward VII are surveyed in Sir S. Lee's *King Edward VII,* which contains a full study of the genesis of the Anglo-French *Entente Cordiale* and may be supplemented by G. P. Gooch's *History of Modern Europe: 1878–1919* (1923), Lord Newton's *Lord Lansdowne* (1929), and H. Nicolson's *Lord Carnock* (1930).

3. *Björkö.* Details of the meeting of William II and Nicholas II are in vol. iv of *British Documents on the Origins of the War* (1929), E. Ludwig's *Kaiser Wilhelm II,* vol. iii of Prince von Bülow's *Memoirs,* vol. ii of Sir S. Lee's *King Edward VII,* and Lord Newton's *Lord Lansdowne;* diplomatic events in G. P. Gooch's *History of Modern Europe: 1878–1919.*

4. *Westminster.* Home politics in vol. ii of J. A. Spender's *Life of Sir Henry Campbell-Bannerman* (1923) and vol. i of J. A. Spender and C. Asquith's *Life of Lord Oxford and Asquith* (1932), supplemented by R. B. Haldane's *Autobiography* (1929) and F. C. Gould's *Political Caricatures* (1903).

1910

Biarritz. General history and personal details in vol. ii of Sir S. Lee's *King Edward VII* and vol. ii of J. A. Spender and C. Asquith's *Life of Lord Oxford and Asquith;* home politics in D. Lloyd George's *The People's Budget* (1909) and *Better Times* (1910), E. T. Raymond's *Mr. Lloyd George* (1922), and vol. ii of Lord Crewe's *Lord Rosebery;* foreign policy in G. P. Gooch's *History of Modern Europe: 1878–1919;* defence questions in Sir I. Hamilton's *Compulsory Service* (1910), R. B. Haldane's *Army Reform* (1909), *Navy League Annual, 1910–11,* and *Taschenbuch der Kriegsflotten, 1911,* retrospectively reviewed in E. L. Woodward's *Great Britain and the German Navy* (1935).

1917

1. *Downing Street.* It would be out of place to attempt a bibliography of the World War; but an admirable outline of its course may be found in *Encyclopædia Britannica* (14th edition, 1929), s.v. *World War;* preliminary diplomacy in vol. xi of *British Documents* (1926); general narratives of its course in C. R. M. F. Cruttwell's *History of the Great War* (1934), J. Buchan's *History of the Great War* (1921), and W.

AUTHORITIES

Churchill's *World Crisis* (1923–7); British operations in France in J. E. Edmond's *Official History of the Great War* (1928 sqq.).

The situation in 1916–17 may be studied in vol. ii of J. A. Spender and C. Asquith's *Life of Lord Oxford and Asquith* and vols. ii and iii of D. Lloyd George's *War Memories* (1934), supplemented by *War Cabinet: Report for the Year 1917* (1918).

2. *Petrograd*. The best narrative in English of the Russian Revolution is vol. i of W. H. Chamberlin's *Russian Revolution, 1917–1921* (1935), supplemented from the point of view of the Provisional Government by A. Kerensky's *Révolution Russe* (1928) and *Crucifixion of Liberty* (1934) and vol. iii of P. Milioukov's *Histoire de Russie*, and from the Bolshevik point of view by vol. i of L. Trotsky's *History of the Russian Revolution* (1932). Invaluable evidence as to the Court is to be found in the Czar's *Journal Intime, 1914–1918* (1934) and *Lettres de l'Impératrice Alexandra Feodorovna à l'Empereur Nicolas II* (1927), supplemented by *Interrogatoires des Ministres, Conseillers, Généraux, Hauts Fonctionnaires de la Cour Impériale Russe par la Commission Extraordinaire du Gouvernement Provisoire de 1917* (1927), M. Paléologue's *Russie des Tsars* (1922), Sir G. Buchanan's *My Mission to Russia* (1923) and M. Buchanan's *Petrograd* (1918). Details as to Lenin in vol. ii of N. K. Krupskaya's *Memories of Lenin*, L. Trotsky's *Lenin* (1925), and vol. xviii of Lenin's *Collected Works*.

3. *Washington, D. C.* The course of American policy and its director is fully traced in vols. iii, iv, and v of R. S. Baker's *Life and Letters of Woodrow Wilson* (1932–5); details in C. Seymour's *Intimate Papers of Colonel House* (1926) and B. J. Hendrick's *Life and Letters of Walter H. Page* (1926); general comment in F. T. Adams' *Epic of America* and vol. ii of C. A. and M. R. Beard's *Rise of American Civilization;* and an excellent, though supercilious, summary in W. Millis' *Road to War: America 1914–1917* (1935).

4. *Smolny*. The progress of the Russian Revolution may be studied in vol. i of W. H. Chamberlin's *Russian Revolution*, A. Kerensky's *Révolution Russe*, L. Trotsky's *History of the Russian Revolution* and *Lenin*, vols. xx and xxi of Lenin's *Collected Works*, and N. Krupskaya's *Memories of Lenin;* details as to the Czar in *Journal Intime de Nicolas II*.

1919

Versailles. The broad history of the Peace Conference and the preceding events is to be found in vols. i and ii of *A History of the Peace Conference of Paris*, (ed. H. W. V. Temperley, 1920), summarised in

AUTHORITIES

G. P. Gooch's *History of Modern Europe, 1878–1919,* and vol. iii of
H. A. L. Fisher's *History of Europe* (1935); personal details in J. M.
Keynes' *Economic Consequences of the Peace* (1920); and the German
experience in V. Schiff's *The Germans at Versailles, 1919* (1930).

1922

Rome. Authorities on Fascism and Mussolini have scarcely passed
the stage of journalism. Mr. Bonar Law's judgment on the *Duce* was
repeated by Mr. Asquith to the present writer on December 15, 1922.

1933

1. *Berlin, NW.* The documentation of Nazi Germany is still pro-
visional and journalistic, apart from the unexpurgated text of A. Hitler's
Mein Kampf in German. Its mental background may be studied in O.
Spengler's *Decline of the West* (translated by C. F. Atkinson, 1926) and
the preceding course of German politics in A. Rosenberg's *History of the
German Republic* (1936); details as to the Reichstag fire in D. Reed's
The Burning of the Reichstag (1934) and *The Brown Book of the Hit-
ler Terror* (1933).

2. *Washington, D. C.* The writer was travelling in the United States
between January and April, 1933. The surface of the previous decade is
brilliantly surveyed in F. L. Allen's *Only Yesterday* (1931).

1936

Westminster. King George's Jubilee and funeral are recorded from
the writer's observation.

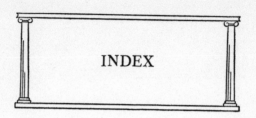

INDEX

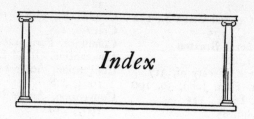

Index

INDEX

INDEX

INDEX

Sullivan, Sir A., 185
Sumter, Fort, 84–96
Sutter's Fort, 41
Sverdloff, 279

Tangier, 215–228
Tel-el-Kebir, 167
Terry, E., 149
Thiers, A., 50, 51, 115, 130, 132
Todleben, General, 143
Trent, U.S.S., 107
Triple Alliance, 180
Trotsky, L., 211, 279, 300, 304, 308, 312
Tsushima, 209, 214

Van Buren, President M., 19–24
Vanderbilt, C., 159
Van der Lubbe, M., 336
Van Horne, W. C., 159
Verdun, 269
Versailles, Treaty of, 317–323
Vicksburg, 94
Victor Emmanuel II, King of Italy, 123, 125
Victoria, Queen, 10–15, 27–35, 38, 53–4, 64, 80, 98–9, 107, 120, 127, 147, 152, 154, 163–4, 167, 169, 173, 184–7, 193, 219, 224, 281

Wellington, F.M. Duke of, 15, 29, 35, 60–2, 64, 100
Werner, A. von, 115–116
Whistler, J. McN., 146
Wilhelmströhe, 130
Wilkes, Captain (U.S.N.), 107
William I, King of Prussia, German Emperor, 106, 114, 116, 118, 125, 126, 129, 130, 134
William II, German Emperor, 152, 164, 178–9, 180, 183, 213–28, 229–33, 248–52, 254, 261, 298
Wilson, Major, 175
Wilson, President W., 271, 290, 291–98, 318–20, 323, 345, 346
Windischgrätz, Prince, 71, 72
Witte, Count, 233
Wörth, 128

Yalu, 209
Young, Brigham, 46

Zola, E., 224

[400]